Denial

DENIAL

How We Hide, Ignore, and
Explain Away Problems

Jared Del Rosso

NEW YORK UNIVERSITY PRESS

New York

NEW YORK UNIVERSITY PRESS
New York
www.nyupress.org

References to Internet websites (URLs) were accurate at the time of writing.
Neither the author nor New York University Press is responsible for URLs
that may have expired or changed since the manuscript was prepared.

Library of Congress Cataloging-in-Publication Data
Names: Del Rosso, Jared, author.
Title: Denial : how we hide, ignore, and explain away problems /
    Jared Del Rosso.
Description: New York : New York University Press, [2022] |
    Includes bibliographical references and index.
Identifiers: LCCN 2021044588 | ISBN 9781479828968 (hardback ; alk.
    paper) | ISBN 9781479815944 (ebook) | ISBN 9781479814565 (ebook
    other)
Subjects: LCSH: Denial (Psychology)—Social aspects. | Self-deception. |
    Problem solving.
Classification: LCC BF175.5.D44 D45 2022 | DDC 155.2—dc23
LC record available at https://lccn.loc.gov/2021044588

New York University Press books are printed on acid-free paper, and their
binding materials are chosen for strength and durability. We strive to use
environmentally responsible suppliers and materials to the greatest extent
possible in publishing our books.

Manufactured in the United States of America

10 9 8 7 6 5 4 3 2 1

Also available as an ebook

To Greg MacAvoy, Gila Hayim, and Stephen Pfohl,

my teachers,

who left me better than they found me.

And to my students,

who so often do the same.

CONTENTS

PREFACE

I T wasn't much, just an offhand remark amid the most forgettable of things, a weather report on Colorado's public radio station. "Highs in the seventies in the Denver metro region," I remember the host announcing. "Sun. A beautiful fall day, even if it's a bit hazy in some places. Crisp."

That late September 2020 morning, I spotted ash drifting over my yard. This was the haze to which the weather report referred. The ash remained stubborn evidence of the state's wildfires. Those fires themselves referred to the enduring drought—caused by both a natural dry cycle and climate change—and extreme heat in the southwest. True, the ash was light that morning. Not nearly as much fell as had a few weeks prior. Not nearly as much fell here, over my home, as blanketed the northwest of the United States that year. But, somewhere, Colorado burned. We could still smell it, the pungent smoke that tested our lungs. The state issued another air-quality advisory, as it had for much of the summer and as it would for much of the autumn. This was our new normal, what passed for a "beautiful fall day" in Colorado. All it took was a bit of disbelief, a sense that we could talk about the weather without mentioning the ash we saw, the smoke we breathed, and the irritation in our throats.

The night before, in the first debate of the 2020 election, President Donald J. Trump had refused to condemn white supremacists.[1] He had also refused to agree to a peaceful transfer of power should US voters support his opponent, former vice president Joe Biden.[2] As outrageous as these statements were, as much as they led the next day's news (and they did), they were well rehearsed and long downplayed by his allies. After all, as a presidential candidate in 2016, Trump had reluctantly and equivocally disavowed David Duke, a former grand wizard of the Ku Klux Klan, after Duke had endorsed him.[3] And, in the third and final presidential debate with Hillary Clinton, Trump refused to commit to accepting the results of that election, saying slyly when pressed on it, "I will tell you at the time. I'll keep you in suspense. OK?"[4] (How honest and tragic his noncommittal proved.)

Two days after his debate with Biden, the day after that "beautiful fall day" in Colorado, President Trump tested positive for COVID-19. For six months, he had minimized the virus, even as it had killed more than two hundred thousand people in the United States by mid-September 2020. In fact, months earlier, Trump had boasted that, like a "miracle," the virus would disappear.[5] Now the president was hospitalized. He suffered "extremely depressed blood oxygen levels at one point and a lung problem associated with pneumonia," according to a February 2021 report in the *New York Times*.[6] He received aggressive, experimental treatments. Some of his political allies hoped the experience would humble the president and that he'd emerge from the hospital empathetic toward the suffering of Americans. Instead, President Trump took a driving tour of a line of supporters, quickly returned to the White House, and boldly tweeted, "Don't be afraid of COVID. Don't let it dominate your life."[7]

Ash in the sky, virus in the air, demagogues in our politics. "A beautiful fall day," secured by that strongest of adhesives, denial.

For nearly a decade and a half, I have been researching and teaching on denial, the social strategies people use to hide, ignore, and explain away problems. As a sociologist, I met these processes through my studies of the politics of US torture.[8] From 2002 to 2008, the George W. Bush administration and its allies routinely downplayed seemingly undeniable evidence of torture, including photographs, human-rights organizations' reports, and the US government's own investigations. Low-profile incidents of detainee abuse and torture—such as at Metropolitan Detention Center (MDC) in Brooklyn, New York, where corrections officers shoved detainees into walls, twisted their arms and hands, and assaulted prisoners with unnecessary body-cavity searches—were overlooked by the media. Politicians, meanwhile, excused the mistreatment of detainees at MDC as the understandable mistakes of well-meaning Americans in the immediate aftermath of the September 11, 2001, terrorist attacks. High-profile incidents—such as at Abu Ghraib prison in Iraq, where US soldiers photographed themselves torturing detainees—were explained away as "isolated incidents" caused by "a few bad apples." Meanwhile, the CIA's so-called enhanced interrogation program, in which agency interrogators were authorized by the Bush administration to torture detainees, was euphemized and justified as necessary for the protection of US national security. None of this was surprising. Torture is a war crime, and virtually no government leader is brazen enough to openly admit its use. The Bush administration's denials largely echoed those that had been used for decades by democracies and dictatorships alike: hide the evidence, then try to ignore it, and, when that fails, explain it away.[9]

But denial is not only for these most global of problems and leaders. Even as I studied the denials of national politicians whose lives and problems were nothing like mine, I was continually returned, by national news, to Pine Bush, the small upstate New York town where I spent most of the first half of my life. In 2012, the public school district that had educated my friends, my siblings, and me was exposed for what it had long kept hidden: deep and enduring anti-Semitism. A suit, by several Jewish families in the school district, alleged that the district had consistently overlooked anti-Semitic graffiti, verbal harassment, and physical assaults. The *New York Times* opened an article on the lawsuit with these descriptions of the allegations.

> The swastikas, the students recalled, seemed to be everywhere: on walls, desks, lockers, textbooks, computer screens, a playground slide—even on a student's face. For some Jewish students in the Pine Bush Central School District in New York State, attending public school has been nothing short of a nightmare. . . . They have reported being pelted with coins, told to retrieve money thrown into garbage

receptacles, shoved and even beaten. They say that on school buses in this rural part of the state, located about 90 minutes north of New York City and once home to a local Ku Klux Klan chapter president, students have chanted "white power" and made Nazi salutes with their arms.[10]

Three years later, Foreign Language Week at the high school was canceled after public outrage regarding the Language Club's reading of the Pledge of Allegiance in Arabic. The local paper and the *Washington Post* both printed a photograph of a car in the high school's parking lot with a xenophobic message on its rear window: "WE LIVE IN AMERICA SPEAK ENGLISH."[11] According to the *Post*, students in the high school verbally harassed the student who read the pledge in Arabic, calling the student a "terrorist" and saying that they "should go to the Middle East."[12]

Then, in 2019, the *New York Times* reported that the school district's own surveys, which a court filing made public, offered evidence that "anti-Semitism remains a stubborn problem at Pine Bush." One-third of middle school and high school students "said they had seen or heard incidents of anti-Semitism in school the previous year."[13]

I realize now that none of this was particularly surprising. As a child, I had thought swastikas to be the normal graffiti of the older kids, as they were commonly carved into bus seats and classroom desks. As far north as New York is, Confederate paraphernalia adorned trucks and cars in town. A long-standing (and unfounded) rumor, revealing of the sympathies of some town residents, still circulated: people in Pine Bush had a conspiratorial connection to John Wilkes Booth and had known about the assassination of Lincoln even before it was reported in the region's newspapers.[14] In the 1970s, before my time, a member of the school board in Pine Bush was an official in the Ku Klux Klan. Her husband, the area's leader of the Klan, worked as an educator at a local prison, recruiting white men and circulating white supremacist literature.[15] Looking back, the legacies of racism and anti-Semitism in Pine Bush and, especially, its schools are obvious. But none of this was discussed openly by the adults in my life; they and I were protected from these horrors by our whiteness and our Christian upbringing.

Despite evidence that white supremacy, anti-Semitism, and Islamophobia festered in Pine Bush, some residents of the town came together to protect its innocence. Following reports on the Jewish students' lawsuit, residents rallied in November 2013. Rather than denounce anti-Semitism and express their support for the students who had sued the school, the town's rally had a defensive tone, as residents spoke against the unfairness of reporting on the allegations.[16] "We are a loving, caring community, and we don't deserve to be painted in such a negative fashion," said one rally participant.[17]

Swastikas on the school walls, Nazi salutes in the buses. A "loving, caring community," secured by that most stubborn of adhesives, denial.

Interpersonal, collective, and social problems threaten our sense of how things are and should be. Denial of these threats offers us a way out. Using denial, we can maintain a sense of normalcy, even when we encounter information to the contrary. Despite drifts of ash and smoke, a fall day can seem beautiful for its sunny sky and seventy degrees. In writing this book, I have tried to identify, categorize, and describe the strategies of denial that people use to maintain the sense that "everything is fine," even when it seems obvious that everything isn't.

These strategies are many and varied. They also differ in their effects, depending on who uses them and how, to what end, and in what contexts. For these reasons, denial frustrates our efforts to precisely and narrowly define it. Rather than pursue, for the sake of coherence, a single form or definition of denial, I treat it broadly in this book, as the range of strategies that people use and the activities that people engage in to efface problems. Some of these activities aim at our awareness of problems; they involve efforts to keep distressing information from intruding into our lives. Other strategies aim at our understanding of problems; when distressing information indeed intrudes, people turn to the rhetoric of denial to downplay or explain away that information.

This broad treatment means that I cover an expansive social terrain. Pursuing denial, I've traveled from the seemingly benign and private interactions between people trying to manage interpersonal troubles to the most public pronouncements, performances, and tweets of influential figures trying to manage scandals. The former occur everywhere—among co-workers avoiding conversations about a supervisor's obvious mistakes, strangers feigning unawareness of the distress of another on a busy city street, and friends who joke about climate change to manage their anxiety about "unseasonably" warm weather. The latter occur everywhere, too. A Hollywood producer invokes his "demons" to excuse his sexual assaults of women. A president claims he was being "sarcastic" after, in all seriousness, he raises the possibility of injecting Americans with bleach in order to control a pandemic.

My hope is that this book will help you identify specific strategies of denial when you encounter them, whether you encounter them in the behaviors of others in your life or in the public maneuvers of the most powerful. I also hope that the arguments presented here can help you understand how denial enables people to cultivate ignorance of social problems. Because even when denied, problems fester. This is denial's paradox. It can seem like a balm, soothing social life and people's anxieties over problems. But it is also an irritant. By smoothing over disturbances, it can actually aggravate them. The causes of social problems remain unresolved, the harms unrecognized. If denial indeed protects us, it only protects *our sense* that social problems don't concern us. It does not protect us or others from those problems themselves.

To give names to our encounters with denial is to bring these experiences, whether familiar or unfamiliar, into language. Giving words and form to denial, we can hold it in common, inspecting and describing it together. This allows us, as the sociologist Charles Lemert writes of all sociological knowledge, to bring experience "out of the dusky realm of the secrets everyone knows but, for fear of the consequences, will not talk about"—and, I'll add, cannot talk about for lack of the right words.[18] I find inspiration for this pursuit, too, in historian and activist Rebecca Solnit's writing on social change: "Calling things by their true names cuts through the lies that excuse, buffer, muddle, disguise, avoid, or encourage inaction, indifference, obliviousness. It's not all there is to changing the world, but it's a key step."[19]

Denial is not all there is to our politics and to our social life. Nor is the naming and exposure of denial all that social change requires of us. Still, let us call denial by its true name. After all, our modern emperors—our film producers, news anchors, corporate and university leaders, and politicians—still parade naked and convince us to disbelieve our eyes. Thankfully, for the rest of us, denial's strength is ultimately its weakness. It works best when it works unnoticed, spending its time casting and then living in the shadows of our world. To notice denial and, then, to speak its name is to undo it.

INTRODUCTION

THE nuances of a language are said to serve the needs of those who use it. One frequently reads, for instance, that there are people who use dozens of words to describe snow, the better to linguistically map their frozen world.[1]

What does it mean, then, that the English language is littered with clichés, idioms, and proverbs to describe the many forms and textures of denial? We use the language of domesticity, describing people "sweeping things under the rug," warning against "washing your dirty laundry in public," and "keeping skeletons in our closets." We invoke the animal world. We keep, impossibly, "elephants in the room." We "let our sleeping dogs lie" and threaten that "curiosity kills the cat." Like ostriches, we "bury our head in the sand."[2] We speak of our perceptual fields and their limits, hiding things "in plain sight," overlooking "open secrets," and keeping still other things "out of sight, out of mind." Using ableist language, we turn a "blind eye" or a "deaf ear"; some people play at being "deaf and dumb." Others cultivate a "willful blindness" to reality. We celebrate that "ignorance is bliss" and that "what you don't know can't hurt you." Both are easier pleasures to pursue when we "bite our tongue" and "don't ask and don't tell." When figurative speech no longer fits, we invent new jargon. We speak of presidents and CEOs who have "plausible deniability" for lacking demonstrable knowledge of the crimes of underlings. We speak of an apathetic citizenry suffering from "compassion fatigue" or "scandal fatigue." Or, owing everything to Freud and Kübler-Ross, we simply say that a person is "in denial."[3]

Perhaps it means that we English speakers are especially prone to, but also aware of, denial. But I suspect that the overgrowth of the language of denial suggests something more fundamental: denial is a core social practice. Perhaps not universal, but nearly so.[4] For wherever people live among other people, there will be those who transgress social norms. Some will be minor. Think of all the embarrassing gaffes that can derail a person's interactions with others. Others will be deeply transgressive. Think of the betrayals of trust, corruption, and crimes that fill the news. Imagine, even, "a society of saints," the French sociologist Emile Durkheim famously wrote. "Crimes . . . will be . . . unknown." But faults and blunders that are normally forgivable "will create there the same scandal that the ordinary offense does" in the typical society.[5] And wherever there is the scandal of fault, of blunder, and of transgression, there will be options. One can hide, ignore, or explain away—that is, deny the transgression. Or one can punish the transgressor. Durkheim emphasized the latter. Yet denial is as basic a social process as is punishment.

Denial and the Social Organization of Attention

We're not used to thinking about denial in this way, as its most familiar form is psychological and pathological: the lone denier, repressing recognition of their troubles.[6] This is the denial of the addict, of the abuser, of those avoiding our inevitable, human encounter with death. But this lone denier is a bit of social scientific fiction. It's not that we don't deny critical truths about ourselves and others. We do, and the ways we do this are legion.

Rather, denial's loneliness is the fiction. Denial is embedded in social life. We learn its ways through socialization, and we maintain it through social interaction. Partly, this has to do with how attention is taught and managed—how it is, in sociological terms, socially organized. People learn from others what they should notice and attend to. People learn, in other words, what they should keep in the foreground of social life. They learn, too, what they should ignore, overlook, and leave in the background. In one of his several deceptively slight books on these issues, the sociologist Eviatar Zerubavel offers a prosaic example of this: that of a child at a zoo, watching the "wrong" animals. Zerubavel writes, "Thus, when young visitors attend to conventionally 'wrong' objects of attention, such as pigeons and squirrels that linger between the zoo's enclosures . . . their parents indeed often try to redirect their attention to the specifically exhibited (and therefore conventionally 'noteworthy') animals."[7] It isn't just the attention of children that is socially organized in these rather simple ways. Like the parent teaching a child how to observe animals at a zoo, experienced birders often redirect the attention of novice birdwatchers from a common bird, the robin or starling, to the uncommon warbler flitting above them. Eventually, the novice birder learns to give the common birds but a perfunctory glance and leave them unreported when others ask what they are watching.

The learning of attention is a lifelong process. In *The Elephant in the Room*, a foundational text on the sociology of denial, Zerubavel notes that professions have "distinctive traditions of paying attention" that "affect what their members notice."[8] These traditions are taught and learned through socialization and professionalization, including apprenticeships, internships, and schooling; probationary periods before promotion; and formal reviews. Through these, those in a profession learn what to attend to and what can be, perhaps even must be, overlooked. Most sociologists, the author included, learn to perceive social structure and to keep inequality in the foreground of their attention. For most of us working in the discipline, other things usually remain undiscussed: genetics, for instance, or the unconscious.

Through everyday socialization and formal training, we learn to attend to some things and not others. What we're taught to leave in the background, and what we indeed allow to remain in the background, is frequently ignored. This is a simple fact of human social development. And it reflects, too, the limits of human attention; we must filter out some, even most, of our environment to attend to the limited portion of it relevant to us at any given moment. Yet this fact takes on a normative, moral dimension whenever the teaching of attention is used to keep inconvenient, disruptive facts from entering the foreground of our lives. When a child, for instance, is taught to avoid drawing attention to the presence of people living on city streets, perhaps admonished that it's not polite to point or stare, homelessness may recede beyond the horizon of the child's perception of a place. Certainly, they've learned that others would prefer them to pretend that they haven't noticed people who are unhoused. When, within their homes, children see that adults do not speak about family members' addictions or violence, they may remain silent out of fear of disturbing the delicate, false peace. But these processes are not the family's alone. Professionalization, too, includes messages about what may or may not be spoken out loud. New hires to a workplace often learn that more senior colleagues' incompetence, indiscretions, abuses of power, even outright crimes are best left undiscussed. In these cases, the social organization of attention operates not as an inevitable method of filtering out extraneous or irrelevant information. Rather, here it appears as denial—a method of backgrounding or effacing information that, if surfaced, could disrupt social interaction, discredit the identities that people claim for themselves, and/or trigger social sanctions.

These processes suggest a partial, sociological definition of denial: it includes the strategies, whether interactional or communicative, that people use to keep troubling information from entering social life in the first place.[9] Importantly, for denial to work, it must be deployed among people. It takes at least two and usually more, a small group of people, to actively collaborate to hush uncomfortable and distressing truths.

The sociologist Kari Marie Norgaard's research into climate change denial illustrates these processes. Norgaard's work largely focuses on denial among climate change *believers*, those who do not explicitly and outright deny either climate change or its human causes. Through interviews and observations in Norway and the United States, Norgaard shows that even these believers practice denial, keeping the smoldering truth of climate change in the background of social life. They do so, Norgaard shows, to manage the powerful and negative emotional responses that they and others have to the threat of climate change. Norgaard's Norwegian interviewees expressed profound insecurity about the future. Parents worried about the world that their children and grandchildren would inherit. Meanwhile, in the United States, discussions among students in Norgaard's courses on the environment veered toward the apocalypse, with students describing the future as resembling eco-Armageddon films like *The Day after Tomorrow*.[10]

We might expect that those who fear the future would take action to fix it. Instead, fear's fellow traveler is helplessness. To many people, the problem of climate change seems too global, too complex, and too deeply rooted in our existing human world to be corrected by individuals. Feelings of helplessness, according to Norgaard, are particularly salient in the United States. Many Americans believe that the causes of most social problems are within individuals and, so, they look for solutions that are similarly individualistic.[11] Climate change stubbornly resists us, no matter our belief in our own individual power. We cannot change our light bulbs and recycle our way out of it. No wonder one of Norgaard's male students described a feeling of "impotence" toward climate change. Another said, "Yeah, I can write my congressman a letter, but in all honesty . . . I am not sure that one person can make such a difference."[12]

Afraid and politically handcuffed by helplessness, Norgaard's interviewees admit that they try to keep climate change in the background of social life. They say that they avoid exposing themselves and others to information about climate change. They avoid talking about the topic at parties and other social events. When they raise the issue, they use humor, joking about the weather, to simultaneously acknowledge their deep fear of climate change and drain it of its emotional power.[13]

The Social Language of Denial

The use of humor suggests a change in how denial operates. Attention-management strategies sometimes fail. Information and, especially, distressing information surfaces. Information, in other words, may become *undeniable* at the level of attention. But this is not the end of denial. Rather, it begins a change in strategies, from those used to keep information out of our collective attention to those used, like humor, to *reinterpret* unavoidable information in ways that disarm it.

Denial, then, is not simply the silence of the unnoticed. It speaks. Or, more accurately, we speak the rhetoric of denial. Here, too, denial is social, as social scientists who have studied the ways people give accounts of themselves have shown. To account for their bad behavior, the seemingly lone denier adapts the "socially approved vocabularies" of denial, to borrow the sociologist Terri L. Orbuch's description of accounts.[14] This vocabulary is highly structured, taking the form of disclaimers, excuses, and justifications. These rhetorical forms, in turn, operate in distinct ways. Deniers use disclaimers to frame potentially discrediting speech and behavior; their hope is that their audiences might interpret their actions in the best possible light.[15] Deniers use excuses, meanwhile, to deny their responsibility for potentially discrediting behavior. And they use justifications to reinterpret potentially discrediting behavior as acceptable or inoffensive.[16]

Each of these forms has myriad subtypes, which I describe in chapter 3. All are highly flexible, too. Observing the latest political or corporate scandal unfold, it can seem that the rhetoric of denial is endlessly adaptable, twisting facts beyond recognition. In reality, the rhetoric of denial features a limited set of linguistic moves. They are, more or less, standardized and, so, predictable in their use. This is because when deniers offer excuses or justifications of their misconduct, they do so in the hope that others will accept their denials as believable and reasonable. In other words, competent deniers must offer explanations for their behaviors that are both believable and unproblematic, though the behaviors themselves may be deeply problematic. The sociologist C. Wright Mills described these rhetorical moves as "vocabularies of motive." These vocabularies are the culturally structured descriptions people give of the ultimate causes of their behavior. Though Mills intended this concept for all explanations, I find that it aptly describes the connections between people's transgressive behavior, their rhetorical denials to minimize that behavior, and social expectations. The rhetoric of denial consists of "relatively stable lingual phrases," to again quote Mills. These relatively stable denials translate the "question of 'why'" someone acted in a problematic way into an "unquestioned answer" for that behavior.[17]

What makes a denial acceptable? What permits it to go "unquestioned"? In a foundational essay on accounts, the sociologists Marvin B. Scott and Stanford M. Lyman provide an answer: an account (and, so, denial) is most likely to be accepted when it is consistent with cultural expectations—commonsensical beliefs about what "everybody knows" to be true of human behavior and, to a lesser extent, the facts of the bad behavior in question.[18] For instance, everybody knows that "accidents happen." Not surprisingly, many a denier claims, "It was an accident." Rhetorical denials are effective when they bridge the gap, to paraphrase Scott and Lyman's theory of accounts, between individual behavior and socially acceptable explanations of that behavior. Whether others accept a person's rhetorical denial is always an empirical question; we need to investigate how audiences respond to the denial and its user. We'd expect, too, that commonsensical beliefs about human conduct change over time and vary by culture. Still, six decades after Scott and Lyman initially theorized accounts, social scientists still find that competent deniers tend to rely on a relatively limited range of claims. This suggests that there may be an enduring structure to people's seemingly idiosyncratic uses of the rhetoric of denial.

Denial, then, takes two forms: attention-management strategies and rhetorical strategies. The former enable us to silence or hide troubling truths and inconvenient facts, keeping them from pressing into social life. The latter, meanwhile, help us to minimize those troubling truths and inconvenient facts when they intrude. These strategies are the main characters of this book. Focusing on them, I hope to show how it is that people deploy denial to obscure or minimize interpersonal and social problems.

The opening three chapters, especially, pursue these strategies. Chapter 1, "How Not to Notice: Overlooking Interpersonal Problems," shows how people use attention-management strategies and a few key rhetorical tricks to manage embarrassment in their interactions with others. Chapter 2, "How to Be a Bystander: Ignoring Public Problems," shows how small groups exert social psychological pressures that keep people from acknowledging and, so, intervening in public emergencies. Chapter 3, "How to Avoid Blame: Explaining Away Problems," focuses on the full set of rhetorical strategies—disclaimers, excuses, and justifications—that people use to explain away their bad behavior.

Scaling Up: From Interpersonal to Collective Denial

Attention-management and rhetorical strategies of denial operate at the everyday, institutional, and collective levels of social life. While similar strategies of denial are used at each level, the distinctions remain vital. Institutional and collective denial is considerably more complex and impactful than is everyday denial. As denial "scales up" through these levels, those using it can mobilize greater resources, involve the active participation and passive acquiescence of more people, and erase more significant social problems than those using denial on the interactional level.

The second half of this book focuses on the different scales at which denial operates. Chapter 4, "How to Conceal Misconduct: Organizations Hiding Problems," shows how organizational actors normalize and then hide corruption, illegality, and immorality. Organizational forms of denial simultaneously enable and protect masses of perpetrators. The scope of the sexual abuse scandals involving Larry Nassar at Michigan State, Jerry Sandusky at Penn State, and Harvey Weinstein at Miramax offers evidence of this. This is because organizations—workplaces, corporations, educational institutions, athletic programs, and the like—tightly organize people into partially closed groups. Organizations can produce their own realities that normalize unethical behavior, integrate their members into those realities, and then cover their tracks, keeping outsiders from learning of their secrets.

At the organizational level, denial becomes more structured and bureaucratic than at the interpersonal level. Organizations socialize their members into states of denial through formal trainings and informal mentorships, as well as with quasi-legal and legal documents (such as those prohibiting public disclosures of organizational activities). Knowledge production, too, is more central to organizational denial than it is to interpersonal denial. On the interpersonal level, people can try to hide information about themselves; they avoid raising certain topics in discussions and manage their personal "paper trails" by deleting texts or social media posts. At the organizational level, however, the effort is more extensive and involves substantially vaster records and people. It can involve strategies to intimidate or ignore whistleblowers, the organizational actors who bring knowledge to the attention of others. It can involve the curation of a paper trail that systematically excludes damaging facts or buries those damaging facts in extraneous information. Organizations also control knowledge by controlling the information that outsiders can access. When all else fails, they can produce junk science, partial truths and outright lies masquerading as facts, as tobacco, opioid, and petroleum companies have done to obscure the dangers of their products. The strategies of attention management, then, are not simply interactional; they also take uniquely organizational forms.

Organizations and institutions go to great lengths to keep their questionable, if not outright criminal, actions hidden. But through the revelations of whistleblowers or investigative journalists, intentional leaks of information, or accidental disclosures, some secrets eventually come to light. Scandals trail such revelations. But like the everyday deniers who turn to excuses when others are no longer satisfied to overlook their bad behavior, those ensnared by scandal have further recourse in denial.

Chapter 5, "How to Avoid Scandal: Elites Managing Problems," follows the processes of scandal management.

Here, the strategies of denial parallel those used at the everyday level. Elite politicians, corporate leaders, and media members use excuses and justifications, just as the rest of us do in our daily lives. They, too, try to change the topic of conversations by pivoting and shaping the agenda of others. One of the core differences, though, is that elite deniers are far better resourced than the rest of us. Their statements are usually scripted by others who are skilled in rhetoric, public relations, and scandal management. Statements that need to be performed live are rehearsed. Elite deniers also perform their denials on stages crafted for the occasion, with flags, photos of family, and other symbols of their righteousness completing their scenes. And they can embed these denials into prerecorded speeches or advertisements.

Elite deniers, to borrow from the work of cultural sociologist Jeffrey Alexander, control the "means of symbolic production," the material and cultural resources necessary to produce effective mass portrayals of problems.[19] This extends to control over information. Just as organizations can shape the contours of what others know about their inner workings, elite actors ensnared in scandals can influence how investigations of those very scandals unfold. This is particularly true of elite political actors, who can appoint allies to conduct investigations, limit the scope of investigations by defining what's in and out of bounds, and set protracted timelines that help dampen public concern.[20]

This does not mean, however, that elite actors are free to use denial in any way that they want. Powerful actors tend to shape their denials to the documentary evidence that reveals their misconduct.[21] They tend to meet anonymous allegations with outright denials. When documentary evidence is more direct and damning, as when video recordings reveal the violence of state actors, elite deniers usually pivot toward reinterpretations and justifications for what the evidence reveals.[22] Unlike everyday deniers, elite deniers must also craft denials that resonate with diverse public audiences. To do this, they frequently stock their denials with references and allusions to collective values and histories. These are usually deployed in predictable ways, in an attempt to tether the elite denier to sacred symbols.[23] And elite deniers must anticipate, preempt, and respond to the counterclaims of their critics, who are invested in revealing the artifice, inconsistencies, and outright lies supporting denial. Scandal management, then, tends to involve a series of moves and countermoves, which shape how elite actors deploy denial.

Finally, organizational and elite denials give enduring shape to the problems being denied. These denials can be embedded in documentary records that describe problems, such as archives, investigations, reports, educational materials, or transcripts. They can also take the shape of cultural objects, such as memorials or museum exhibits. In these ways, present-day denial may become historical and collective denial, as cultural and textual artifacts become part of a collective memory in which problems have been erased or minimized. For instance, here in Colorado, the 1864 massacre of Cheyenne and Arapaho people at Sand Creek was long downplayed on a monument outside the state's capitol in Denver. The monument listed the event as one of many military "battles" that Colorado soldiers participated in during the Civil War. Erected in 1909 and designed by a member of the cavalry that committed the massacre, the monument's rendition remained for ninety years, when an interpretive marker was added to the monument to clarify that the "battle" was, in fact, a massacre. (The statue was toppled by protesters in June 2020, and the state intends to replace it with a memorial to the victims of the Sand Creek massacre.)[24]

In the end, the divides between everyday, organizational, and collective denials of problems are not as stark as these previous paragraphs make them seem. Organizational and collective denial flow down through everyday interactions, contributing to the socialization of attention and the everyday rhetoric of denial. Denial's fate, then, is to return to everyday life. Chapter 6, "How to Hide in Plain Sight: Denying Racism," addresses, as chapter 1 does, the everyday uses of denial. But rather than focus on interpersonal problems—mistakes, embarrassment, and the various blunders associated with living life in real time—chapter 6 shows how everyday forms of denial are deployed to erase or downplay genuinely collective problems.

There is a complex interplay between everyday, organizational, and collective denials of social problems.[25] On one hand, organizational and collective denials of problems structure everyday encounters with denial, as when students learn from textbooks specifically designed by educational boards and publishers to erase certain claims about historical events. On the other hand, in their everyday denials of problems, people creatively deploy collective denial. In private conversations, for instance, people may explain away problems by adapting the excuses and justifications that politicians and media claims makers also use.[26] And everyday denial can itself be a creative, generative process, socializing people into the denial of problems even before they encounter institutional or collective denials.

Across chapters 1–5, I take a broad and synthetic approach to denial, drawing on research into a range of interpersonal and collective problems. Unlike many books on denial, which focus on a particular case (climate change or torture, to name two), these chapters focus on not a particular problem but the more general types of denial and their various examples. I do so to reveal how a lot of different people are using the same tools of denial to address different situations, to paraphrase the sociologist Joel Best's case for using multiple examples to illustrate social phenomena.[27] I follow, too, Zerubavel's approach to studying "conspiracies of silence" in *The Elephant in the Room*. Like Zerubavel, I try to "highlight general patterns that transcend any particular social situation," and I "deliberately oscillate" among widely different examples and cases "to emphasize the distinctly generic properties" of denial.[28]

By contrast, chapter 6 addresses the everyday denial of one particular problem: racism. Even as this chapter narrows its focus, it also illustrates two general processes that occur across the denial of social problems. The first entails the interplay between institutional, collective, and everyday denial. Institutional and collective processes of denial structure everyday uses of denial. They do so by withholding information from or framing it for everyday actors, shaping their understanding of social problems. They also provide rhetorical templates for use to minimize social problems in everyday discourse. For instance, in chapter 6, we see how educational institutions cultivate curricula that whitewash the history of racism, keeping some students from adequately understanding systemic racism's living legacies. We see, too, how the disclaimers and excuses of political elites who deny racism reappear in everyday discourse. The second process is that by which people—often, though not exclusively, white people—adapt the generic forms of denial, described in the previous chapters, and fit them for use to deny a specific problem. These processes are endemic to our everyday negotiations of social problems and, so, this chapter is meant to help the reader see and anticipate this process across problems.

But I do not intend to dissolve the denial of racism into the broader study of denial. Rather, my intent is to bring the analytic vocabulary of the sociology of denial to scholarship on white privilege and racial domination. Doing so, the chapter shows how both attention-management and rhetorical strategies of denial efface the reality of systemic racism and serve as a central tool in its maintenance.

* * *

Denial can feel like a force with its own volition, erasing problems so thoroughly that ignorance of those problems is automatic and awareness, by contrast, impossible. For this reason, social scientists sometime speak of *states* of denial, as if denial is a semipermanent reality independent of human activities and the cultural artifacts people produce.[29] I'm tempted by this language, too. Throughout this book, I'll describe denial as if it is agentic, as if a force called "denial" itself does the denying. But I mean such descriptions figuratively, and I offer them to keep the focus on the *strategies* of denial, rather than on the myriad examples, with their casts of characters, presented in each chapter.

In fact, the interplay between organizational, collective, and everyday denial suggest that "states" of denial must be continually maintained. Denial is a moment-by-moment achievement, if we can call it that, of interpersonal, organizational, and collective actions. Through these actions, groups of people push distressing facts into the background of everyday life or downplay them when they do intrude.

Certainly, this is the case, at least, in relatively open and pluralistic societies, in which multiple perspectives on problems persist and people compete to foreground or background particular problems. Under these conditions, the achievement of anything like a collective state of denial is precariously maintained, moment by moment, interaction by interaction. It requires vigilance to keep that which is denied indeed denied.

It is impossible to underestimate denial. People have strategies to deny any and all things, no matter how credibly demonstrated those things are. But we must not overestimate denial. It belongs to us and to our collective life. It only does the work that we ask of it.

1

HOW NOT TO NOTICE

Overlooking Interpersonal Problems

THE elementary forms of denial are those that you and I use, every day, to manage embarrassment in our encounters with others. Here, denial appears at its lightest. It aims at minor disruptions, the proverbial "food in the teeth" of a speaker. It mingles with humor, the laughter we use to make light of our mistakes. And it serves us well, protecting our relationships while doing relatively little harm to social life.

Consider, for instance, this scene. Each year, for the past several, I've intentionally bungled my first-day performance in my sociology of denial course. Once, I buttoned my shirt incorrectly, the right side tugged upward by the wayward button. The next year, I donned an inside-out sweater, the seams showing and the tag, too. The year after that, I introduced myself to students while wearing a smear of ketchup across my face. Most recently, as a remote educator, I angled my webcam badly, so only the top of my head was visible to students as I delivered my first-day lecture.

These sorts of "norm violation" exercises are typical of sociology and criminology courses.[1] They allow sociologists and their students to observe, describe, and analyze how others respond to unexpected, embarrassing events. But what we typically find is not so dramatic. When faced with the unexpected behavior of another, most people will try to appear as if they haven't noticed.

At least that's what I find, year after year. As I meander through my scripted, first-day lecture, students try to pretend that they haven't noticed my mistakes. Those seated at the front of my physical classrooms work especially hard as they remain, mercilessly, under my gaze. They maintain uncommonly disciplined eye contact, the better to keep their eyes from appearing to notice that something's amiss. If I dare step toward them, they look down. Or else they try the opposite: a stare straight through me at the PowerPoint slides projected at the front of the room. Those at the back of the room smother the suggestion of a smirk.

It usually takes forty minutes or more for some courageous student to draw attention to my mistake. And this usually happens only after I've helped the intervention along by asking students to offer familiar phrases for denial. "Head in the sand," they say. "Hidden in plain sight," they offer. The phrases all seem to allude to my blunder and, as we share them, it becomes increasingly difficult for students to avoid speaking about the elephant in the room.

These responses are not unusual. In fact, my exercise in embarrassment merely replicates the work of sociologists Shane Sharp and Gregory T. Kordsmeier, who conducted the (awkwardly titled) "shirt-weenie" exercise to teach students at the University of Wisconsin–Madison about the uses of tact. (What's a "shirt-weenie"? It's when the bottom of a dress shirt is threaded and then zippered through the fly of one's pants. It's not, as far as I'm aware, a common mistake people make when dressing.[2]) Nor are these responses limited to the artificial environment of the classroom. Every day, we encounter mildly uncomfortable situations: a supervisor with an undone zipper; co-workers with something vague, yet still off-putting, visible in their noses; and public speakers with meals squirreled away in the gaps of teeth, edges of mouths, or facial hair. Advice on how to confront these situations abounds. Those who give the advice suggest that we act with care and tact, the better to avoid drawing prolonged attention to these problems and their people.[3]

But why should such minor issues provoke such weak responses from us? Why are we so unlikely to help, to ease the collective discomfort by simply letting each other know of our blunders? Why would we, in other words, prefer to deny the obvious mistakes of others?

Erving Goffman and the Denial of Embarrassment

The problem, the Canadian sociologist Erving Goffman discovered over a half-century ago, is that embarrassment threatens to undo so much: our identities, our senses of each other, and our shared sense of how to act within social situations.[4] Rather than confront embarrassment directly, we sidle up to it, hoping it won't notice us noticing. Much of what we call denial is simply our individual and collective willingness to pretend that something disturbing, if only mildly so, has not, in fact, occurred.

Goffman revealed this by closely attending to the ways that people interact with each other. But he went further, intentionally embarrassing colleagues, students, and acquaintances to watch their responses.[5] Indeed, Goffman's academic influence might only have been matched by his notoriety. The sociologist John Irwin, a close friend of Goffman, contended that Goffman's work might "stand as the most important body of sociology produced in the 60s and 70s."[6] Yet even Irwin left Goffman off his own dissertation committee because of Goffman's reputation for giving graduate students—and note the vagueness of Irwin's words here as its own kind of denial—"a lot of trouble."[7] Goffman was known to insult friends, colleagues, even those he'd just met. He'd untactfully comment on others' apparent weaknesses, professional achievements, or tastes in clothing, music, furniture, even spouses.[8] He could undo social gatherings, publicly eviscerating hosts of parties and interrogating guests.[9]

I recall, twenty years on now, a story that my undergraduate social theory professor shared with the class. While at the University of Pennsylvania in the 1970s and early 1980s, Goffman might offer a hostess of a faculty party a pittance for her efforts, a handful of small bills on the way out of the party. The insult was double: to rudely turn the evening into a cold, commercial exchange and to do so with just a few dollars, suggesting the cheapness of the event.[10] That these parties were meant to signal so much—the (usually) male faculty member's social standing and, given the gender and economic roles of the time, his choice of a wife—added insult to insult.[11]

Was Goffman staging difficult interactions to observe, as a sociologist would, what unfolds? Maybe. Or perhaps it was a provocation. The sociologist John Lofland, another friend of Goffman, describes Goffman as using his "exquisitely cruel" wit as a "social catalyst" to electrify social events.[12] According to others, Goffman bristled at both the rules of social engagement and those whom they benefited, those whom Goffman famously described as "normals"—the "young, married, white, urban, northern, heterosexual Protestant father of college education, fully employed, of good complexion, weight, and height, and a recent record in sports."[13] According to those who knew Goffman, the roots of this opposition were deep. Goffman grew up Jewish in provincial Canada, at a time of rampant anti-Semitism.[14] He stood around 5'3" and was often the shortest man in the room.[15] He studied the mechanics of interaction, at a time when seemingly more serious concerns of social structure dominated sociology. In a field of competitors, each trying to dominate others, Goffman sided with the underdogs of social life.[16]

So, embarrassment was central to both Goffman's biography and his research. But if we are to make anything of Goffman's life, perhaps it should be that his sister, Frances Bay, was a successful television and film actress for nearly a half-century. Bay is best known as a character actor, playing the role that her physical appearance most seemed to embody: grandmothers (to *Happy Days*'s Fonzie and Adam Sandler's *Happy Gilmore*) and various "old ladies" (as "Mabel," the so-called Marble Rye Lady, in *Seinfeld*, for instance).[17] When Goffman theorized social interaction, he turned his work, much as his sister had, to the theater. His was a dramaturgical theory of social life, in which people "perform" their identities, much as actors perform roles, for their audiences. To understand embarrassment and our efforts to deny it, we first need to understand the ways that people perform for others.

Embarrassment and the Performance of Self

The departure point for Goffman's theory of identity is the performance, for it is through acting in social performances that people create and sustain their identities. It isn't clear if Goffman meant that people are literally actors, or rather metaphorical ones, on the social stage. In fact, he seemed to have us as both. "All the world is not, of course, a stage, but the crucial ways in which it isn't are not easy to specify," he wrote.[18]

But whether we are actors or merely *like* actors, so much depends on our ability to act. With our very selves at stake, we rarely leave things to chance. Rather, we plan and rehearse performances, particularly those with high stakes. We do this in what Goffman referred to as our back stage, a setting where we are out of sight and earshot of our audiences.[19] There, we try on what Goffman referred to as our "personal fronts," the "expressive equipment . . . that we most intimately identify" with our self, such as outfits and accessories, makeup and hairstyles, even gestures and expressions.[20] We may rehearse a script of the verbal elements of our performances. We think through the (clever?) turns of phrases we'll deploy and the (enthralling?) anecdotes we'll share. Perhaps we'll even script the entire thing, reading and rehearsing until the written words seem to emerge spontaneously. We gather the props for our performances, objects that we can use to embellish our actions. Once ready—or once required—we enter the front stage. There, we find ourselves open to the gaze of an audience. There, we perform.[21]

Our performances succeed when we give the impression of having mastered—or, if the audience is generous enough, nearly mastered—all of this. We hope, in other words, that the self we perform appears to pour from our very being. By way of example, let's stay, for only a while longer, with the character who opened this chapter: the professor, preparing and performing for a class. In my classes, I try to manage my students' impressions of me as a college professor. I try, in other words, to perform this role in a way that elicits from students the response that I want: that they treat me as if I'm a competent college professor, someone capable of leading a classroom of students through an hour of lecture and discussion about the sociology of this or that. As Goffman would have it, this identity isn't securely stored inside me, as we usually think it is. Rather, my identity as a college professor is imputed, or attributed, to me by my audience of students, depending on how effectively I perform my role vis-à-vis their expectations for it.[22]

Knowing this, back stage, protected from watchful students, I prepare. I plan my time with them, drafting and practicing the (riveting?) lectures, (provoking?) discussion questions, and (engaging?) activities. I build my most important props, tinkering with PowerPoint slides and composing handouts. If there's time, I'll visit the setting of my performance, arranging desks or my Zoom background and checking that other key props, such as the overhead projector that will show my slides or my webcam, work. Despite these efforts, and despite my decade of experience in the classroom, this performance can still go wrong. Here's a partial list of blunders that, mercifully, are rare enough and usually occur singularly.

I can mismanage my personal front. I sometimes spill my cup of tea on my desk, my shoes, and my lecture notes. Once, I choked on a sip of water and no amount of physical work could make the choking stop. I'm not the only unlucky one. A colleague reports she showed up to class with the size sticker still stuck to a new shirt. Another reports having been caught in a downpour while biking to class and having to teach in his intramural basketball uniform instead of in his expected, professorial costume.

I can mishandle my props. I sometimes leave my lecture notes or outline in my office. Or I forget to reorder a PowerPoint presentation to match it to my lecture notes; I find myself looking back, aghast, as it displays a different concept than the one I'm describing. Absentmindedly, I leave my bag in the path that I usually pace and, even more absentmindedly, I step through its straps, stumbling.

I can lack what Goffman called "dramaturgical discipline," the ability or focus needed to execute the planned performance.[23] As I deliver the lecture, I forget my lines. As I deliver my lecture, I deliver the correct lines but badly, a hitch in my voice when I arrive at a polysyllabic word. Teaching over Zoom, I leave myself muted as I respond to a student's question. Back in the classroom, I forget a student's name and realize this too late, having called on the student, opened my mouth, and found only another's name forthcoming. Or I manage time badly, finding myself left with far more than a responsible instructor should be or running out mid–.

And so on. There may be no limit to the ways our performances can go wrong. Embarrassment stalks us, our often cleverer, sometimes cruder, and always crueler shadow.

Usually, we can quickly and with little work recover from our mistakes. If I remain poised after realizing I've lost my lecture notes, I might pose a discussion question to the class, sneak out as students talk in small groups, and recover a copy from my office. But some blunders endure, with palpable consequences. Goffman describes the effects of a disrupted performance well: "The social interaction . . . may come to an embarrassed and confused halt; the situation may cease to be defined, previous positions may become no longer tenable, and participants may find themselves without a charted course of action. The participants typically sense a false note in the situation and come to feel awkward, flustered, and, literally, out of countenance."[24]

If you have ever sat in a room as a speaker or teacher attempts to force a projector to display their computer screen, you've probably felt this. As it occurs to the unfortunate presenter that the prop may never work, they realize that the performance cannot go on, though it must. The prop was too central; the presenter's notes, meanwhile, too thin to support a spontaneous presentation. The presenter feels their face getting warm. They wonder if they're blushing and, if they are, whether those in the audience have noticed. They murmur something meant to deflate the tension in the room. But the audience, silent, swats it away, unsure of what to do to salvage the situation and increasingly annoyed that the speaker has put them in this position. No one knows what will happen next.

Embarrassment threatens the identity that performers claim for themselves. But it does more than that. Embarrassment, like other emotions, is contagious.[25] Another's poor performance can feel like it also belongs to the audience. Audience members might blush on behalf of the performer. They may want to look away, cover their eyes, or flee. Or they may sense that they can no longer passively watch the main actor. Rather, they need to improvise and help the struggling actor salvage their performance.[26] If a professor so badly flubs their performance that they no longer appear up to that role, then students, too, are corrupted. After all, the performative role of the student is predicated on the professor competently performing their role. Acute embarrassment, then, can undo an entire situation. The façade of social life—shared expectations and scripted roles that are easy to perform—comes down. In its place, embarrassment or worse, a disorienting unease, moves in.[27]

Denial as Antidote: On the Management of Embarrassment

Both actors and their audiences, then, have a stake in managing disruptions to performances. And both have strategies to do this. Goffman referred to these strategies, which are both verbal and nonverbal, as face work. Face work, according to Goffman, has two functions. We use face work to defend ourselves from embarrassment (defensive face work) and to protect others from it (protective face work). Importantly, the line between defensive and protective face work is porous. If embarrassment is contagious, then our protection of others often involves efforts to inoculate ourselves from "catching" their embarrassment, so to speak.

Goffman's primary interest was in social interaction, not denial. But, in my view, the face-work strategies that he first described are indeed the elementary forms of denial. Face-work strategies allow people to (pretend to) overlook or minimize potentially embarrassing disruptions in everyday interactions with others. When deployed effectively, face-work strategies allow people to either keep embarrassment in the background of social life or minimize it when it steps into the foreground. In this way, such uses of denial do two laudable things at once. They prevent minor blunders from ruining people's social identities. And they allow people to preserve smooth social interactions in the face of disruptions.

Sociologists working in Goffman's intellectual wake have shown how both defensive and protective face work can be used to keep embarrassing behavior and mistakes in the background of social interactions. They've also revealed how face-work strategies can be used to minimize those mistakes when they intrude into social life. The former are interactional strategies of attention management. These allow us to avoid, hide, or overlook embarrassment, preventing it from entering collective attention in the first place. The latter are behavioral and communicative strategies to minimize information. These allow the embarrassing event into the foreground of social life, but they reframe and, so, weaken it. Both strategies can be used defensively, to save oneself from embarrassment, or protectively, to bail out others.

Attention-Management Strategies: Avoiding, Hiding, and Overlooking Embarrassment

A preemptive way to defend against embarrassment is to use avoidance, dodging situations in which it's likely to occur.[28] For instance, students who expect to receive a poor grade on an exam might decide not to attend the class when graded exams are returned, avoiding face-to-face encounters with other students. Those brave enough to attend class and receive their exams may immediately use hiding techniques, stuffing tests into bags overflowing with papers. This allows students who have bombed an exam to feign ignorance of their grades and pretend it is forever lost if another student asks them how they did.[29] Similarly, consumer research suggests that customers at grocery stores bury purchases that they feel are embarrassing, such as condoms, in carts filled with other goods.[30]

Brown bagging, the act of publicly drinking liquor from a paper bag, is another common form of hiding. Unlike the bag, the act itself is transparent. Everyone knows what drinking from a container in a paper bag means. Still, "brown-baggin' your beer allows cops"—and other pedestrians, passersby, and public transit riders, too—"to ignore you and pretend that there could be anything in that paper bag."[31] But brown bagging is not just for drinkers. In the early 1970s, David Karp, a sociologist at Boston College, described brown bags as "shields" for men who made purchases at pornographic bookstores.[32] Even bingo players brown bag. Despite the game's association with churches and wholesome retirees, bingo is, technically, a form of gambling, and many players prefer to keep their bingo habits to themselves. Kim M. King, a sociologist who studied face-work strategies among bingo players, describes one player hiding her seemingly harmless chips and stamps in brown paper bags. "I don't want my neighbors to know that I play bingo," this player told King. "It's not something to brag about."[33]

Typically, hiding and avoidance techniques are defensive forms of face work. But, to do their defensive work, they require a tactful audience and so involve protective forms as well.[34] For the student who bombed their test to successfully "hide" it, classmates must play along that the exam is indeed lost. Cashiers must not linger on the mildly embarrassing item as they scan it. And others must not inquire too much of the brown bagger.

Today, technology helps our efforts to avoid or hide from potentially embarrassing situations, dodging the risks of living life among others in real time.[35] Learning-management systems, such as Canvas or Blackboard, deliver grades to students impersonally. Self-checkouts at grocery stores allow customers to avoid potentially embarrassing interactions with cashiers. But why even leave one's home to shop? Nearly every consumer product, no matter how mortifying, can be purchased from an online retailer. These purchases, in turn, are dropped on empty doorsteps in smiling brown boxes that advertise the retailer, not the wares within. Even still, technology users, particularly those of social media, find ways to discredit themselves. They may desperately "hide" their offense by deleting a social media post, only to find that the web remembers all.

Stalling is a related face-work strategy. Like avoidance, stalling is used by public performers who anticipate embarrassment. However, stalling is used when the performer must, in fact, perform. By stalling, we wait out embarrassment by filling the time in which it might appear onstage with us. For instance, performers who realize that they don't know their next line often use verbal ploys to stall until they can will it into existence. Freestyle rappers use "canned resources" of set lines and rhymes to buy time when their next line resists them.[36] Public speakers do something similar. "Have some ready transitions to use in any presentation," *Forbes* advises.[37] Unskilled ones, however, might find stalling does little to salvage their performances, as too many "umms," "uhhs," and false starts overwhelm even a generous audience.

If we cannot wait out embarrassment, we may try redirection, shifting attention away from our mortification, hiding it, so to speak, in plain sight. In conversations, we change the subject, leaving potentially embarrassing topics behind. Savvy audiences, meanwhile, may use protective forms of redirection to support others. When a freestyle rapper finds himself stalling for too long, his words falling off and his filler failing too, another rapper may interrupt, offering the next line, and drawing attention to herself.[38] Teachers often do this for students who seem to have lost the meaning of their words during a classroom discussion. In these cases, we'll gently interrupt students, restate their points, tether their points to class themes, and move the discussion along. All the while, the class's attention snaps from the floundering student to the teacher in the front of the room. I regularly use this strategy when a guest speaker's technology fails in my classroom. Stepping to the front of a room, I'll say to my students, "As we allow Professor So-and-So to set up their slides, I want to talk about this week's assignments." Behind me, in the sort of back stage I've created through redirection, the guest presenter's body sheds its stress. My students, meanwhile, interact with me, rather than staring, stone-faced, at a professor failing in their effort at using basic technology.

Performers can also use poise to mask embarrassing or discrediting behavior, controlling or hiding those "parts" of their front that might give away their inner feelings. Public speakers, for instance, hide their trembling hands behind a podium until the nerves pass. They'll likely avoid displaying them, too, by, say, picking up a glass of water, which would surely exaggerate and also reveal the shaking.[39] (My first experiences teaching were like this. I could hardly stand to drink my coffee, my hands were trembling so much with anxiety.) Goffman knew this well, telling Sherri Cavan, a grad student of his in the 1960s, not to smoke during an oral exam because, "when you go to light your cigarette, your hands are going to shake, and then everyone will know how nervous you are."[40] Goffman, in his typical (and naively?) tactless way, gave the advice right before Cavan was to take the exam, ensuring maximum anxiety.

Poise, as a form of defensive face work, implies its protective twin: tactful obliviousness.[41] Goffman describes this as a "studied nonobservance" to the source of embarrassment.[42] Remaining tactfully oblivious, we appear as if we have not noticed an obviously noticeable, embarrassing thing about or committed by another person. We keep on a face that shows no recognition of the blunder. Perhaps we maintain eye contact, sometimes an unnatural amount, to avoid having our eyes roam over the trouble. Conversationally, we stay on topic, never allowing our words to wander over to the mistake. But should we decide to intervene, even our efforts at helping are tactful. To avoid drawing unnecessary attention to the source of embarrassment, we often let others' obvious mistakes stand until, in private, we can correct them.

Reframing Embarrassment: Alibis, Humor, and Demonstrative Displays

If we can't avoid, hide from, or wait out embarrassment, we can try to reframe it. We admit, at least implicitly, that the troubling event occurred. We just deny its nature, transforming it into something that doesn't threaten us: normal behavior, comedy, or an opportunity to correct oneself.

To reframe potentially discrediting behavior, we may develop an alibi, using behaviors and alternative accounts to explain away our actions. Using an alibi, people try to reframe a potentially damaging event as something benign. Linguistically, one offers a credible, alternative explanation for one's behavior. For instance, a student, suffering from a hangover, tells his professor he has a migraine or stomach bug, which is, frankly, true enough.

Our audiences can also protectively provide us an alibi, downplaying our blunders and reframing them as minor mistakes that might happen to anyone. This is typical of student responses to the breaching exercise I use on the first day of my denial course. Students who inform me of my faux pas try to protect me from embarrassment even as they draw attention to my mistake. One year, a student (correctly) imputed knowledge and motive to my inside-out sweater, drawing attention to it in front of the class while also asking if I did it as a class exercise. This student provided me an alibi. Had I not intended my shirt to be inside-out, I could pretend that I had, transforming my unadorned shame into an appropriate class topic by invoking the student's alibi of the "class exercise." I suspect, too, that the student was engaging in a bit of defensive face work for themselves. After all, it's generally taboo to comment on the appearance of other people, particularly authority figures, in the middle of public performances. This student framed their comments as appropriate classroom conversation, making them less about my appearance and more about the pedagogical purpose of it.

Anticipating the need to account for ourselves, we can also build alibis into our behavior. Doing so, we transform behavior that threatens our identity into "acceptable" or normal behavior. For instance, a visitor to Colorado, curious about but still uncomfortable with marijuana, might seem to enter a pot shop at random, but only after window shopping through a full block of stores hawking hats, t-shirts, and pot, too.[43] Here, the tourist, if called to account for their visit to the shop or let alone a purchase, can claim benign consumer curiosity and deflect from their interest in the not-yet-fully-destigmatized drug.

Humor, though, may be the most powerful way to reframe and thereby downplay mistakes and blunders. You've probably seen it: the sly smile and chuckle given by the pedestrian who stumbles while crossing an intersection or wipes out, feet over head, on a patch of ice.[44] Punch lines may follow. "Gravity still works," one may announce. Or "I meant to do that. Want to see me do it again?"[45] Those who experience particularly powerful embarrassments—having a chair break under one's weight, for instance—might lose themselves and their audiences in laughter, allowing that visceral response, rather than the more threatening embarrassment, to go viral. It is as if we are in on the gag, as if we have planned this bit of physical comedy the whole time. Our mistakes, we convey, should not be taken seriously.[46]

It's a robust thing, humor. Spencer Cahill, whose work on social interaction extended Goffman's, documented people's use of humor in a number of potentially distressing or embarrassing situations. Writing with a team of undergraduates who had studied public restroom behavior, Cahill notes that people use humor to manage the embarrassing smells they leave in bathrooms. "Something died in there," one restroom user says to another, the former having, in Cahill's careful words, "filled the bathroom with a strong fecal odor."[47]

In another study, Cahill and Robin Eggleston examine the emotional work of wheelchair users who often confront and then need to manage difficult social encounters with strangers. When the built environment, their bodies, or their chairs do not cooperate, wheelchair users sometimes fend off embarrassment, as well as others' anxieties, by transforming distressing situations into comedy. Eggleston, herself a wheelchair user, describes one such situation:

> I wheeled up to the entrance to a dressing room while my friend held a number of garments. I forgot to set the brakes on my chair, so when I started to raise myself up with my crutches the chair went rolling backwards while I went falling forward onto the floor. My friend stood there with this look of alarm until I started laughing. The two of us started laughing, and then a saleswoman came rushing over: "My goodness, are you all right?" I answered "Yes, I'm fine" while still laughing. Her facial expression went from alarm to unconcern in a flash, once she realized we were laughing.[48]

For humor to do its face work, we need our audiences to protectively play (or laugh) along with us. If they respond with silence, then humor will have failed to do its corrective work. In such cases, embarrassment is doubled. The original embarrassment stands, but now, too, we experience an awkward discomfort for our failed comedy routine. One wheelchair user recounted to Cahill and Eggleston her experience in a mall restroom:

> There was a whole line of people waiting to get into these two stalls. It was packed. And I'm trying to back up and not doing a very good job of it and having to start over again, bumping into the washbasin. I finally get myself around, with all these people obviously watching me. There was dead silence. So I finally got myself out, and I looked up at all these people and I went "Now, I would like a big round of applause, please." Nobody did anything. It was like you can't make a joke about this stuff. I thought "Give me a break."[49]

A person can also use humor to protect another's self-image, even as the former knowingly risks embarrassing the latter. David A. Snow, Cherylon Robinson, and Patricia McCall's 1991 ethnography of singles bars shows how women use protective face work to simultaneously reject heterosexual men's advances while avoiding embarrassing those men. If, as Goffman suggests, an embarrassed person may lash out, this risk is particularly acute, severe, and real for women in their encounters with heterosexual men.[50] And, so, a woman may try to reverse the flow of shame, using self-deprecating humor to reject a man, while leaving that man feeling unrejected and his sense of his masculine self intact.[51]

If humor signals that we're "in on the joke" of ours or others' embarrassment, disciplinary displays allow us to signal that we're "in on the norms" that our behavior violated.[52] Disciplinary displays convey that we're aware of our mistakes. Others, then, need not correct or sanction us. By signaling awareness, we seem to side with our audience against ourselves. Cahill puts this well, writing, "offending individuals metaphorically split themselves in two: a sacred self that assigns blame and a blameworthy . . . self. Because the offending individual assigns blame, moreover, there is no need for others to do so."[53]

Using disciplinary displays, we flirt with embarrassment. Doing so, we may briefly sacrifice our role in a situation. But we do so with a purpose. Following the sacrifice comes an act of redemption. Condemning ourselves, we demonstrate that we are "disturbed by the fact" of our failure, as Goffman puts it, and, so, "may prove worthy at another time."[54] A speaker who stumbles on a word exaggerates the mistake, haltingly spitting the sentence that follows. Those who stumble cast blame by peering down at their feet. Those who walk into a bathroom labeled for the "wrong" gender may shake their heads and mumble a condemnation to themselves as they walk out, letting others know that they, too, realize something is wrong. After using a stall and leaving, again, that "strong fecal odor," a person may "facially display disgust."[55]

People may also use disciplinary displays when they sense that others view them as the lead actors, responsible for the behavior of supporting actors: parents for children, dog owners for their pets, and adult children for their elderly parents, for example. Used on behalf of another, disciplinary displays, such as instructing a child that "it's not polite to stare" or compelling a dog to sit after it has lunged at a passerby, do several things at once.[56] They may socialize the supporting actor (the child or the pet), helping this actor become a competent social performer. But like disciplinary displays more generally, they do defensive face work for the lead actors, allowing them to signal to aggrieved others that they, indeed, respect the rules of social interaction.[57] And though disciplinary displays draw attention to the shortcomings of the supporting actor, these tactics offer a bit of protective face work. Using a disciplinary display, the leading actor downplays the supporting actor's behavior. The display does so by suggesting to the audience that the supporting actor is redeemable; their shortcomings are not inherent, but rather a developmental stage to be corrected with additional socialization.

* * *

Denial, when it takes the form of face work, can be a balm, soothing social interactions inflamed by blunders, stumbles, and other embarrassing mistakes. In this way, these everyday uses of denial are a special case. Their pro-social effects allow us to pretend that minor disruptions to social life didn't happen or aren't, in fact, disruptions at all. It allows us and our social life to survive. We can pretend that struggling performers are competent, allowing them to *become* competent again and permitting us to set the nearly ruined situation right.

But everyday denial has a shadow side. We are uneasy around situations that threaten to embarrass us. We are also just a bit too capable of feigning that we haven't noticed genuine emergencies. Together, these allow us to withdraw from the suffering of others. And they can promote the appearance of apathy, an apathy often thought endemic to contemporary urban life: that of the bystander.

2

HOW TO BE A BYSTANDER

Ignoring Public Problems

I F not for a predawn encounter between strangers, Friday, March 13, 1964, might have remained a bit player in the collective drama of 1960s America. The front page of the next day's *New York Times* reports but minor developments in major histories: a change in US strategy toward North Vietnam, maneuvers by Senate Democrats to advance civil rights legislation, and the beginning of the end of the trial of Jack Ruby, the assassin of John F. Kennedy's assassin.

Deeper in the day's paper, one finds a record of that predawn encounter. Still, that article is easily overlooked. Its neighbors on the paper's twenty-sixth page, a hodgepodge of religious announcements, overwhelm the brief story. Their larger, noisier headlines loom over these words: "Queens Woman Is Stabbed to Death in Front of Home." The article's opening sentences only hint at the story's eventual legacy: "A 28-year-old Queens woman was stabbed to death early yesterday morning outside her apartment in Kew Gardens. Neighbors who were awakened by her screams found the woman, Miss Catherine Genovese of 82–70 Austin Street, shortly after 3 am in front of a building three doors from her home."[1]

Catherine Genovese, better known to history as Kitty Genovese, closed Ev's 11th Hour, a Queens bar where she worked, a little earlier than usual in the early morning that Friday, owing to a lack of customers. As Genovese got into her car, Winston Moseley, who was stalking Queens for a potential victim, spotted her. In his own car, Moseley followed Genovese to her neighborhood, Kew Gardens. There, he attacked her. There, in the stairwell of an apartment not far from her own home, he killed her.[2]

As is apparent from the *New York Times'* initial coverage, the paper and its metro editor, A. M. Rosenthal, were unmoved by Genovese's death. Later in the year, Rosenthal would publish a brief book on the murder. Even then, with an opportunity to account for the blasé coverage of Genovese's death, Rosenthal was unapologetic: "I have no recollection whatever of that four-paragraph story being assigned or written. Early in the job I had come to the delightful rationalization that I could not occupy myself with every little story that came in during the course of the day."[3] He continues,

> The truth also is that if Miss Genovese had been killed on Park Avenue or Madison Avenue an assistant would have called the story to my attention, I would have assigned a top man, and quite possibly we would have had a front-page story the next morning. . . . I can find no philosophical excuse for giving the murder of a middle-class Queens woman less attention than the murder of a Park Avenue broker but

journalistically no apologies are offered—news is not philosophy or theology but what certain human beings, reporters and editors, know will have meaning and interest to other human beings, readers.[4]

It would take two more weeks for Catherine Genovese to become history's Kitty Genovese. And that would take the story coming to matter to Rosenthal. On March 23, Rosenthal had dinner with Michael Joseph Murphy, then the police commissioner of New York City. During the meal, Rosenthal asked the commissioner about Moseley, who, after his arrest for the Genovese murder, had confessed to two other murders. It was a fraught question, and Rosenthal must have known that. The New York Police Department (NYPD) had already made an arrest for one of those other murders and extracted a confession, apparently false, from the suspect.

Instead of admitting that the NYPD coerced a false confession from the wrong person, Murphy used redirection, changing the topic to the apparent bystanders to Genovese's murder. "That Queens story is something else," Murphy told Rosenthal. "Remember, we talk about apathy, public apathy toward law enforcement? Brother, that Queens story is one for the books."[5] Murphy then told Rosenthal that thirty-eight people had witnessed Genovese's attack and yet hadn't called police. Rosenthal recounts: "I experienced then that most familiar of newspapermen's reaction— vicarious shock . . . the realization that what you are seeing or hearing will startle a reader."[6] Murphy's redirection, in other words, had its intended effect. Rather than pursuing an investigation of the NYPD's interrogation practices, Rosenthal pursued a story about citizens' apathy toward law enforcement. (Lost on Rosenthal was this: Public apathy toward the NYPD might be, at least partially, explained by the fact that the city's police were extracting false confessions to murder, allowing the perpetrator to remain free and kill again.)

On Friday, March 27, the *Times* featured a new account of the attack, written by Marty Gansberg, on its front page. This time, the headline blares "37 Who Saw Murder Didn't Call the Police."[7] A large photograph of Kew Gardens, taken from above, dramatizes the attack. Locations where Genovese first noticed Moseley and where he subsequently attacked her are numbered, one through four. The image powerfully illustrates just how close Genovese was to help that never came. The attacks took place right outside an apartment complex, thickly settled, as evidenced by the full parking lot outside of it. And the article opens with these seemingly definitive sentences:

> For more than half an hour 38 respectable, law-abiding citizens in Queens watched a killer stalk and stab a woman in three separate attacks in Kew Gardens. Twice the sound of their voices and the sudden glow of their bedroom lights interrupted him and frightened him off. Each time he returned, sought her out and stabbed her again. Not one person telephoned the police during the assault; one witness called after the woman was dead.[8]

Thus began the story of a now-familiar figure: the apathetic, urban bystander. Today, nearly sixty years later, this figure remains with us. It reminds us of what can happen when we use our facility in feigning ignorance not to protect another from some minor embarrassment, but to close ourselves to others, to deny both their calls for aid and our responsibility for providing it.

The Pathologies of the Urbanite

People use tactful obliviousness to protect others from embarrassment. They have, as described in chapter 1, their motives: they hope to avoid the contagion of embarrassment. And they have their interactional strategies of denial. Passive bystanders, too, have their motives and their strategies for remaining uninvolved in others' troubles. Soon after his dinner with Murphy, Rosenthal sought those motives, tasking another reporter, Charles Mohr, with speaking with New York–area social scientists about urban apathy. Rosenthal remembers the article for the little it offered: "I am fascinated, now, by the threads that ran through the 'reaction' from our professional sources. . . . The reaction of almost every one of these social physicians was to admit total failure on their part to understand, or to look for a comforting bit of jargon, or to reach out for a target."[9]

In fact, for decades, social scientists had prefigured the apathetic bystander in their commentary on urban life. At the start of the twentieth century, Georg Simmel, a German sociologist, offered an influential analysis of contemporary cities, in which he described the "mental attitude" of urban dwellers as one of "reserve." By this, Simmel meant that urban dwellers display a mixture of withdrawal and worried caution toward others. He reasoned that, because of the size and scale of cities, our contacts with others are brief and usually forgettable. "We do not know by sight neighbours of years," Simmel noted. And so we remain strangers.[10] Then he pushed deeper into the psyche of the urban dweller. "The inner side of this external reserve is not only indifference," he concludes, "but more frequently than we believe, it is a slight aversion, a mutual strangeness and repulsion."[11]

Sixty years later, Howard Becker reached a similar conclusion.[12] Borrowing Simmel's notion of reserve, Becker describes the city dweller as one who "minds his own business and does nothing about rule infractions" and crime.[13] Beyond the sheer quantity of interactions in a city, Becker identified two other factors that contribute to urban reserve. One is urban dwellers' attitudes toward the policing, in the broadest sense, of public life. Becker contended that urban dwellers believe that it isn't their responsibility for intervening in the emergencies of their cities. That's the job of police, EMTs, and firefighters—those trained to intervene. And we tend to believe that more enduring problems, the kinds that smolder for years, are the purview of social workers, mental health professionals, policymakers, nonprofits, charities, and citizen-volunteers.[14]

Becker also argued that urban dwellers are less likely to share beliefs, values, and norms than are people who live in smaller, more homogeneous communities. This diversity, many sociologists of the first half of the twentieth century believed, undercut social norms and their enforcement.[15] City dwellers often do not share expectations of how others will act or, even, what others consider normal or appropriate.[16] It follows that a would-be helper can't be sure that others, even those involved in an apparent emergency, need, want, or would welcome help.

Becker's writing on urban life appeared in his classic work on deviance, *Outsiders*. The book was first published in 1963, the year before Genovese's murder. Amid his broad, sociological discussion of reserve is an even more prescient description of the bystander. Becker, offhand and, of course, unaware of what the next year would bring, writes, "Several years ago, a national magazine published a series of pictures illustrating urban reserve. A man lay unconscious on a busy city street. Picture after picture showed pedestrians either ignoring his existence or noticing him and then turning aside to go about their business."[17]

Reserved urbanites have reason to remain reserved. They also have their strategies for remaining reserved. As usual, Erving Goffman, sociology's great observer of everyday behavior, aptly described how people pull off urban reserve. In urban settings, interactions among strangers are marked by what Goffman referred to as civil inattention. Passing strangers give each other brief looks to affirm one's respect for the other's existence. But this visual attention is quickly broken, the passing strangers signaling that no further interaction is needed or desired.[18] Civil inattention gives the impression of urban callousness, if not apathy. Strangers seem to barely register each other's presence. But civil inattention is a central and probably necessary ritual of public life in densely populated areas. Giving and then withdrawing an unobtrusive, brief glance, one passerby affirms the existence of the other, as well as the other's right to be left alone.

When civil inattention turns into what Goffman called non-person treatment, it becomes an uneasy denial of others and their requests for help. When we use non-person treatment, we withdraw visual recognition of the humanity of the other. Like tactful obliviousness, non-person treatment involves the studious appearance of not having noticed something we indeed noticed. But unlike tactful obliviousness, non-person treatment does not function to protect another from embarrassment. Rather, non-person treatment allows its users to erase others from social settings. The user of non-person treatment transforms the other into part of the physical landscape of public life, "as objects not worthy of a glance," rather than as a human whose presence might require something of them.[19] For instance, housed residents of and visitors to cities often use non-person treatment to erase unhoused people.[20] In this, the use of non-person treatment supports everyday denial of an obvious, widespread, and enduring social problem.

The "Discovery" of the Urban Bystander

Even before Rosenthal sent his reporters to investigate the "thirty-eight witnesses," social scientists had described and explained urban apathy. But it's undeniable that Genovese's murder was a tipping point in social scientific research of bystander behavior. This turn of attention to the bystander is its own lesson in denial. Research typically lags behind public attention to problems, and the public usually doesn't recognize latent problems as they stew.[21] We're often caught off guard when an enduring problem takes the form of a horror story, a singular, often violent, and just as often extreme form of the "worst of the worst" of a problem.[22]

Genovese's murder and the "thirty-eight witnesses" provided Rosenthal with just such a horror story. The story affirmed what many already believed: urban dwellers are apathetic, callous, and desensitized to the suffering of others. Recall, after all, Murphy's preface to his story to Rosenthal: "Remember, we talk about apathy, public apathy . . . ." But the story of "thirty-eight witnesses" focused and amplified this assumption, transforming it into a tragic fact. Apathy now burned with the quantifiable intensity of the thirty-eight who did nothing. No matter that reporting, decades later, would reveal that the "thirty-eight" contained a mixture of fact and fiction. There was no definitive list of the witnesses. None of those who witnessed the attack had voyeuristically watched Moseley stalk and kill Genovese. Most of those who could see the attack had limited, obscured, and brief views of an ambiguous confrontation in the street. But most could only hear the attack and didn't know what the sounds, deep in the night, meant. And some witnesses did intervene. One yelled at Moseley to leave Genovese alone, briefly interrupting the assault. Others, in fact, called the police or at least tried to. One—Sophia Farrar, a neighbor and friend of

Genovese—came to Genovese's aid when learning of the attack, comforting her until an ambulance arrived.[23]

Better, then, to think of the thirty-eight witnesses as a parable of the contemporary bystander, not as a factual representation of it, according to psychologists Rachel Manning, Mark Levine, and Alan Collins.[24] It is a story, albeit one with a tragic and too real core, that gestures toward meaning. After the *New York Times* published their parable of the thirty-eight witnesses, social psychologists pursued the moral of the story. What they discovered was the bystander effect, a robust principle of human behavior: people in groups are less likely to help others than are those who are alone.

Two New York City social psychologists were at the vanguard of research into bystander behavior. In the late 1960s, Bibb Latané and John M. Darley, then at Columbia University and New York University (NYU), respectively, ran a series of experiments that revealed people's unwillingness to intervene in emergencies, particularly when the would-be helper is in the presence of others. Latané and Darley's experiments involved nearly 5,000 subjects. Many were unsuspecting college students, left in rooms while all sorts of simulated disasters befall them and others: fires, thefts, falls, and seizures. Other experiments involved strangers in New York City, who were asked to give small amounts of money, time, or information to strangers or to report "thefts" of beer to liquor-store employees.

In 1970, Latané and Darley reported on their experiments in a brief book, *The Unresponsive Bystander: Why Doesn't He Help?* In it, they challenge the prevailing wisdom that urban bystanders are apathetic to those whom they encounter. Rather, they show that people, when alone, will often help and usually fairly quickly. It's when others enter the scene that the potential helper, the proverbial Good Samaritan, becomes the urban bystander. Bystanders are immobilized not by callous indifference or the repulsion that Simmel suspected they harbor. Rather, basic interactional processes freeze them.

Latané and Darley's explanation of bystander behavior begins with the obvious. Before potential helpers can decide whether to act or not in an emergency, they need to notice the incident. But noticing isn't so simple. In a busy setting, one's attention necessarily focuses on what one deems pertinent. Much of the surrounding environment doesn't satisfy that standard and is filtered out.[25] But there are also strategies to intentionally narrow one's attention. Bystanders to an emergency may use non-person treatment of others, withdrawing attention from troubling situations before consciously noticing or, at least, having to admit to themselves or others that they noticed something wrong. This, in turn, keeps bystanders from having to make a decision about intervening in the first place. One of Latané and Darley's experiments, in which students were placed in a room with a confederate who "stole" cash from the experimenters, suggests this. (Confederates, which I'll reference in my discussions of several experiments, are people involved in experiments who pretend to be research subjects. In reality, they're collaborating with the experimenter, who is testing how research subjects respond to the behavior of the confederates.) Those who did not report the theft were asked why they hadn't. Many simply said that they hadn't noticed it, despite, Latané and Darley write, the "obviousness of the theft and the lack of other things to distract their attention."[26]

Noticing an emergency is only the start. If a person is to intervene in a situation, they need to assess it as an actual emergency that requires their action. In a crowd, confronting a potential emergency, people look around to see how others define the situation. With Goffman, we might expect that those witnessing an emergency will use tactful obliviousness, maintaining an appearance of not having noticed the distressing event. Bystanders might do so for two reasons. They might believe that, by feigning obliviousness, they are protecting those involved in the emergency from embarrassment. But they may also do so to defend themselves from appearing deeply involved in an unpredictable, and potentially dangerous, social encounter. As tactful obliviousness washes over faces in a crowd, it drains the situation of urgency. The potential helper, looking around at faces that show little concern, assumes that no concern is warranted.

Latané and Darley refer to this process as pluralistic ignorance.[27] To illustrate it, they ran an experiment in which research subjects (Columbia University undergraduates) waited in a room, allegedly to participate in an interview about urban experiences. As they waited, the room slowly filled with smoke. In one version of the experiment, the subject sat alone. In another, the subject sat with two confederates, students who were also part of the research team. The confederates sat, passively and indifferently, as the room filled with smoke. When alone, the subjects left the waiting room to report the "emergency" 75 percent of the time. When waiting amid the indifferent actors, the report rate dropped to just 10 percent. The presence of other bystanders, unconcerned by the smoke, was sufficient to dull the "emergency."

Why should the presence of others matter? Again, it seems to come down to our fear of humiliation. Pluralistic ignorance promotes what Latané and Darley refer to as audience inhibition. If others seem to define the situation to be a nonemergency, the potential helper becomes unsure of their appraisal of the situation. This is especially so of ambiguous situations, ones that don't appear to be obvious emergencies.[28] In these cases, potential helpers worry that if they *were* to act, others might judge them for misinterpreting the situation.

Others' nonresponses to emergencies inhibit helping. So, too, does the size of the group, or what researchers call diffusion of responsibility. As the size of a group witnessing an emergency increases, the amount of responsibility that each witness feels decreases. Alone, facing an emergency, the would-be Good Samaritan bears all the guilt of inaction. In a group, others lighten his load.[29]

Again, Darley and Latané simulated an emergency to illustrate this. This time, they recruited NYU undergraduates to participate in an experiment allegedly about personal problems. The research subjects were placed in a room with an intercom; they were told that they'd communicate with other students in separate rooms through it. Subjects were further told that only one microphone could be on at a time. Thus, while one student spoke, others could not communicate with the speaker or with the others.

In one version of the experiment, the research subject was paired with a single other "student." This "student" was actually a recording of a student, who first admitted to suffering from seizures and, later, seemed to experience a seizure. In another version, the research subject believed themselves to be in a group of three with one other potential "helper" (also recordings of students, performing a script) and the student stricken by a seizure. A third version increased the group size further, with four other potential helpers and the stricken student. Again, all were recordings of students. In version one, research subjects believed that they were the only potential helper. In version two, they believed that they were one of two potential helpers. And in version three, they believed that they were one of five potential helpers. As the number of potential helpers increased, both the rate and speed of helping decreased. When subjects believed they were the only helper, they responded, on average, within a minute to the "seizure," and 85 percent of those in this scenario tried to provide help. When subjects believed they were one of two helpers, their response time increased to about a minute and a half, and the rate of helping dropped to 62 percent. In the largest groups, subjects took over two and a half minutes to respond and only 31 percent provided help.[30]

From Latané and Darley's initial experiments emerged a fully formed literature on bystander behavior. By 2011, when a team of psychologists in Germany, Austria, England, and the United States conducted a meta-analysis of this research, there was nearly a half-century of work, involving nearly 8,000 research subjects, to consider. That work supports Latané and Darley's initial discovery. People in groups usually intervene less frequently and less quickly to emergencies than do those who are alone.[31] Two caveats, from the meta-analysis, are in order. First, the ambiguity surrounding the emergency is particularly impactful; the bystander effect weakens as the severity and obviousness of the emergency increases.[32] Second, there is evidence that the bystander effect has weakened over time.

This latter trend is especially important. It suggests that people are becoming more willing to intervene in emergencies. We may, the authors of the meta-analysis speculate, owe this to the notoriety of the "thirty-eight witnesses" to Genovese's murder and the amplification of the parable in popular culture. One encounters lessons about bystanders and, even, direct references to the murder of Genovese in films and television shows, such as *Boondock Saints*, *Law & Order*, *Law & Order: SVU*, *Girls*, and *Black Mirror*.[33] On Wikipedia, a lengthy entry describes the bystander effect.[34] On YouTube, pages upon pages of videos describe or simulate the effect. Genovese's murder and the bystander effect are also featured in most popular psychology textbooks, and an estimated 1.2 to 1.6 million undergraduates take introductory psychology classes in the United States each year.[35] One study, conducted in the late 1970s, foreshadowed the abating effect of familiarity with the effect itself. In it, researchers tested students' behavior after the students heard either a lecture on bystander behavior or an unrelated topic. Students who heard the lecture on bystander behavior were more likely to offer help to a person in need than those who heard the unrelated one.[36]

Complicating the Urban Bystander: Cautionary Tales

Despite the enduring power of bystander research, there are reasons to approach this work with care and caution. Bystander research doesn't do justice to the experiences of members of marginalized communities and groups, who are rarely afforded civil inattention in public or protected from would-be "Samaritans."

There are, for instance, the seemingly well-meaning, but ultimately intrusive and hostile "Samaritans." Cahill and Eggleston found that wheelchair users often encounter this "helper," who offers unwanted, unnecessary, and even disruptive aid. Strangers may insist on helping a wheelchair user fold a wheelchair and put it in the user's car, even though the wheelchair user alone can do it more deftly and quickly. At the same time, some "helpers" respond rudely when wheelchair users rebuff offers of help, forcing wheelchair users to endure "help" or risk a hostile social interaction.[37]

Others who breach civil inattention don't do so with the intention of helping. In public, boys and men often harass others—cis- and transgender girls and women; boys and men whose self-presentations don't conform to dominant expectations of masculinity; and transgender boys and men. Street harassment takes many forms, including aggressive, dehumanizing, and objectifying looks; sexist, homophobic, and/or transphobic calls and comments; and threats of and outright violence, including unwanted touching, groping, and other forms of sexual violence.[38] Those who experience street harassment bear the burden of managing it. For instance, Carol Brooks Gardner, in a foundational study of women's experiences of street harassment, describes several strategies women use to minimize their exposure to it. Women often avoid places where harassment has occurred in the past or is likely to occur. They may manage their personal fronts to limit unwanted social interactions by, for instance, wearing dark sunglasses to close themselves to others. They may also adopt direct, brisk, and purposeful walking styles that limit others' ability to approach them. And, when compelled to wait with others, they may wall off their own attention by focusing on books, magazines, and cellphones.[39]

Even bystander interventions have a dark side. We're used to thinking of the unhelpful bystander as the social ill, the problem we need to understand and fix. But there is a thin line between the Good Samaritan who comes to the aid of a person in need and the self-appointed and state-sanctioned white "watchmen" and "watchwomen" of public places. White Americans often "intervene" when they witness other Americans barbequing, swimming, babysitting, waiting, napping, birding, or simply existing "while black."[40] The mundaneness of the activities that prompt actions—such as calls to 911, demands for names and identification, verbal harassment, and physical assaults—highlights the fact that this watchperson defines the presence of a person of color, not the situation itself, as the emergency. It also suggests that the right of "being unknown" in a community, as the sociologist Freeden Blume Oeur describes it, is racialized.[41] Goffman's civil attention, in other words, is a privilege most authentically enjoyed by white Americans and white cisgender men at that.

Of course, these are not the types of interventions that bystander researchers have in mind when they conduct their experiments. Even so, bystander researchers have largely ignored the effect of race and racism on bystander behavior. In their studies, we find many references to how gender shapes bystander interventions. Rarely do we find meaningful discussions of race. Works that do address race, such as Samuel L. Gaertner's studies of race, racism, and helping, are often minimized by other scholars in the field.[42] Latané, writing with Steve Nida, gave work on race and the bystander effect a half-paragraph treatment in a 1981 review of the literature. They punctuate that half-paragraph rather flippantly, stating that "it is difficult to evaluate" the meaningfulness of studies of race and bystander behavior, "since they are so rare and since little rationale has been offered for their existence."[43]

In the same article, Latané and Nida treat gender and age at length and with seriousness. In Latané's earlier work with Darley, even physical attractiveness, particularly of the female students involved in bystander research, elicits commentary. Of the female confederates who participated in one of their landmark studies, Latané and Darley wrote that they were "all at least moderately attractive," basing this, it seems, on their own assessments of the women who worked for them.[44] Though seemingly made offhand, Latané and Darley's remark suggests that they consider, or expect that their reader considers, the attractiveness of women as an independent variable that might explain the behavior of bystanders. Needless to say, one finds, in their work, little rationale for the existence of this discussion. The 2011 meta-analysis, meanwhile, contains little more commentary on race than did Latané's earlier review. Only one of Gaertner's studies, dating to the early 1980s, is referenced in a ten-word discussion of race.

Before addressing what is known about race and the bystander effect, it's worth considering why this exclusion, this denial of the relevance of race, exists. Part of the answer may be in something typical to most professions, what Eviatar Zerubavel refers to as "rules of relevance." These rules, usually learned through advanced study and practice, separate what practitioners in any field need to attend to from what they may safely ignore.[45] Bystander research emphasizes that features of situations, such as the number of bystanders present and the reaction of those bystanders, largely predict whether or not someone intervenes in an emergency. "Norms," "values," and characteristics of personalities, all of which get us close to bias (implicit or explicit) and racism, are held to be inadequate to explain interventions in emergencies. "Norms do not seem very useful to the scientist," Latané and Darley wrote, "because they are so vague, unspecific, and conflicting. For the same reasons, they may be of little use to an individual trying to decide what course of action to take in a specific situation."[46] It's also likely that the experiences of people of color remained beyond the horizon of many white bystander researchers' intellectual and political imaginations.

The same year that Latané and Nida published their review discounting the effects of race, Jane Allyn Piliavin, John F. Dovidio, Gaertner, and Russell D. Clark III offered a competing vision of bystander behavior, building a theoretical framework for helping, rather than passive, behavior. Their framework emphasized the costs, to witnesses of public emergencies, of providing or not providing help. Drawing on a robust set of studies of helping behavior and race, they argued that race has ambiguous effects on bystander helping. But these ambiguous results are explainable. When white bystanders face unambiguous situations—when, in other words, the emergency is clear—they are as likely to help a Black person in need as they are a white person. The same holds when white bystanders know they are the only potential helper. However, in ambiguous situations or in large groups, white bystanders helped white people more frequently and more quickly than they helped Black people. Piliavin, Dovidio, Gaertner, and Clark argue that in unambiguous emergencies or when there are no other potential helpers, white bystanders cannot justify nonintervention for a person of color without admitting that racial preference mattered. The situation provides no other intervening variable, so to speak, that they can use to explain away discriminatory feelings and actions. And this is a cost too great for many potential helpers to bear. On the other hand, in ambiguous situations or when there are other potential helpers, white bystanders can effectively rationalize nonintervention by telling themselves that the situation wasn't *really* an emergency or that someone else would help. Apparently, the broader social context of race indeed shapes interventions.[47]

But these studies largely address helping behavior. Does race matter to interventions when there is an apparent "perpetrator" of "criminal" behavior or ambiguously "threatening" behavior? Here, the research is less well developed. Most bystander studies do not stage emergencies involving ambiguous conflicts or obvious perpetrators. Emergencies like a person falling or suffering a medical event are more common.[48] As far as I know, those bystander studies that stage crimes involving a "perpetrator" do not meaningfully examine whether the race of the perpetrator matters to interventions.[49]

Even so, there's credible evidence that white Americans are more likely to view a situation, even an ambiguous one, as an "emergency" that demands an intervention if a person of color is involved as an apparent "perpetrator" (in the eyes of the white observer). Experimental research suggests that white research subjects are more likely to interpret the ambiguous behavior of a Black person to be violent than they are the similar behavior of a white person. Experimental studies have further found that white research subjects are also more likely to misperceive common tools as guns when those tools are proximate to a Black person than when they are near a white person. And in a video-game simulation of the decision to shoot or not shoot potential "target" individuals, white research participants "shot" armed Black people more quickly than they "shot" armed white people. They also mistakenly "shot" unarmed Black people more often than they did unarmed white people.[50]

These studies suggest that many white Americans associate people of color, especially Black Americans, with aggression, violence, and crime. This association is often implicit. Even so, it leads us to expect that some white Americans will be more likely to view ambiguous situations as emergencies when they believe a Black person is an antagonist in those situations. It would follow, then, that they're also more likely to intervene—directly themselves or indirectly, by alerting others to the "threat"—in situations in which they view a person of color as an "antagonist" or "perpetrator." There's credible evidence of this as well. Victimization studies find that crimes involving perpetrators of color are reported at higher rates to police than are crimes involving white perpetrators.[51]

And, of course, there is the long history of violence, sometimes perpetrated by groups of white Americans, other times by the lone bystander, against people of color.[52] Twenty years after Genovese's murder gave bystander researchers their violent origin story, New York City offered another tragic and too real parable of the violence of anonymous strangers. On December 22, 1984, Bernhard Goetz, a white New Yorker, shot four Black teenagers on a crowded New York City subway. No passive bystander, Goetz claimed he thought the teenagers were going to mug him, after one of the four asked him for money and, according to Goetz, the four surrounded him.

Unlike Genovese's murder, the *New York Times* immediately featured the shooting on their front page. It appeared there through much of December. And the paper would return the story to prominence in early 1985, after Goetz surrendered to police, and throughout the spring and summer of 1987, during Goetz's trial and sentencing. On talk radio and in op-eds, commentators alternatively described Goetz as a hero, an unjustified vigilante, or, in a resigned mood, a New Yorker doing his best to survive in a subway system overrun by crime.[53] Despite its prominence, we find no social psychological research paradigm forged from the shooting, little effort to understand how the typically reserved subway rider could, in the brief time Goetz was on the train, assess a situation as an emergency requiring a nearly lethal intervention.

* * *

The passive bystander contains multitudes. It is made, at least partly, of the urban legends surrounding the tragic murder of Genovese. But its figure is cut from a cloth that excludes so much—to be left alone in public spaces is a right, but one that is most fully the privilege of the white men who first described this bystander.

And yet there's a social psychological truth at the bystander's core: the presence of others exerts a pressure on people not to intervene in genuine emergencies. But even this bystander is more complex than it at first appeared. It is not the apathetic or callous bystander that so concerned Rosenthal. Rather, this figure is frozen by fear and sometimes a meager fear at that, of embarrassment. This bystander is also immobilized by the uncertainty that the situation is not, in fact, an emergency. And it is frozen, too, by denial of responsibility, a belief that someone else will, or should, or is better able to help. These worries, not apathy, render us passive.

But this only explains unresponsive bystanders; it does not absolve them. Questioned about their inaction, as Genovese's neighbors were by the *Times*, bystanders offer their own explanations: "We thought it was a lover's quarrel"; "Frankly, we were afraid"; "I was tired . . . I went back to bed."[54]

Here, then, is denial's next move.

When others refuse to ignore a transgression, when they call the transgressor to account for it, the transgressor turns to the alchemy of language. Here are the disclaimers, excuses, and justifications, the turns with words that transform the seemingly undeniable into something others may abide.

3

HOW TO AVOID BLAME

Explaining Away Problems

THERE are times when we can no longer keep discrediting information in the background of social life. Perhaps the attention-management strategies of denial, which allow us to pretend that we haven't noticed others' mistakes, fail. Perhaps others refuse to use those strategies on our behalf, bringing our mistakes, blunders, or bad behavior into the foreground of social life. In these moments, denial undergoes a metamorphosis. Now, the denier uses language itself to try to transform problematic speech or actions into harmless, acceptable behavior.

For instance, in my decade or so of teaching, I've received emails—emails upon emails, then more emails still—from students who've missed classes. In these messages, students offer many explanations for their absences. They cite forces outside their control: car troubles, contagious or debilitating illnesses, injuries, and family emergencies. They cite nonnegotiable commitments: medical appointments, interviews for jobs, and funerals.

When they write these emails to me, students rely on what I'll call the rhetoric of denial. Think of the rhetoric of denial as verbal bridges that people build to span the gap between a transgression of a social expectation and the expectation itself.[1] By offering an excuse, say that of car troubles, a student spans the gap between the missed class and their commitment to their education. The absent student says, in other words, "if not for these car troubles, I would be with you, learning. This is not a choice I made against education, but rather one forced by circumstances beyond my control. As you know, I'm a committed student. Don't hold this absence against me." Doing this, the absent student engages in defensive and *rhetorical* face work, neutralizing their transgressions and defending their social identities as responsible students.

Are these explanations always true? I doubt it. I find that stomach flus and food poisoning are particularly virulent on Monday mornings, and survey research suggests that students use excuses fraudulently as often as they do legitimately.[2] Even still, there's a reason students use these explanations instead of . . . well, a (sometimes) more honest one: "Hey Prof Jared, I won't be in class today. I'd rather spend my time skiing than with you. See you next week." This explanation fails, and gratuitously so, because it doesn't bind the student's absence to the value that the absence transgressed: the prioritization of education. As a rhetorical bridge, it's shoddy. As usual, Goffman put this best: "True accounts are often good, but false accounts are sometimes better."[3]

For the rhetoric of denial to do its defensive face work, it must align its user's behavior with commonsense modes of reasoning. Otherwise, the recipient of the denial is not likely to accept it. Because of this, the rhetoric of denial consists of a stockpile of standardized and socially acceptable disclaimers, excuses, and justifications. Disclaimers are phrases that people typically use to reframe problematic speech or behavior. Usually, disclaimers are prefaces, preceding problematic speech in order to manage others' responses to it. Excuses and justifications are subtypes of what sociologists refer to as accounts, or explanations for one's behavior. A person who uses an excuse downplays or denies their responsibility for that behavior. A person who uses a justification denies the wrongness of their behavior, in hopes that it appears appropriate, normal, or acceptable.

Disclaimers: Rhetorical Strategies to Reframe Speech

Frequently, we anticipate that others will respond badly to what we're about to say. Rather than allow that to happen, we use disclaimers to reframe our speech in ways that manage our audience's assessments of it. Ultimately, we're trying to lead our audiences from negative evaluations of us to neutral or even positive ones.[4] Successful disclaimers, then, do defensive face work for a speaker. They allow speakers to make a potentially discrediting or controversial remark without having their social selves discredited.

"This May Sound Crazy": Cognitive Disclaimers

Several springs ago, my mother-in-law went missing from our house. No note, no comment, her phone left behind, and her usually pampered Shih Tzu left outside. None of this made sense. Fearing the worst, my partner and I went door-to-door through our new neighborhood, each of us greeting unfamiliar neighbors with some variant of "I know this sounds crazy, but have you seen . . . ?" (My mother-in-law was, in fact, just visiting with neighbors.)

Cognitive disclaimers like this often preface statements that may test a listener's confidence in the speaker's sense of reality. In my case, I anticipated that my neighbors would judge me as just a bit off, for having seemed to have "misplaced" a family member and gone looking for her in strangers' homes. Indeed, when we worry that our words or behaviors will open what sociologists call a "reality disjuncture," gaps between ours and others' senses of reality, we turn to cognitive disclaimers.[5] Guillermo del Toro, writer and director of a heap of serious and award-winning films, admits to having seen a UFO: "I know this is horrible. . . . You sound like a complete lunatic, but I saw a UFO."[6] Cognitive disclaimers indicate to our listeners that we remain on their side of reality. We recognize what is *likely* real and unreal, even as our words bend toward the latter.[7] Using them, we perform defensive face work, assuring ourselves and our audiences that our mental faculties and cognitive abilities hold, even as we say or do things that suggest otherwise.

Cognitive disclaimers are robust, adaptable to a range of other, less surreal uses. When speakers worry that their words may lead others to doubt their judgment, mental fitness, or intellectual abilities, they may use cognitive disclaimers. Amid a brainstorming session, a colleague, worried that their idea may be badly received, might open with "This may be *too far* out of the box, but . . . ."

One cognitive disclaimer is a favorite of students everywhere: "I know this is a stupid question, but . . . ." Students use this disclaimer to defend their identities as competent and intelligent, even while speaking words that they think others may see as contradicting that identity. (In my experience, what usually follows those words is perfectly intelligent and, so, the disclaimer's use reveals insecurities about competence and intelligence—and perhaps worries about how educators wield authority in classrooms—not actual lacks.) This disclaimer is also an implicit invitation. Directed to an instructor, it asks for protective face work. And many instructors are generous enough to provide aid, offering, "No, there are no stupid questions" or some other variant that affirms the value of the question.

The use of this disclaimer can also reveal structural inequalities in education. A teacher in a New York City school district recounts how an elementary school student who had "dropped out" of a reading program was struggling with a standardized exam that included passages about a "typical" beach scene. The student had lived in an urban environment his entire life. The beach scene was not so typical, and the words to describe it alien. "I know this is a stupid question," the student asked his teacher, "but what is a 'sand dollar'? What is 'tide'?"[8] Though young, this student knew that the inclusion of these words on an exam meant that they are part of others' common knowledge. By using a cognitive disclaimer, he hoped his teacher would not judge him as deficient because he didn't already possess that knowledge.

As forms of defensive face work, cognitive disclaimers are similar to the disciplinary displays discussed in chapter 1. Those using cognitive disclaimers condemn themselves before others can. Their words suggest that no further judgment from the audience is necessary. And even as a speaker makes potentially discrediting remarks, they can use cognitive disclaimers to remain on the side of their audience. Speakers and audiences alike remain entrenched in their sense of the normal and acceptable, even as speakers draw their (potentially) deviant views near.

"With All Due Respect": Affective Disclaimers

To shape an audience's emotional response to remarks, a speaker can use an affective disclaimer. "I know you might get upset," a person says, before unleashing upsetting remarks.[9] This disclaimer signals the speaker's awareness of the nature of their remarks. But this awareness, in turn, is meant to signal something deeper—that they aren't recklessly or thoughtlessly upsetting those to whom they speak. They've considered, perhaps even carefully, the content of their speech and how others might respond to it. And by bracing the listener for the affective response, the speaker hopes to mitigate it.

Similarly, a speaker might open a remark with one of these brief phrases: "With all due respect" or "No offense, but . . . ." These familiar prefaces attempt to separate the speaker's intent for their remark from the listener's perception of it. If the words that follow carry disrespect or offense, the speaker has already denied intent.

Care, though, must be taken when using this disclaimer. If there is asymmetry between the disclaimer and the subsequent statement, the disclaimer may sound insincere or farcical. For instance, in 2012, Vice President Joe Biden wanted to criticize his Republican challenger, Paul Ryan, for the Romney-Ryan campaign's statements on the tragic, terrorist attack on the US embassy in Benghazi. Biden began his critique with "With all due respect . . . ." But then he finished with "that's a bunch of malarkey."[10] Biden's use of the word "malarkey," a relatively uncommon and aurally unserious word, suggested intent in Biden's put-down. And so the affective disclaimer, "with all due respect," failed to neutralize that interpretation of Biden's remarks. It should be obvious: you can't start a sentence with "with all due respect" and then say "that's a bunch of malarkey."[11] Put differently, someone who respects you won't usually call your ideas malarkey and especially not publicly, before a vast audience. Indeed, Biden likely meant the malarkey more than his respect. The moment, after all, went viral. And it fit with public perceptions of Biden as both an uncommonly straight-talking politician and a bit rogue.

Speakers may go farther to effect the affective responses of audience members. Most supervisors know to give positive praise before "constructive" criticism of subordinates. The much-maligned "compliment sandwich," criticism wedged between two pieces of unrelated praise, is meant to provide protective face work, guarding the self-image of the recipient of the criticism.[12] For those giving the criticisms, compliment sandwiches likely perform defensive face work as well. By readying the recipient for the critique that's coming, the compliment may make it less likely that employees will lash out at their supervisors. It also suggests that supervisors, even the critical ones, are not so bad after all, for they recognize their employees' valuable qualities alongside the lackluster ones. Similarly, professors are advised to open written feedback on student writing with compliments, before digging in to the "constructive criticism."[13]

"I May Be Wrong": Hedging Disclaimers

A favorite of professors and other (supposed) experts everywhere, hedging allows us to assert a fact or view on a topic while also signaling the weakness of our commitment to that fact or view.[14] When students ask questions that require faculty to speak about topics outside their expertise, faculty often hedge. Rather than admit a gap in their knowledge and risk calling into question their identity as the "sage on the stage," professors will often answer the question with some dimly remembered fact, while simultaneously signaling that the fact may be wrong. My own favorite hedging technique is to tell my students, "Don't quote on me on this . . . ." This hedge signals that I'm not confident in what I'm about to say, and I don't want them offering my statement to others, particularly other faculty members, as proof of anything. (I admit—it's a terrible teaching strategy. Better, instead, to open a response with questions: "How might we know this?

What kind of research would we need to conduct? What kind of evidence would we need?")

Similar forms of hedging abound. Pressed to share one's view of a topic, one might say, "I'm no expert, but . . . ." One might also try, "I may be wrong, but . . ." or even a simple "I think," followed by a long, wavering pause. These forms of hedging signal speakers' "minimal commitment" to their statements and their "willingness to receive discrepant information, change opinions, be persuaded otherwise, or be better informed."[15] This use of hedging allows those performing expert roles to assert their expertise. At the same time, it allows them, if proven incorrect, to change their minds or admit that they were wrong without discrediting their claim to competency.

"I Can Say This, Because . . .": Credentialing Disclaimers

When a speaker claims a special privilege to make a controversial remark, they're engaging in credentialing. For instance, when Greg Cote, a journalist for the *Miami Herald*, wanted to criticize the romantic undertones of a Smokey Robinson concert, he did so while using credentialing. Aware that he could be accused of displaying ageism against the then seventy-nine-year-old singer, whom he had deemed too old to display sensuality, Cote offered, "I'm old, so I'm allowed to blaspheme fellow elderly . . . ."[16] Similarly, comedians take and, typically, are given more leeway to tell deprecating jokes about groups to which they claim membership.[17]

(Credentialing has a well-documented history in the denial of a racism; I take up this topic in chapter 6.)

Accounts, or How We Explain Away Our Transgressions

People use disclaimers to frame problematic remarks in ways that downplay those remarks' problematic nature. People use accounts, on the other hand, to explain problematic behaviors in ways that downplay those behaviors' problematic nature. One can, of course, explain all behaviors. Accounts, then, need not bend toward denial. However, in practice, we rarely account for ourselves when we meet others' expectations. We're also not likely to ask others to account for themselves when they meet ours. Returning to my earlier example of students explaining absences, it's worth noting that I never receive emails from students who want to account for their presence in my classes. Nor do I ask for accounts of their presence. Most of us, most of the time, take conformity to norms for granted, and we ask no explanation for that conformity.

The accounts that concern us most, then, are those we give for conduct that potentially discredits us: our mistakes, poor behavior, affronts and wrongs to others, even crimes. Asked to account for these, we often turn to excuses and justifications, which (respectively) allow us to deny responsibility for our behavior and for the wrongness of it in the first place.

Excuses, or How to Deny Responsibility

A person using an excuse admits two things, but denies a third. The excuse maker admits that they engaged in offending or discrediting behavior. They also admit, if only implicitly, that the behavior was indeed offensive or discrediting. But the excuse maker denies responsibility for that behavior, by using one of three types of excuses. The accused may claim that the offending behavior was an accident, unintended, or out of their control.

"IT WAS AN ACCIDENT . . ."

This is perhaps the most common and familiar excuse. One claims that the alleged wrong was, simply, an accident. To excuse an absence or late arrival to class, students claim that their alarm failed or that they overslept it. To excuse late submissions of work, students claim that they left the papers in their rooms or, if the submission is online, accidentally submitted the wrong paper.[18]

One can claim "accident" in a wide range of situations. Most of us, most of the time, only break or lose another's prized possession accidentally. Most of us, most of the time, only get into fender-benders accidentally.[19] And many of us, much of the time, will also honor the claim of "accident." Accidents, as we know, happen.[20]

But one must not overrely on accidents as excuses. The power of this claim is that accidents are inevitable. At the same time, they're understood to be statistical anomalies. If one claims "accident" too often, one becomes, in the eyes of others, a clumsy, negligent, or careless person, a person uniquely prone to accidents. Or they risk being viewed as a liar, who fraudulently claims that their bad behavior is accidental.[21] The claim, in these cases, no longer does defensive face work. A student who oversleeps an alarm might be able to use the account once or twice and still have it "work"— that is, do the necessary defensive face work so that a professor does not view them as a chronically late or absent student. Beyond that, the account fails, even if it is true. The student is likely to transform, in the eyes of the professor, into someone who is insufficiently committed to the professor's class.

"I DIDN'T MEAN TO . . ."

Another common excuse is to claim lack of intent. One says the outcome of one's behavior was unintended, unforeseeable, or incidental to their planned action. If others accept this claim, the accused may face diminished consequences for their actions.

We're likely to see this claim when there is an asymmetry, perhaps especially a profound one, between the meaning of an action for the person committing it and those evaluating it. For instance, a person may claim that their harmful action was really meant as a prank; its outcomes were meant to be interpreted as humorous and unserious.[22] A story from my hometown of Pine Bush, New York, illustrates this. Barely a month after the September 11, 2001, attacks, just ninety miles outside New York City, with the country gripped by a series of anthrax attacks, a manager of my town's local grocery store filled an employee's paycheck with baby powder. When the employee tried to cash the paycheck at a nearby bank, the white powder spilled onto the bank's counter. The entirety of the town's emergency workers responded. So, too, did the county's hazmat team. And the FBI. Bank workers and customers were quarantined and decontaminated.[23] Federal charges followed. In late October 2001, the *New York Times* reported that the store's manager "was charged under a provision of the Federal Anti-Terrorism and Effective Death Penalty Act of 1996 that makes it a felony to threaten to use a weapon of mass destruction. It can carry a sentence of up to life in prison." The manager's lawyer admitted that the manager "now realized something that would have been comical on Sept. 10 is not very funny anymore."[24] I don't think it requires us to stretch our imaginations very far to imagine that the store manager didn't, in fact, intend for others to *believe* and *act on the belief* that the white powder, smelling of baby powder, was a weapon of mass destruction.

Claims of "lack of intent" have other, more systematic and, so, harmful uses. Men accused of sexual harassment or assault often use this claim, exploiting the gap between their (alleged) intent for and others' understanding of their behavior. In 2019, former vice president Joe Biden confronted allegations that he forced unwanted hugs, kisses, and other violations of physical autonomy on female politicians. "I'm sorry I didn't understand more," Biden admitted. But then, Biden betrayed his profound lack of reflexivity: "I'm not sorry for any of my intentions. I'm not sorry for anything that I have ever done. I've never been disrespectful intentionally to a man or a woman."[25] Similarly, Louis C.K. responded to revelations that he'd exposed his penis to several female comedians by admitting that "these stories are true. At the time, I said to myself that what I did was O.K. because I never showed a woman my dick without asking first, which is also true. But what I learned later in life, too late, is that when you have power over another person, asking them to look at your dick isn't a question."[26] Both men admitted that their acts were wrong when understood through contemporary norms or from the perspective of women. But both also denied acting, originally, with guilty intent.

"I COULDN'T HELP IT . . ."

A third common excuse is to claim that forces outside one's control are to blame for the offending behavior. Marvin B. Scott and Stanford M. Lyman, sociologists who co-wrote the foundational essay on accounts, call this the excuse of fatalistic forces.[27] In offering this excuse, account givers portray themselves as powerless to change the course of events because of an overwhelming internal or external force.

On the everyday level, we're familiar with a range of common "forces" that can prevent a person from meeting others' expectations. Traffic or car troubles excuse late arrivals to meetings. Troubles with technologies, a force that many of us accept is outside the control of ordinary users, excuse late submissions of work for both employees and students. Invoking crashes, corrupted files, or, for PC users, the notorious "blue screen of death," we portray our personal technologies as almost supernatural forces to explain away whatever work we were unable to finish.[28]

The "personal" or "family" emergency is a catch-all excuse that suggests that an unspecified and inscrutable event outside the control of the account giver explains the offending behavior. The excuse is too intimate and private to be scrutinized by most tactful recipients of it. And yet it's general enough to cover all sorts of failures: rescheduled meetings, absences, missed work, and so forth.[29]

Perpetrators of serious and highly stigmatized crimes will often use fatalistic forces to purge the crime from their self-image. Research of men convicted of sexual crime reveals that they often try to excuse their violence as expressions of urges, disorders, or addictions. Rapists and child molesters frequently claim that alcohol or drugs caused their crimes. They may also cite past traumas and mental health problems.[30] Here, perpetrators attempt to split the "real" self from the criminal self; the former condemns the latter and protects itself from its own critical evaluation, if not the evaluations of others.

THE PROSPECTIVE USE OF EXCUSES

Excuses are usually used retrospectively, to deny responsibility for something that has already occurred. But they can also be used prospectively, prior, even, to the behavior that requires the excuse. It is not unusual for a student to warn me that they may need to step out of a class because of an illness or that they may be distracted and looking at their phone due to a family emergency. An audience member at a public talk might similarly tell the speaker that they need to leave early for some reason out of their control. In these cases, the excuse as a warning performs both kinds of face work. It defends the person giving the excuse from the negative assessments of others; the person leaving a talk early is not rude but is compelled by other obligations. The excuse as a warning also protects its recipient from the embarrassment that might follow when they notice an audience member on the phone or departing early.[31]

Justifications, or How We Deny the Wrongness of the Wrong

Using excuses, we deny responsibility for our actions. But we leave untouched their wrongness. When using justifications, on the other hand, people admit responsibility for their behaviors; however, they claim that special circumstances void the usual prohibitions on those behaviors. A justified act is no longer wrong; it appears, instead, appropriate, legitimate, perhaps legal, maybe even moral.

The strategies of justification can be endlessly adapted to specific behaviors and offenses. However, the most common, powerful, and corrosive justifications are two strategies: denial of victim and denial of harm.

"THEY DESERVED IT . . ."

When a person accused of wrongdoing claims that their victim deserved what they got, they're using the denial of victim justification.[32] This is the familiar schoolyard cry, "They started it." Students who commit violence against their peers often justify that violence as defense against alleged bullies. Parents often condone this justification. They do so prospectively, as when they tell their children, "If you need to protect yourself, then you do what you need to do. And we'll deal with it after."[33] And they may also use it retrospectively, to justify acts of violence against alleged bullies.

Social scientific research about rapists and rape culture reveals that men frequently use denial of victim to justify sexual assaults, relying on rape myths in an attempt to explain away their violence. Rapists describe women as seductresses who instigate sexual encounters. Rapists also claim that women who reject their sexual advances consent, in fact, to sex; a woman who says "no," they say, is being modest, as they believe women "should" be. According to rapists, these women need to be "convinced" of sex. But these rape myths do not belong to rapists alone. Bystanders, law enforcement agents, and legal actors may also believe them and fail to intervene in situations involving rape or to take seriously the claims of women who have been raped.[34]

Denial of victim also appears in the defenses of police officers and ordinary citizens accused of murdering people of color. These defenses usually introduce a second subtype of the denial of victim: that of necessity or self-defense. When this claim is introduced, perpetrators try to transform the victim of their violence into the aggressor, reversing the flow of responsibility for the perpetrators' behavior. This claim further draws its power from racist stereotypes about the criminality of people of color and, especially, men of color. These stereotypes make it more likely that audiences, particularly but not exclusively white audiences, will accept the account.[35]

The 1986–1987 trial of Bernhard Goetz illustrates this. During Goetz's trial for the attempted murder of the four Black teenagers whom he shot on a New York City subway, Goetz testified that he did not think the teenagers had a gun. He also testified that none of the four teenagers displayed a weapon before he began shooting.[36] Still, he claimed to have believed they were going to mug him. A Manhattan jury largely accepted the defense, acquitting Goetz of attempted murder and assault charges and finding him guilty of only a single charge, of illegal possession of a weapon.[37]

A similar set of denials contributed to George Zimmerman's acquittal for the 2012 killing of Trayvon Martin. On the evening of February 26, 2012, Zimmerman, an armed neighborhood watch coordinator in Sanford, Florida, stalked Trayvon Martin, an unarmed Black teenager, through Sanford. Zimmerman did so even after alerting 911 to Martin's presence and being instructed to stand down. When Martin ran, Zimmerman pursued. That pursuit ended when Zimmerman fatally shot Martin, during a physical struggle that Zimmerman himself, through his pursuit and confrontation of Martin, instigated. Even so, a jury of six women—five of whom were white—acquitted Zimmerman, accepting the defense's claim that Zimmerman acted in self-defense.[38]

"NO ONE WAS HURT . . ."

Denial of harm involves claims that the alleged act didn't cause injury or harm to the victim.[39] The person giving this account hopes that others, then, will see the act as something inconsequential, worth neither concern nor sanction.

Typically, denial of harm involves an implicit denial of victim. If no harm comes from one's behavior, then it follows that there is also no victim. Shoplifters, for instance, may justify their behavior by saying that a chain grocery store can afford the marginal loss of the stolen item. This justification may be combined with an explicit denial of victim, with the shoplifter arguing that the store is the real thief, given the prices they charge for basic necessities.[40]

Euphemisms, a subtype of denial of harm, are commonly used to minimize the reality of abuse, harassment, and violence. Violence in schools is merely "bullying," a word that conjures cartoonish images of students jostling, absconding with lunch money, or kicking another's sand castles.[41] To some parents, the verbal abuse and harassment that many female students experience in schools are "only words," and "words can't hurt you," the cliché goes.[42]

Research about domestic and child abuse reveals that perpetrators frequently rely on denial of harm to justify their violence. A man who physically assaults his partner might say that the two were merely having a "disagreement."[43] Likewise, parents "spank" children, which is different, one is supposed to think, from assaulting, beating, or abusing them.

Euphemistic denials of harm usually minimize the wrongness of the act. Other efforts at denial of harm attempt more stark transformations. Here, I have in mind denials of harm that involve an attempt to relabel acts, particularly of abusive practices or even violence, as in the best interest of those who suffer those acts. I refer to this as the "discourse of care."[44] The claim of "tough love," which college coaches who rely on verbal abuse, intimidation, and physical abuse sometimes invoke, is of this type.[45] Similarly, parents and teachers who use corporal punishment say their intent is to teach children the difference between right and wrong—or that it's for their own good. The violence, then, is said to benefit children who need to learn valuable lessons about personal conduct at a young age.[46]

* * *

So these are the tools of everyday denial, documented in this and in chapters 1 and 2: attention-management strategies that allow people to feign ignorance of distressing events and rhetorical ones that allow people to downplay their bad behavior when others refuse to look away. For many of us, much of the time, these tools are just another way to get by. We use the techniques of everyday denial to mend social relationships frayed by the inevitable accidents, blunders, and mistakes of living among others in real time.

But denial soon transforms. Face work gives way to bystander behavior. Excuses and justification, when unchallenged, empower perpetrators and allow harms, inequities, and injustices to fester. Eventually, denial burrows into the places we pool resources, power, and people: workplaces, schools, governments. Once institutionalized, denial becomes a parasite, infecting many and making victims out of more still.

4

HOW TO CONCEAL MISCONDUCT

Organizations Hiding Problems

IN the mid-1950s, Solomon Asch, a psychologist at Swarthmore College, ran a seemingly mundane series of experiments. Research subjects were shown two cards. One had a single line drawn on it. The other showed three lines of various lengths. Subjects were asked to identify which of those three lines matched the first. There was, it appeared, no trick to it. Subjects in a control group, who did the matching by themselves, correctly identified lines of the same length 99 percent of the time.[1]

But Asch wasn't interested in people's ability to assess the lengths of lines. His experimental situation had research subjects matching the lines in groups with seven to nine other "research subjects." In fact, there was only ever one research subject. The other group members were part of the experiment, participating in it as "confederates" pretending to be research subjects. As the group went through a series of trials, the confederates occasionally and unanimously misidentified the matching line. They did so before the genuine research subjects had opportunities to announce their selections. This meant that research subjects heard the incorrect consensus before they made their choice. In this experimental situation, subjects were frequently swayed by the incorrect assessments of the group, conforming to the majority opinion about one-third of the time.[2]

Asch's experiments revealed how even a loosely organized and weakly bonded group can lead its members to suppress their awareness of an obvious fact: that the group was mis-identifying the correct lines. But unless we are engineers or architects, lines, their length, and group consensuses about them rarely concern us. Rather, we take notice when group cultures arc toward fraud and other financial malfeasance; toward the harassment of students, employees, or clients; or toward outright violence. The examples are legion, and any list risks being badly incomplete. Here are some, perhaps only the now better known, perhaps only those that come to mind today, as I write: Wells Fargo bankers defrauded its customers, opening credit cards and other banking products in their names; Purdue Pharma illegally marketed opioids, flooding US communities with its highly addictive and lethal drugs; Michigan State harbored a pedophile in its gymnastics program, despite years of accusations against him; Miramax protected Harvey Weinstein, as he sexually harassed, abused, and assaulted women; for decades, petroleum and tobacco companies suppressed knowledge of their products' harms from the public; and the US military, the CIA, members of Congress, and the executive branch protected torturers, at Abu Ghraib, Guantánamo, and myriad secret CIA black sites. Reading of each case—and, I suspect, reading of the next organization gone wrong—we wonder this: how could so many people participate in or simply tolerate that kind of bad? Or else: how could so many people not know what their co-workers were doing?

Denial provides a partial answer to these questions. Organizations gradually socialize new members into attention-management strategies that keep guilty knowledge of wrongdoing in the background of organizational life. Rhetorical strategies of denial, meanwhile, construct a veneer of normalcy over that wrongdoing, allowing organizational members to euphemize theirs and others' misconduct. And information is withheld from outsiders, so that those who might investigate and expose misconduct are stymied; this, in turn, keeps misconduct out of collective attention and public discourse. Together, these processes make it possible for organizations and their members to harm others, while simultaneously denying those harms.

How Wrong Comes to Seem Right: Habituation and Desensitization

Few people arrive at their workplaces prepared to abide fraud, abuse, or violence. To those not used to such things, organizational realities arrive as shocks, perhaps undeniable ones. Quoting Javal Davis, a US reservist stationed at Abu Ghraib prison in Iraq, the journalist Philip Gourevitch describes the confusion of US soldiers during their first tour of the prison.

> By way of orientation, the soldiers of the 372nd who were assigned guard duty at the hard site were given a tour of

the place. They saw the . . . highly restricted M.I. [Military Intelligence] block, where the most "high value" security detainees were held. . . . "That's when I saw the nakedness," Javal Davis said. "I'm like, 'Hey, Sarge, why is everyone naked?' You know—'Hey, that's the M.I. That's what the M.I. does. That's the M.I. thing. I don't know.' 'Why do these guys have on women's panties?' Like—'It's to break them.'" Davis was wide-eyed. "Guys handcuffed in stress positions, in cells, no lights, no windows. . . . It's like, Whoa, what is that? What the hell is up with all this stuff? Something's not right here."[3]

Davis knew something was wrong at Abu Ghraib. But, soon after arriving, it seemed a little less strange. A little less appalling, too. Charged with preparing detainees of special interest for interrogations, Davis abused and tortured the unarmed, defenseless men in his custody. He withheld food, deprived detainees of sleep, put them in stress positions, submerged them in ice water and then made their cells cold by leaving windows open. "Open a window while it was, like, forty degrees outside and watch them disappear into themselves . . . before they go into shock," he recounted to the documentary filmmaker Errol Morris.[4] According to other military police, Davis would threaten detainees with rape, after telling them he'd raped their wives or mothers. And he allegedly beat newly arrived detainees, punching them in the kidneys during in-processing.[5] (As far as I know, Davis did not admit to these latter accusations in his interviews with Morris, suggesting that he downplayed his active involvement in torturing detainees, even as he admitted *some* involvement. I suspect this is because Davis sees the violence that others accuse him of as more direct, active, and, in the case of threats of rape, sadistic than those to which he admits.) Abu Ghraib changed Davis, who adapted to his conditions with denial—of both the harms of and his responsibility for the violence he committed. "We are at war, this is Military Intelligence, this is what they do—and it's just a job," he told Morris. "So you become numb to it, and it's nothing. . . . You see it—that sucks. It sucks to be him. And that's it. You move on."[6]

Davis's introduction to torture is not unusual. Most perpetrators of torture go through a similar process, learning from more experienced interrogators and guards before they themselves start torturing others.[7] But it's not just torturers. Veteran members of most corrupt organizations know that new initiates can't be trusted with organizational malpractice.[8] Like Davis at Abu Ghraib, most new initiates will sense that "something's not right here" if exposed to malpractice and corruption too quickly. Veterans deliberately and slowly introduce new members to organizational misconduct. After an initial exposure, like Davis's tour of Abu Ghraib, initiates may be ordered to observe and then engage in token instances of misconduct. This entangles initiates in organizational corruption, ensuring they feel complicit in it and, so, remain silent about it.[9]

This begins a process that social scientists call habituation. As organizational members are repeatedly exposed to questionable, if not obviously unethical, situations, they may gradually come to see these situations as normal. A second process—desensitization—often occurs alongside, or after, habituation. It occurs when organizational members are exposed to increasingly severe violations of norms, policies, or laws. Together, these processes weaken initiates' responses to those violations and season them in the rancid organizational culture.[10] Eventually, they come to deny that very rancidness. This normalization of deviance, as the organizational sociologist Diane Vaughan calls it, changes an organization's standards of behavior.[11] What previously seemed unethical or illegal now appears permissible, ethical, and perhaps even necessary.

Research of police socialization into corruption shows how this happens. New police officers may be idealistic, harboring a seemingly inflexible sense of right and wrong. The normal, everyday corruption in some departments shocks them, and veteran officers know it. "Say an old timer will have a new man working with him and he'll tell you, 'You've got to watch him, because he's honest,'" an ex-officer explained to the sociologist Ellwyn R. Stoddard.[12]

But habituation and desensitization can bend the rookie. Through a series of compromises—small ones giving way to larger ones—the new officer may turn. Mort Stern, a former editor with the *Denver Post*, documented how this happens in a 1961 interview with a Denver police officer. That year, a widespread corruption scandal in Denver made national news. Over forty officers and a sheriff, as well as deputies, private detectives, and civilians, had been implicated in burglaries of local stores, gambling, prostitution, and myriad other criminal activities.[13] Stern's anonymous interviewee describes how he was introduced to the police department's culture of corruption. New officers, he told Stern, might first witness veterans accepting small items from storeowners—cigarettes, for instance.[14] This was habituation, by the book.

> The older [officer] stops at a bar, comes out with some packages of cigarettes. He does this several times. He explains that this is part of the job, getting cigarettes free from proprietors to re-sell and that as part of the rookie's training it is his turn to "make the butts." So he goes in to a Skid Row bar and stands uncomfortably at the end waiting for the bar-tender to acknowledge his presence and disdainfully toss him two packages of butts.[15]

But this was only the start. Habituation gave way to desensitization, as new officers grew used to receiving increasingly valuable "gifts."

> One thing leads to another for the rookies. After six months they have become conditioned to accept free meals, a few packs of cigarettes, turkeys at Thanksgiving and liquor at Christmas from the respectable people in their district. The rule book forbids all this. But it isn't enforced. It's winked at, at all levels. So the rookies say to themselves that this is okay, that all the men accept these things, that it is a far cry from stealing and they can still be good policemen.[16]

And then?

> And then this kind of thing may happen: One night [the
> novice officer] is sent to cover in on a "Code 26"—a silent
> burglar alarm. This may mean that a burglar has broken into
> a business place. He and his partner go in to investigate.
> The burglar is gone.... [After] they get back in the car his
> partner pulls out four $10 bills and hands him two. "Burglar
> got careless," says the partner. The young cop who isn't in-
> volved himself soon learns that this kind of thing goes on.
> He may even find himself covering in on a burglary call, say
> to a drug store, and see some officers there eyeing him pecu-
> liarly. Maybe at this point the young cop feels the pressure
> to belong so strongly that he reaches over and picks up some-
> thing, cigars perhaps. Then he's "in," and the others can do
> what they wish.[17]

Small steps and eventually officers in Denver were staging
elaborate burglaries of city stores that they'd then themselves
investigate and wipe of evidence.[18] These activities went on
for at least a decade. They only ended when some officers became just a bit too desensitized to their crimes. Brazenness,
then sloppiness, followed. In August 1960, Art Winstanley, a
young officer just a few years out of the academy, was arrested
after a stolen "safe literally fell out of his car trunk and into
the path of a police cruiser," as he fled a burglary.[19]

Sixty years later, these processes still hold: rookie police may be socialized into organizational cultures in which

misconduct, including violence, appears normal, acceptable, and necessary. Reporting on the 2020 murder of George Floyd, by Derek Chauvin, revealed how this occurred in the Minneapolis Police Department. Chauvin, a veteran Minneapolis police officer, murdered George Floyd during an arrest, kneeling on Floyd's neck for over nine minutes, ignoring Floyd's cries for help and the protests of bystanders, some of whom videotaped the killing. Chauvin also ignored the weak interventions of other law enforcement officers at the scene; a rookie cop, whom Chauvin supervised, suggested that Floyd be turned on his side. But bystander video shows that the other officers present at the scene took no direct action to stop Chauvin from killing Floyd.

Subsequent reporting on Minneapolis policing revealed how veteran officers in the city socialize rookies, normalizing the use and abuse of force. The process begins with messaging. Veteran officers send a consistent message to the new officers they supervise: "forget everything you learned at the academy." (This message has been part and parcel of police socialization for decades.[20]) Other messages fill the void left by this forced forgetting. According to Andrew Arashiba, a former Minneapolis officer, "training officers told him not to activate his body camera at times when it was required unless he had notified other officers first." That training officer "also once scolded him for not using force against a drunken older man they had encountered, according to the lawsuit. 'You missed a free slap,'" the veteran officer told him.[21] Many of Minneapolis's officers, like many of the country's officers, also took so-called warrior trainings. These trainings emphasize that every police encounter with citizens is a potentially fatal one, involving "those who need killing—the 'gang-bangers,' terrorists, and mass murderers."[22]

Through socialization, new police officers may come to see the use and abuse of force as a normal, necessary, and acceptable part of their job. Many also come to believe that their loyalty to other officers overrides their commitment to the rule of law and civil liberties. The "blue code of silence" offers police officers justifications for hiding—from investigators, judges, and juries—corruption and the criminal use of violence, even if it means lying during sworn testimony. This code of silence is a subtype of a form of denial that criminologists refer to as the appeal to higher loyalties; people who invoke this appeal claim that their commitments to others—friends, teammates, families, or co-workers—justify their misconduct or crimes.

The blue code of silence protects officers from the legal repercussions of their crimes. Even those who want to expose wrongdoing may be silenced; intimidation, threats, and retributive violence protect the blue code of silence from would-be whistleblowers.[23] Arguably, it also affects how officers use violence, emboldening some and leading others to become bystanders. Thirty years before Floyd's killing, a passerby's video recording of Los Angeles police officers brutally beating and tasing Rodney King similarly revealed the dynamics of violence and inaction. Of the video, Jerome Skolnick, professor emeritus of law at the University of California at Berkeley, wrote,

The televised beating of Rodney King by Los Angeles police was broadcast by CNN around the world. I was asked by CNN to interpret the beating, and was also asked by the *Los Angeles Times* to write a guest editorial. For both media, I pointed out that while most viewers were focused on and appalled by the beating—as I was—I was at least as attuned to the dozen Los Angeles police officers who could be seen watching, and doing nothing to end it. I thought of how this televised event so well illustrated the power of ties of loyalty among the police[. . . .] Because so many other officers stood by and watched the beating of King, those who participated must have believed that they could count on their colleagues to lie in case of an investigation.[24]

Euphemisms and the Sanitation of Corruption

Socialization into corruption teaches new organizational members that such corruption is normal and necessary. It also teaches them to protect, or intimidates them into protecting those who commit corrupt and criminal acts from the scrutiny of outsiders. But it involves other lessons. Particularly impactful are lessons in language, in the euphemisms that cleanse corruption of its rankness. Euphemisms, as George Orwell famously wrote, allow people "to name things without calling up mental pictures of them."[25] This is particularly true of what Albert Bandura, a Stanford psychologist who's studied human aggression and atrocity, calls sanitizing euphemisms.[26] These are euphemisms that linguistically—and, so, perhaps also cognitively—suppress the most repugnant qualities of organizational corruption.

For instance, there are many names for police corruption, few of which call up mental pictures of crime and illegality. Stern's young interviewee was told to "make the butts," and the more general term for this—"mooch"—is far from the language of theft or bribery.[27] In a 1968 article on "blue coat" crime, Ellwyn R. Stoddard lists several other, equally endearing euphemisms for police corruption. Police engage in "chiseling," demanding free admission to events. They go "shopping," "picking up"—that is, stealing—"small items such as candy bars, gum, or cigarettes" at closed stores.[28] Police officers also "coop" (which is also referred to as "huddling" or "going down"); these phrases obscure a simple act—sleeping while on duty. Bankers, meanwhile, may engage in "gaming," which sounds far more fun and more benign, too, than fraud, which is what the term refers to. People who steal and embezzle from their employers often describe themselves as "borrowing" the valuable resources.[29]

Violence depends on sanitizing euphemisms, as the bleached language of euphemism helps perpetrators live with violence and its consequences. Recall the veteran Minneapolis officer's admonishment that Andrew Arashiba had missed a "free slap," a nearly innocuous phrase that denies the harm and criminality of police violence. In 1997, an NYPD officer, Justin A. Volpe, tortured Abner Louima, raping him with a broomstick in a bathroom in an NYPD station. "I took a man down tonight," Volpe allegedly told a sergeant about the attack, using not a single descriptive word in his boast. Other officers at the station failed to prevent the assault, despite witnessing Volpe marching Louima "around the station house with his pants around his ankles."[30] Again, the blue code of silence created bystanders and emboldened a criminal. Still others were complicit in the assault on Louima, having previously "driven him to a deserted lot and beaten him," after (wrongly) arresting him for punching Volpe during a brawl at a Brooklyn nightclub.[31] According to Skolnick, the initial assault, which mixes retribution with "a lesson in compliance" is referred to as a "tune up" in police lexicon.[32] (But let us call it by its true name: torture—and what the political scientist Darius Rejali refers to as civic discipline torture.[33])

The history of state violence is written in sanitizing euphemisms. In the United States, torture masquerades as "enhanced interrogation," which sounds like a scientific or upgraded form of a normal interrogation. Water torture, meanwhile, went by "waterboarding," which sounds like a beachside leisure activity.

Argentinian torturers, meanwhile, used a domestic vocabulary to efface their atrocities. The sociologist Stanley Cohen writes of these, in his classic *States of Denial*, with images that destabilize the euphemisms.

> *Assado* (a barbecue) is now a bonfire to burn dead bodies; *la parilla*, the grill for cooking meat, becomes the metal table on which victims are laid out for torture; *Comida de Pescado* (fish food) describes the prisoners thrown from planes into the sea, either drugged or dead, with their stomachs split

open. *Submarino* was not a submarine, or a sandwich, or a traditional children's treat of a chocolate bar melting in milk, but repeatedly holding the victim's head under foul water (often containing urine or feces), stopping each time short of suffocation.[34]

Sanitizing euphemisms also allow perpetrators to deny the victims of their violence. In Cambodia, the Khmer Rouge, a Communist regime that ruled the country from 1975 to 1979, spoke and wrote of smashing, destroying, or discarding their enemies.[35] For perpetrators, it is arguably easier to do those things to other humans than it is to admit that one is killing them. "Smash" and "destroy" suggest the physical breakdown of something immaterial and unhuman, denying the humanity of victims. It also denies the violent criminality, as well as the ethical problems, of the act of killing. This is what Van Naath, a survivor of the Khmer Rouge's notorious S-21 prison, told perpetrators in Rithy Panh's 2003 documentary, *S-21: The Khmer Rouge Killing Machine*: "In the word 'kill,' there still seems to be a moral aspect. In 'destruction,' there's nothing human left. We become dust, just particles blowing in the wind. In 'kill,' there was still . . . we still had a certain value. 'Destruction' is the end. Even for animals you don't speak of destroying, but of killing. We become dust in the wind. There's no humanity left."[36]

The discourse of care, too, euphemizes institutional violence. Rejali, in his encyclopedic *Torture and Democracy*, provides one example. In the 1980s, some New Yorkers used the discourse of care to justify police's use of electrical torture (with stun guns) to extract false confessions from teenage boys of color. A neighbor of one boy suspected of dealing drugs told a reporter, "Sometimes, they deserve it. . . . I think they need some of that lesson when they are 10 and 12 years old, when they're smoking and hanging out, because in 10 years you can't tell them anything."[37] Here, the classic form of denial of victim—"they deserve it"—is combined with the discourse of care to relabel state violence as, merely, a lesson.

Institutional and state actors have used the discourse of care in especially pernicious ways. In the nineteenth and twentieth centuries, the US and Canadian governments forcibly removed indigenous children from their families and communities, placing them in boarding schools. There, some teachers neglected, abused, and tortured indigenous youths. Many died from mistreatment, lack of adequate care, or illness. Many who survived found themselves torn asunder. Their cultural identity had been destroyed. Teachers had assigned them new names and denied them the opportunity to use their native languages.[38] And yet white Americans and Canadians used a discourse of care— humanistic, civilizing, and missionary—to justify the existence of these schools. The most notorious example comes from Richard Pratt, an army officer who founded Carlisle Indian Industrial School. Pratt gave voice to the belief that the schools were in the best interest of indigenous peoples: "A great general has said that the only good Indian is a dead one. . . . In a sense, I agree with the sentiment, but only in this: that all the Indian there is in the race should be dead. Kill the Indian in him, and save the man."[39]

How We Come to Believe That No One's at Fault

Euphemisms have still another effect on organizational action: they permit denial of responsibility when things go terribly wrong. According to Javal Davis, interrogators at Abu Ghraib told military police (MPs) to "loosen" up detainees; they also told MPs to make sure detainees have "a bad night" or that they get "the treatment."[40] Military intelligence (MIs) had the authority to give these orders because of recommendations issued by General Geoffrey Miller in the summer of 2003. Miller, who was then the commander of Guantánamo, had been sent to Iraq to advise on detention and interrogation. He recommended that MPs like Davis be subordinate to MIs, rather than independent, as military policies prescribe. The goal, for Miller, was for MPs to be "actively engaged in *setting the conditions* for successful exploitation of the internees."[41]

MPs like Davis understood this trash heap of language to mean one thing: abuse and torture detainees, until they're willing to talk during interrogations. Of course, when investigators came looking for accountability at Abu Ghraib, neither military interrogators nor General Miller admitted this meaning to their words. The ambiguity itself may be the point. These phrases are two-faced. They can mean something mundane, if not benign; they can also mean torture. Miller's recommendation that military police "set the conditions" for "successful exploitation" of detainees might simply mean, as a military lawyer told a Senate committee investigating Abu Ghraib, that MPs and MIs "talk about . . .

the environment that those prisoners are in day in and day out" and the questions of whether a "detainee [is] having a good day or bad? Has he been quiet, or has he been talking?"[42] MI orders could similarly have been misunderstood by MPs, according to military investigators. For instance, MPs claimed that interrogators ordered MPs to "strip them out and PT them"—"them" meaning detainees. Of these phrases, military investigators wrote, "Whether 'strip out' meant to remove clothing or to isolate we couldn't determine. Whether 'PT them' meant physical stress or abuse can't be determined. The vagueness of this order could, however, have led to any subsequent abuse."[43] The vagueness, more likely, was the point.

Organizational denials of responsibility exceed the use of euphemisms. In his analysis of the bureaucratic processes underlying the Holocaust, the social theorist Zygmunt Bauman concluded that "the organization as a whole is an instrument to obliterate responsibility."[44] This is due to the structure of organizations, which dilute responsibility for action. From the top of organizations drift policies, rules, guidelines, and orders. These are typically ambiguous enough—sometimes intentionally, but often not—to allow their issuers to deny responsibility for the unethical or criminal behavior of subordinates.[45] Nearer the bottom, employees try implementing—or following, if they view themselves as particularly obedient— those policies. Whatever they do, then, seems to them to have been authorized, if not ordered, by those above them.

Technical jargon contributes to this, though it may not be specifically or intentionally developed to obliterate responsibility. Jargon is typical of work in a complex institution. Procedures, policies, and rules are articulated in a highly specialized, context-dependent language that only insiders can understand.[46] In this way, it differs from euphemisms, which are often consciously and intentionally used to efface the more repugnant qualities of organizational corruption. And euphemisms are often ordinary, even benign words and phrases, the better to build a façade of normalcy over crime and cruelty. But like euphemisms, technical jargon tends to sanitize organizational work, keeping the reality of it at arm's length. In part, this is because the meaning of technical jargon is often unclear. When organizational workers interpret the jargon, they may have to guess at its meaning or, else, how to best transform it into action.

The gaps between those giving and those receiving orders create other opportunities for things to go badly and for denial to cover it all up. Those at the top of an organization rarely understand conditions on the ground. Their directives, in turn, can be poorly suited for the worlds in which employees or subordinates work. Policies, practices, and orders, then, may strain the organizational reality itself. Employees may be told to reduce costs or earn profit at nearly impossible rates.[47] Interrogators may be pressured to collect intelligence from recalcitrant—and often innocent and, so, ignorant—detainees. Facing impossible situations, each may turn to questionable, if not outright illegal, if not wholly immoral, practices to accomplish what's expected of them. Still, one searches in vain for accountability, finding only denials of responsibility in its place.

Wells Fargo's well-documented descent into fraud illustrates several of these processes. In 1997, Dick Kovacevich, the bank's CEO, established a new company slogan and, by extension, bankwide goal: "Going for Gr-Eight." (Why? John Stumpf, Kovacevich's successor, insightfully explained, "Because eight rhymes with great.") The slogan required individual banks and their bankers to sell eight products—credit cards, ATM cards, and loans, for instance—to each customer. On its face, it's a benign-enough phrase. But for bankers at Wells Fargo, there was an inevitable problem. Despite the cuteness of its rhyme, the goal was too ambitious, too disconnected from the reality that bankers faced. In an exposé in *Vanity Fair*, Bethany McLean highlights the troubles in St. Helena, California, where "there were only about 11,500 potential customers in the area, and 11 other financial institutions. The quotas for the bankers at Guitron's branch totaled 12,000 Daily Solutions [the bank's term for products] each year, including almost 3,000 new checking accounts. Without fraud, the math didn't work."[48]

Employees of Wells Fargo responded by gaming the system. Bankers pressured customers, who rarely understood the technicalities, into opening unwanted loans. They deceived others, often the elderly or those who were not fluent in English, into opening unnecessary accounts. Or bankers used outright fraud to accomplish the same thing, using forged signatures and fake email addresses to open accounts in customers' names without those customers' knowledge. In total, Wells Fargo found that, between 2011 and 2015, more than 1.5 million accounts and half a million credit-card accounts had been opened by the bank that may not have been authorized by its consumers.[49] The bank also charged customers for life insurance they never purchased and foisted unnecessary car insurance plans on customers who took out car loans with them.[50] In 2020, the bank agreed to a $3 billion settlement with the Securities and Exchange Commission for defrauding customers and the bank's investors. This was, the *New York Times* reported, "not even the largest" sanction of Wells Fargo; the bank had settled an investigation into its mortgage-lending practices, which contributed to the 2008 fiscal crisis, for $5.35 billion. "The bank has paid more than $18 billion in fines for misconduct since the financial crisis," the *Times* laconically concluded.[51]

Where was responsibility for the fraud? Certainly, the "Going for Gr-Eight" approach to banking exerted pressure on bankers. It introduced what criminologists refer to as strain, an imbalance between organizational goals and the legitimate—that is, ethical and legal—means available to pursue those goals.[52] Wells Fargo's bankers simply could not meet organizational quotas through legal, ethical practices. In the face of strain, they innovated, inflating sale numbers through fraud. And yet neither Kovacevich nor Stumpf meant for the "Going for Gr-Eight" approach to be license to defraud. And, of course, the bank does not formally abide fraud. (Few legitimate organizations do, and still . . . .) Stumpf, meanwhile, remained in stubborn disbelief of the problems at Wells Fargo. According to the bank's own investigation, Stumpf's nature as an "optimistic executive" kept him from perceiving systemic problems, instead blaming a "few bad employees" for trouble within the bank.[53]

Responsibility? Perhaps, then, it's at the bottom of the bank, among the individual bankers. But individual bankers, the ones committing fraud, thought they knew what Kovacevich, Stumpf, Wells Fargo's board, and the layers of middle managers wanted done: meet sales goals, at any cost and by any means necessary. Managers sent this message by ignoring bankers' concerns about fraud, allegedly berating bankers who had not met sales goals, pressuring bankers to sell products to customers who could not use or appropriately manage those products, and suggesting that bankers make sales goals by "achieving 'solutions'"—note the sanitizing jargon—"through family members."[54] Employees who failed to make quotas were compelled to work late or on weekends.

Bank managers often did the same. And they faced their own pressures. Managers of banks were under constant scrutiny from district managers, "motivated" to make sales quotas through daily emails, meetings, and more. One regional president allegedly organized a "running" of the "gauntlet." District managers dressed in "themed costumes," forming lines through which managers ran down until they reached a whiteboard on which they'd scribble the number of sales they achieved. This regional president also allegedly suggested "to subordinates that they encourage customers to sign up for products regardless of need."[55] In this sort of work environment, it's not surprising that employees believed superiors want them to "sell" by any means necessary. The emphasis on outcomes and the relative indifferences to how those outcomes are achieved can feel like a wink and a nod by supervisors to fraud.[56] It's also not surprising that those very superiors could themselves plausibly deny responsibility for what their subordinates did. The pressure to sell, after all, can be defended as just that—not an implicit authorization of unethical practices, but an expression of ambition and aspiration. It's an affirmation, too, of healthy competition.

Denial of Knowledge, or How No One Knows

Organizations obliterate not only responsibility. They also obliterate knowledge, particularly guilty knowledge, of misconduct and wrongdoing. In part, this is a result of the fragmentation of action. Orders come from above, are passed along by middle management, and are enacted by workers in circumstances that don't always fit those orders. Organizational actors may not, in fact, genuinely know what the end result of all their meager contributions are. But one can cultivate strategic and willful ignorance to what others are up to.[57] One simply does not inquire. Stockholders, for instance, may vote to not have certain facts about corporate behavior disclosed to them.[58] Or investors can be kept in the dark. Wells Fargo, according to prosecutors, allegedly hid fraudulent banking practices "from investors by changing its public descriptions of its sales practices over several years."[59] Subordinates, meanwhile, may know or even simply sense that they *ought not* bring certain facts to the attention of supervisors, all the better for maintaining the plausible deniability of those supervisors.[60] Still others, who might resist organizational misconduct, are prevented from learning about it by being excluded from meetings or memo chains. Or they're ignored, then fired, like Yesenia Guitron, a Wells Fargo banker who documented fraud and warned bank managers about it.

But the structural secrecy of organizations is not merely an outcome of knowing too little. Paradoxically, it can also be the outcome of knowing too much. "Rules that guarantee wide distribution of information can increase the amount to the point that a lot is not read," writes Vaughan, in her study of the Challenger shuttle disaster.[61] Organizations may also intentionally use the glut of information to bury evidence of wrongdoing. This is how Michigan State University allegedly responded to requests for documents by William Forsyth, whom the Michigan attorney general appointed to investigate Michigan State's handling of sexual assault accusations against Dr. Larry Nassar. In a 2018 update on the investigation, Forsyth describes how the university frustrated the investigation by "drowning investigators in irrelevant documents," including documents describing bed-bug management procedures and a "seemingly endless (and duplicative) supply of emails from news-clipping services containing publicly available articles."[62]

Denial of knowledge is not just a problem within organizations. There are significant barriers that confound regulators', the press's, and the public's efforts to learn of organizational misconduct. Regulators, though tasked with the responsibility to uncover "guilty knowledge," are highly dependent on the organizations that they're meant to monitor. Most cannot access the places, information, and people needed to expose wrongdoing without coordinating with the organization itself.[63] This dependence leads to a predictable difficulty. Organizations often know when regulators or outside observers will visit and audit them. Because of this, they can manipulate the conditions of audits, hiding incriminating information.

For instance, at Abu Ghraib, the US military prevented International Committee of the Red Cross (ICRC) monitors from interviewing some detainees, particularly those held by the CIA. (The ICRC is tasked, by the Geneva Conventions, with monitoring detention conditions during war.) Some detainees—known as "ghost detainees"—remained unregistered at Abu Ghraib and were moved constantly throughout the facility. This prevented the ICRC from knowing of their detention there. Meanwhile, the US military denied the ICRC access to a number of detainees during January and March 2004 visits to the facility.[64]

Perpetrators of torture further confound the ability of outsiders to discover torture through their use of stealth—that is, nonscarring and, in some cases, even nonbruising—techniques.[65] Robert H. Willoughby, a student of Erving Goffman's, noted this practice among attendants in mental hospitals in the 1950s. Citing Willoughby's unpublished thesis, Goffman describes how patients may be "necked"—again, note the euphemism—or choked "into submission" with a wet towel "that leaves no visible evidence of mistreatment." "Absence of mistreatment can be faked," Goffman ominously concludes, but "not order."[66]

While organizations that torture are singularly committed to hiding their crimes, these problems are not limited to them. Some organizations confound regulators, monitors, and other external observers by simply not creating paper trails. According to a lawsuit brought by the State of New York, the Sackler family, owners of Purdue Pharma, the maker of the opioid OxyContin, "abolished quarterly reports" and "insisted that numbers be recounted only orally to board members."[67] This might have had two effects. One was to preserve the plausible deniability of board members for Purdue Pharma's role in the opioid crisis. In the absence of a paper trail, outsiders wouldn't know for sure what Purdue Pharma's board indeed knew about the risks and sales of their drug. The other was to thin out Purdue Pharma's paper trail, making that role more difficult to discover in the first place. Distributors of opioids, meanwhile, allegedly "warned pharmacies when their monthly opioid limits were approaching, then helped them manipulate the timing and volume of orders to circumvent the limits. On the rare occasion when a distributor would conduct 'surprise' audits of its customers, it would often alert them in advance, the complaint says."[68]

Organizations can also suppress information and evidence, keeping it out of the public eye. For decades, tobacco companies did just this, keeping studies that pointed to the harmful effects of tobacco use from becoming public.[69] They can also disguise incriminating information. For the better part of three decades, petroleum companies, particularly ExxonMobil, appear to have misled the public about the link between their products and climate change. While the company's scientists produced reports, some of which were indeed published and discussed publicly, affirming the link between carbon emissions and climate change, the company published ads and funded think tanks that denied the link, intentionally sowing uncertainty and hiding climate change in the plain sight of information overload and in the fog of climate change skepticism.[70]

Organizational misconduct, as well as the misconduct of employees, can also be kept out of the public eye through agreements that prevent employees, even victims, from divulging what they know. The tobacco company Philip Morris, for instance, required its scientists to sign lifelong agreements not to discuss their work in public. It was only after the company "released them from that pledge," at the request of the US Subcommittee on Health and the Environment, that the scientists could discuss with Congress their research on the addictiveness of tobacco.[71]

Even more pernicious are the nondisclosure agreements (NDAs) that prevent victims from speaking about their experiences publicly. Miramax, the production company founded by Harvey and Bob Weinstein, pressured some of the women whom the former had mistreated, harassed, and assaulted to sign NDAs during settlements. Miramax also required employees to sign NDAs that prevented employees from "disclosing any information" about the two founders.[72] These agreements isolate victims, preventing them from learning that their experiences are not theirs alone, but part of a pattern of abuse. It prevents the public from understanding the same. In this way, NDAs can contribute to the perpetuation of organizational misconduct. Evidence of wrongdoing remains fragmented, experiences remain unrecognized, victims remain isolated, and, in the end, perpetrators remain empowered to continue acting with relative impunity.[73] Not surprisingly, powerful serial sexual harassers and abusers often make NDAs part of their terror.

The Bush administration popularized a relatively obscure word—"redaction"—that makes the suppression of evidence of state crimes both literal and symbolic. It's literal, for the word refers to the blacking out of information in released documents, allegedly for national security reasons. It's also symbolic, because redactions gesture beyond what's kept from the public and toward the fact of the state's power to control information. A single word or phrase might appear on an otherwise redacted page on a government report. "Cables indicate that Agency interrogators [redacted word] applied the waterboard technique to Khalid Shaykh Muhammed" appears on page 45 of the CIA inspector general's report ("Counterterrorism Detention and Interrogation Activities") on the CIA's interrogation program.[74] This sentence fragment is surrounded by an ocean of blacked-out text. Other pages of the report look the same—blocks of blacked-out text, cracked to expose nearly meaningless combinations of words: "waterboard on Abu Zubaydah," for instance.[75]

Mass redactions actually seem fairly sophisticated when compared with the CIA's destruction of videotapes of its interrogations. The CIA decided to destroy the tapes, some of which recorded the use of waterboarding, after the release of the Abu Ghraib photographs in April 2004. According to

Jose Rodriguez, the agency official who ordered the destruction of the tapes, the decision was about "getting rid of some ugly visuals."[76] The decision, however, did more than that. To this day, waterboarding remains the most controversial of the CIA's practices. In part, this is because supporters of the practice have claimed that it can be used with restraint and care, denials of harm that could have been checked against the visual record.[77]

All of this assumes that outside observers want to know the truth. But this is not always the case. Through the end of March and all of April 2020, no interviewer had asked the eventual Democratic nominee, Joe Biden, about Tara Reade's allegations that he sexually assaulted her in 1993.[78] Reporting on Harvey Weinstein's sexual assaults and Donald J. Trump's misuse of campaign funds taught the public a new euphemism, "catch and kill." The phrase refers to the practice of news organizations, in this case the company that owns the *National Enquirer*, to protect powerful people—often, men—by acquiring exclusive rights to damaging stories about them and then never publishing the stories.[79]

* * *

These efforts to suppress knowledge of organizational wrongdoing point to an apparent contradiction. On one hand, organizational members are socialized into accepting wrongdoing, seeing it as normal, perhaps necessary, even justified. But the close control over information—internally, to keep some in the organization protected from guilty knowledge, and externally, to keep the public ignorant, too—points to how partial denial always is. The organization that hides evidence of its wrongdoing remains convinced of its own illegality and immorality. They know, in other words, that they have something to hide.

The fear is this: secrets rarely stay so. Most organizations have a "compulsive bureaucratic urge to record every detail, no matter how loathsome," Cohen writes in *States of Denial*.[80] Whistleblowers exploit the urge, leaking internal reports, damning communications, or, rarely but most spectacularly, photographs and video evidence to the press. Some will testify publicly, bravely putting a name to their disclosures. What was only sensed is converted—first into knowledge and perhaps, eventually, into truth.[81]

But once more, denial. It stalks the secrets, chases down the whistleblowers, and speaks, convincingly, for the accused.

5

HOW TO AVOID SCANDAL

Elites Managing Problems

A VIDEO is released of a US presidential candidate bragging about sexually assaulting women. Women testify to the media that the candidate had indeed sexually assaulted them. The candidate is elected still.

A decade prior, in the months before another presidential election, a sitting president is embroiled in the country's first torture scandal in over a century. Still, he's reelected and his defense secretary, who had put his name to a memo authorizing torture, keeps his job.

Before that, a president lies to Congress about a sexual relationship with a White House intern. He's impeached by the House but acquitted by the Senate. He finishes his second term with enduring support among his political party and finds a pile of riches waiting for him: book contracts, speaking engagements, and honorary degrees.

Scandals represent a peculiar transformation in denial. At their onset, they seem to signal the end of denial. Collective attention finally turns, in spectacular ways, toward personal misconduct, abuses of power, and social problems. Suddenly, open secrets become acknowledged and secret secrets burst into public view. Investigators investigate; politicians politick; protesters organize. Change seems within reach.

But then comes the response. Those who are most likely to be enmeshed in scandals are also the most skilled at extracting themselves from scandals. The discourse of crisis management comes naturally to most political, corporate, and media elites. The powerful are also the best resourced, helped along by masters of denial, apology, and law. Facing scandal, they rhetorically stutter-step. Scandal lunges, stumbles, and recovers itself, only empty-handed.

In fact, for all the attention given to them, for all their power to draw the public in, scandals often do not result in meaningful political or social change. They don't even always damage the reputations of those embroiled in them, though Andrew Cuomo, the former governor of New York, might beg to differ.[1] Now and then, a scandal costs a middling government official, a college administrator, or a CEO a job. Seen more clearly, however, scandal's meager burden is this: to bring attention, for a time, to a transgression of social norms or even laws. This attention can itself have beneficial, collective effects, according to John Thompson, a British sociologist who's studied political scandals. Thompson writes that scandals force the public to confront "the shortcomings and transgressions" of public officials and work "through the sometimes painful process of disclosure, denunciation, and retribution." Both sorts of reckonings, Thompson reasons, can reinforce "the norms, conventions, and institutions" the scandal-inducing transgression initially threatened.[2]

Scandal provides us with another opportunity, too: to observe denial in its most conspicuous forms. Responses to scandal are now so highly formulaic—scripted, rehearsed, and often stiffly performed—that these forms are easily detectable. This chapter identifies, defines, and illustrates these forms, the better to anticipate the next effort of a president, member of Congress, media talking head, or corporate leader to extricate themselves from the self-set trap of scandal.

Scandal, Doubled

Scandal begins with the transformation of a previously overlooked, ignored, or unknown transgression into a public allegation. The shock of the revelation itself scandalizes and, in the early stages of scandal, spokespeople often explain or apologize for the revelation as much as what's revealed.

We can see this in the very first report on the Abu Ghraib photographs, which aired on CBS's *60 Minutes II* program on April 28, 2004. Near the end of the fifteen-minute report on Abu Ghraib, Dan Rather, the show's host, questioned General Mark Kimmitt, then deputy director of coalition operations in Iraq, about a particularly disturbing photograph. The photo in question showed the corpse of an Iraqi detainee, later identified as Manadel al-Jamadi.

> RATHER: And then there is this picture of an Iraqi man who appears to be dead and badly beaten.
>
> KIMMITT: It's reprehensible that anybody'd be taking a picture of that situation.

RATHER: It'd be reprehensible that he'd be taking a picture of that situation. What about the situation itself?[3]

KIMMITT: Well, I don't know the facts around what caused the bruising and the bleeding. Um, if that is also one of the charges being brought against the soldiers— that, too, is absolutely unacceptable and completely— uh—outside of what we expect of our soldiers and our guards at the prison.

Confronted with a photograph of a dead detainee, injuries to his face obvious, Kimmitt's instinct was to condemn the evidence, the photograph, and the photographer who produced them—not those who had committed the murder. But Kimmitt was not alone. Days later, Secretary of Defense Donald Rumsfeld gave a public apology during a congressional hearing on Abu Ghraib. But Rumsfeld's apology largely focused on the scandal of the revelation itself, expressing remorse for failing to convey to the president, Congress, and the public "the gravity of this before we saw it in the media."[4]

The scandal of Abu Ghraib was two scandals at once. It was a torture scandal, which was *revealed* by the release of the photographs. But it was also the scandal *of* the photographs. On one hand, their existence was scandalous, for they revealed that those who took them had become so desensitized to torture, or so titillated by it, that they wanted souvenirs of their violence.[5] On the other hand, the publication of the photographs, seemingly out of nowhere, was itself a scandal. The leak of the photographs revealed that the US military, the Department of Defense, and the Bush administration had failed to oversee detention and interrogation at Abu Ghraib. The failure was such that President George W. Bush and the US Congress were all apparently unaware of the photographs' existence and impending release by CBS.

But Abu Ghraib is unusual. Rarely does a scandal arrive as fully formed, as it did in the spring of 2004. No surprise, then, that the photographs ruptured US politics. More common, however, are scandals that arrive through the slow leak of information. Even still, many of these scandals are themselves doubled. They are scandals of initial transgressions; they are scandals, too, of cover-up. As I initially drafted this chapter in September 2019, the *New Yorker* published (another) article by Ronan Farrow that illustrates the double nature of scandal. Farrow, who'd previously investigated Harvey Weinstein's crimes and Weinstein's efforts to hide them, now reported on the MIT Media Lab and the lab's then—but soon to be former—director, Joi Ito. Farrow's article detailed how Ito solicited funding and other forms of financial support from Jeffrey Epstein. This relationship continued even after the latter had pled guilty to "state charges of solicitation of prostitution and procurement of minors for prostitution" and been disqualified by MIT from giving donations.[6]

Ito's relationship with Epstein was bad enough. But Farrow's reporting that Ito and Peter Cohen, the lab's director of development and strategy, had actively covered up their work with Epstein deepened the scandal and led to Ito's resignation the day after the article's publication. Farrow's investigation revealed myriad strategies of effacement and cover-up. Epstein was referred to only by his initials in Ito's calendar;

full names of other high-profile guests of the lab were typical. Epstein's donations were listed as "anonymous." His name was scrubbed from records of donations that he himself solicited from other wealthy donors. Cohen, meanwhile, tried to keep at least one faculty member, Ethan Zuckerman, who opposed the lab's relationship with Epstein, from knowing about the latter's visits to the lab. Farrow writes, "In 2015, as Epstein's visit drew near, Cohen instructed his staff to insure that Zuckerman, if he unexpectedly arrived while Epstein was present, be kept away from the glass-walled office in which Epstein would be conducting meetings." The revelation of the cover-up, as much or perhaps even more than what was covered up, doomed Ito.

There is, then, the scandal of transgression and the scandal of transgression's concealment. Thompson helpfully distinguishes between these, calling them first-order and second-order transgressions.[7] First-order transgressions are the initial actions that violate norms or laws. This is the torture committed at Abu Ghraib. It is Ito's solicitation of money and support from Epstein, even after MIT had prohibited financial relationships with him. Second-order transgressions are all the efforts—often within the law, though sometimes barely—to keep those first-order transgressions from becoming public in the first place.

Both forms of scandal are visible in media coverage and the US House's investigation of President Trump's dealings with Ukrainian president Volodymyr Zelensky, which eventually led to Trump's first impeachment. First-order transgressions, such as Trump's request that Ukraine investigate the Bidens in exchange for US aid, were at the center of this scandal. (The sudden cultural currency of the phrase "quid pro quo" is evidence of this.) But certainly the initial power of the scandal also involved second-order transgressions, such as the revelation that Trump's phone call with Zelensky had been covered up, inappropriately classified in order to protect Trump.

Even if legal, second-order transgressions scandalize for a few reasons. By trying to hide first-order transgressions, people reveal that they realize those transgressions are discrediting, improper, even unethical or illegal, all claims to ignorance of criminality or innocent intentions aside. Additionally, second-order transgressions are often betrayals of public trust and the rule of law. Particularly in liberal democracies, power—political power certainly and to a lesser extent economic and institutional power—is meant to be wielded openly and transparently.[8] Ironically, then, the concealment of a first-order transgression, particularly by elected officials, can be more damaging than the first-order transgression itself. Former president Bill Clinton, for instance, found himself impeached for perjury and obstruction of justice— that is, for *lying* about his affair with Monica Lewinsky—not for the more famous and better-remembered affair itself.[9]

Evidence and the "Undeniable" Scandal

First-order transgressions are typically concealed. It usually takes a disclosure, seemingly out of nowhere, to transform the hidden transgression into a public scandal. Sometimes, scandal arrives in the form of an allegation—one or sometimes several accounts by those privy to the transgression. But a single allegation, even a few allegations of those in the know, is vulnerable to the outright denials of the accused. Stanley Cohen, in *States of Denial*, refers to this as literal denial. Those using literal denial claim that alleged transgressions did not occur. Bill Clinton's infamous lie, "I did not have sexual relations with that woman," is an example of this. Clinton issued his defiant denial in January 1998. At the time, reports of his affair with then–White House intern Monica Lewinsky were based solely on the statements of Linda Tripp, a confidante of Lewinsky, as well as media reports of rumors that Lewinsky possessed a dress stained with the president's semen. When, in July 1998, Lewinsky began cooperating with Special Prosecutor Kenneth Starr's investigation and produced the dress, Clinton was compelled to admit that he indeed had a "relationship" with Lewinsky that was "not appropriate."[10]

Scandals that don't exceed initial allegations are likely to stall. Or they're likely to give the upper hand to those with the most institutional and social power. We saw this dramatically in the testimony that Judge Brett M. Kavanaugh, then President Trump's nominee to the Supreme Court, gave to the Senate Judiciary Committee in September 2018. After an initial and fairly standard nomination hearing before the Judiciary Committee, Kavanaugh returned to address accusations made by Dr. Christine Blasey Ford that Kavanaugh had sexually assaulted her during a party in the summer of 1982. Using literal denial, Kavanaugh denied being at the party at which the alleged assault happened; he also denied having assaulted Ford. In support of his denials, Kavanaugh cited the statements of four other people who, according to Ford, were allegedly at the party. All, Kavanaugh said, did not recall the assault. One, a friend of Ford, had "no recollection of ever being at a party or gathering" where Kavanaugh was present.[11]

In his testimony to the Senate Judiciary Committee, Kavanaugh dramatically performed his denials, expressing righteous indignation, anger, and despair at the potential derailment of his career and public reputation. Because there was no compelling, *documentary* evidence to support Ford's accusation, Kavanaugh had the performative space to execute his outrage.[12] Indeed, the most important documentary evidence, a calendar that Kavanaugh kept during the summer of 1982, neither proved nor disproved Ford's allegations. No doubt, Kavanaugh understood that the political and media allies would allow him to address the scandal in "he said / she said" terms.

Beyond Allegations: The Potency of Documentary Evidence

More potent than allegations are documentary forms of evidence, particularly incriminating letters or emails, photographs, tape-recorded conversations, and, now, texts and social media communications. Documentary evidence preserves back-stage words, actions, and events that are otherwise ephemeral. This, then, gives them their revelatory power: documentary evidence seems to bring the private into public view.[13]

These forms of evidence are especially powerful for several reasons. They're highly reproducible and can be quickly disseminated through the media. They are also compelling props for the performance of scandals. Documents can be held up during congressional testimony and dramatically read. Audio recordings can be played aloud for witnesses. Photographs can run on the covers of newspapers, on protest signs, or behind news anchors as they deliver reports.

Documentary forms of evidence also act as checks on denial, though only in a rather narrow sense. Credible documentary forms of evidence often foreclose literal denial, the outright denial of an alleged transgression. This is particularly true of direct forms of evidence, such as photographs, video recordings, and audio recordings. These forms of evidence seem to reproduce a first-order transgression as it had occurred or in a way that seems to directly capture the transgression.

After the release of the Abu Ghraib photographs, it became impossible for the Bush administration to outright deny that detainees were being mistreated by US soldiers, at least at a single detention facility in Iraq. Rumsfeld, for instance, said of the photos, "We have taken a beating in the world for things we were not doing that were alleged to be done. Now we're taking a beating, understandably, for things that did, in fact, happen."[14] Confronting the photographs, a politician would seem a step or two outside the "reality-based community," to borrow the infamous phrase attributed to Karl Rove, if they outright denied what the photographs showed: naked detainees, some in stress positions, others being forced to simulate sexual acts, others jeered at by US soldiers.[15]

Cellphone and body-camera videos of police officers beating or killing Black men and boys have proven undeniable in another sense: they can act as direct checks on officers' descriptions of those killings. For instance, in October 2014, Jason Van Dyke, an officer with the Chicago police, fatally shot Laquan McDonald, a seventeen-year-old African American teenager. Officer accounts and official reports of the shooting claimed McDonald, who was carrying a knife with a three-inch blade, attempted to stab officers before the shooting. This account held up for over a year, until a county judge ordered Chicago to release dashboard-camera footage of the shooting. On November 24, 2015, hours before the video was released, Van Dyke was charged with first-degree murder. The released footage showed McDonald walking near but not toward officers. And the footage contradicted officers' claims that McDonald had attempted to attack them. Ultimately, the video acted as a check on the public denials of the Chicago police department and eventually contributed to the 2018 conviction of Van Dyke for the murder of McDonald.[16]

Similarly, cellphone footage that showed Michael T. Slager, a white police officer in North Charleston, South Carolina, shooting Walter L. Scott in the back contradicted Slager's official account of the 2015 shooting. The release of the footage, taken by Feidin Santana, a bystander, eventually led to Slager's federal prosecution for violating Scott's civil rights and a twenty-year sentence.[17]

More recently, bystander video proved critical to the prosecution and eventual conviction of Derek Chauvin for the 2020 murder of George Floyd in Minneapolis, Minnesota. The Minneapolis Police Department's initial account described Floyd's death as caused by a "medical incident" that occurred during Floyd's arrest. Bystander video, by contrast, revealed that Chauvin kneeled on Floyd's neck for nine and a half minutes, ignoring Floyd's pleas and a crowd of witnesses' protests.

Video recordings can undercut law enforcements' accounts of how that violence occurred. But they do not guarantee a conviction of officers or an end to denial. In 1992, a jury acquitted the Los Angeles police officers involved in the brutal beating and tasing of Rodney King, despite the recorded evidence of the assault. Over two decades later, a New York grand jury declined to bring criminal charges against Officer Daniel Pantaleo of the New York Police Department after Pantaleo killed Eric Garner during a video-recorded confrontation on a Staten Island sidewalk.[18] Though literally undeniable, these recordings and others like them remain vulnerable to officers' claims of necessity and self-defense, as well as the US legal system's willingness to legitimize those claims.

Photographs and video recordings seem to be a special case of documentary evidence. They offer a singular form of directness and objectivity, in that the devices that produce them record whatever appears before them, independent of the subjective intentions of the person operating those devices. (This assumes the images have not been modified or faked.) The French philosopher Roland Barthes put this quality of visual records best in his writing on photography: "In Photography, I can never deny that the thing has been there."[19]

Audio recordings come close to this level of directness. Richard Nixon, Thompson argues, was done in by the presence of *undeniable*—again, in that literal sense—recordings that incriminated him in the Watergate break-in.[20] The Trump administration's handling of "transcripts" of the president's call with President Zelensky of Ukraine speaks, though only in an oblique way, to this quality of audio records.[21] The Trump administration released a document they—and many in the media—referred to as a transcript of the call. But the incompleteness of the document, and its potential partiality toward the president, became caught in processes of claims making and counterclaims making. The document was, in fact, a "memorandum" and not a "verbatim transcript" of the phone call. (The document itself said this, and yet it was still referred to as a transcript.) No doubt, the release of an actual audio recording of Trump's call would have been received differently by the media and public.

But even written documents can offer a seemingly local perspective on first-order transgressions. This is particularly so of written documents that are richly descriptive, so as to provide the proverbial "thousand words" a photograph is said to be worth. Such documents have particular power when their authors are insiders to the organizations, corporations, or institutions that committed the transgressions. When authors are aligned with those who committed the first–order transgressions, readers are often more willing to treat those written accounts as credible, even objective.

For instance, human-rights organizations produce vitally important investigations of torture. These investigations document torture's use; its physical, psychological, and social effects on victims; and even its effect on perpetrators. These investigations chip away at denial, by bringing hidden acts to public attention. By promoting a political culture of monitoring and accountability, they also may contain the use of torture.[22] But these investigations are vulnerable. Government officials who authorize torture, their allies in the media, and their supporters among the public often deeply mistrust human-rights and civil liberties organizations. They accuse these organizations of bias (against the country, an administration, or a regime). Or of naiveté (for trusting the country's enemies to provide honest accounts of torture). These two claims are part of the literal denial package.[23] Political officials alleged to have authorized or ignored torture use these claims to discredit those making the allegations. If these claims work, the allegation, no matter how well documented, may disappear. But when government officials, national security officials, soldiers, or interrogators themselves document torture, the effects are far more unsettling to the political status quo.[24] Simply put, it's much more difficult to discredit these actors, who serve the very country and institutions implicated in torture.

This is how the US detention facility at Guantánamo became a scandal. In 2004, when Abu Ghraib threatened to consume the Bush administration, Guantánamo stood out as a contrasting success story. Members of Congress, particularly Republicans, praised the interrogations that occurred at the facility. They did so, in part, to downplay concerns that there were systemic problems of detainee abuse and torture in the United States' war on terror. This was possible because there was not yet an official, documentary record of abuse and torture at Guantánamo. Human-rights organizations had been raising concerns about the facility since its opening in 2002. They had, however, raised them in a political culture unwilling to listen. Members of Congress downplayed concerns about the facility; some even labeled criticisms of the facility as un-American.[25] More frequently, these concerns were simply ignored.

Then, in December 2004, the Department of Justice released emails and memos written by FBI agents who had been stationed at Guantánamo. In these documents, FBI agents expressed serious concerns about military interrogations at the facility. One described the interrogations as involving "torture techniques."[26] Another described the treatment of detainees in excruciating detail, offering the sort of local depiction more typical of photographs. (For ease of reading, I've added periods to the end of sentences in the email; these appear lost from the copy of the email released by the Department of Justice.)

On a couple of occasions, I entered interview rooms to find a detainee chained hand and foot in a fetal position to the floor, with no chair, food or water. Most times they had urinated and defecated on themselves and had been left there for 18 to 24 hours or more. On one occasion, the air conditioning had been turned so far down and the temperature was so cold in the room that the barefooted detainee was shaking with cold. On another occasion, the air conditioning had been turned off, making the temperature in the unventilated room probably well over 100 degrees. The detainee was almost unconscious on the floor, with a pile of hair lying next to him. He had apparently literally been pulling his own hair out throughout the night.[27]

In 2005, a *Time* magazine article included excerpts of another official document—a military interrogation log of Mohammed al-Qahtani, then still classified—that offered a play-by-play account of abuse and torture at the facility.[28] Investigations again followed. Congressional hearings, too. Eventually, both political parties largely abandoned their support of the facility. The public and political image of Guantánamo would never recover (though its use to hold detainees indefinitely endures to this day).

Local accounts are powerful scandal makers. There are several reasons for this. On one hand, local accounts typically describe first-order transgressions in narrative form. Transgressors can be figured as perpetrators, even villains. These are familiar, easily understood characters.[29] By identifying these characters, local accounts aid in the pursuit of accountability and closure to the breach in the moral order. They do so by figuring the *cause* of a problem or scandal in the form of a few people, at whom blame can be directed or laws enforced, rather than in opaque institutions or the seemingly inscrutable social structure by which sociologists explain collective ills.

Local accounts may also identify and describe the suffering of victims. This can take evocative form, as in the FBI email above. These descriptions help readers empathize with victims. They may also provoke outrage. No surprise, then, that human-rights organizations tell stories, often of the suffering of *one*, when attempting to engage the public.[30]

Local accounts, too, also transform enduring, often systemic, problems into digestible episodes. In so doing, they affirm the agency of individual actors and, especially, whistleblowers that interrupt, interfere, or prevent transgressions. They suggest, in other words, that a few right-minded, courageous people can reveal, even stop, abuses of power. Joseph Darby, a US reservist, helped end the nightmare of Abu Ghraib by passing compact discs of digital photographs to a military investigator. Alberto Mora, a navy lawyer, meanwhile recorded his opposition to the Bush administration's interrogation policies; doing so, he pressured the Department of Defense to change those policies. Whistleblowers, too, figure prominently in the 2019 House investigations of Trump's dealings with Ukraine. To be sure, most whistleblowers are initially, if not enduringly, reviled, particularly by those whose power they threaten. But when a scandal converts enough of the public and the powerful, whistleblowers often become heroes.

Conversely, local accounts can also instruct by revealing the individuals who failed to act; these are the stories of bystanders who might have prevented brewing trouble from bubbling over. Thus the power of the fable of the "thirty-eight witnesses" to Genovese's murder. We read of the passive bystanders—those who failed to take action, those who became complicit through inaction—in accounts of sexual violence at Penn State and Miramax.[31]

In all these ways, local accounts affirm the agency and power of individuals. They resonate, then, with common-sense understandings, especially in the United States, about the causes and solutions to political and social problems.[32] They background intractable factors that produce first-order transgressions—permissive policies, government or corporate secrecy, social and economic power, to name a few. This is its own sort of denial. But certainly part of the scandalizing power of local accounts is that they render problems intelligible, even solvable, to the public.

On the Limits of Evidence

But evidence takes us only so far. We risk overestimating evidence, particularly photographic evidence, when we claim it is "undeniable." A photograph, or an audio recording, or even a written account may seem to give us a window on the back-stage dealings and crimes of the powerful. But we still need to describe what we see. We need to understand it. And we need to discover what's just beyond the horizon. The release of some particularly scandalous bit of evidence signals, then, not the end of politics, but the beginning. Likewise, it is not the end of denial, but a phase beyond *outright*, or literal, denial.

Choose a scandal, any scandal, instigated by the release of visual evidence, and this is quickly apparent. As a candidate and president, Donald Trump outright denied that he's sexually assaulted, sexually harassed, or mistreated women. But following the release of the *Access Hollywood* footage of an off-screen conversation between him and host Billy Bush, Trump could not outright deny that he spoke these words about women: "You know, I'm automatically attracted to beautiful . . .—I just start kissing them. It's like a magnet. Just kiss. I don't even wait. And when you're a star, they let you do it. You can do anything." And these: "Grab 'em by the pussy. You can do anything."[33]

Rather than manage the scandal of these comments with literal denial, Trump relied on what Cohen calls interpretive denial.[34] This is a rhetorical strategy through which the denier relabels a first-order transgression. Usually, the denier relabels the transgression with a less serious term. For instance, Trump used interpretive denial to relabel his words as "locker room talk."[35] They reflected, he suggested, not a description of actual actions—sexual assaults—but masculine bluster. This use of interpretive denial attempts two things at once. On one hand, Trump attempted to normalize his speech, suggesting it's typical of how most heterosexual men speak, to each other and about women, behind closed doors. On the other hand, he also tried to transform the talk into talk only, rather than a description of a reality in which he indeed sexually assaults women, as critics construed the taped confession.

But what of evidence of actual events, not words? The Abu Ghraib photographs were undeniable at a literal level. But the release of them precipitated a competition to label what they showed. Most politicians and many media members referred to the "abuse" or "mistreatment" of detainees at Abu Ghraib, rather than the "torture."[36] Some did so seemingly by default, not arguing against the use of the label "torture" per se, but still avoiding the word. In the first report on the Abu Ghraib photographs, the news anchor Dan Rather referred to US soldiers as having "mistreated" detainees, and *60 Minutes II*'s initial reporting on Abu Ghraib used the word "abuse," not torture.[37] Others, like Rumsfeld, were more explicit and intentional in their use of interpretive denial. Responding to a question about whether *torture* occurred at Abu Ghraib, Rumsfeld answered, "I think that—I'm not a lawyer. My impression is that what has been charged thus far is abuse, which I believe technically is different from torture. I don't know if the—it is correct to say what you just said, that torture has taken place, or that there's been a conviction for torture. And therefore I'm not going to address the torture word."[38]

Later, some of the techniques photographed at Abu Ghraib—keeping detainees in painful stress positions, for instance—would be reinterpreted in a different way. When it turned out that the Bush administration had authorized the CIA to use techniques like stress positions, beatings, and waterboarding, torture went from merely "abuse," which still remains a crime, to (allegedly) acceptable, professional, sophisticated "enhanced interrogation" techniques. In this case, interpretive denial reworks the illegality and immorality of torture, drawing it into the sphere of legitimate discourse and policy through the use of a sanitizing euphemism.[39]

Interpretive denial allows claims makers to do two things at once: acknowledge the literal existence of whatever problem or scandal is under scrutiny, while denying its problematic or scandalous nature. Empirically cornered by compelling evidence and public pressure, those using interpretive denial first place themselves within the reality-based community of their critics. They admit, if even only implicitly, the validity of that compelling evidence. But then they void it by renaming what the evidence shows.

Interpretive denial is often combined with what Cohen refers to as implicatory denial.[40] These are the justifications that deflate scandals; most are similar to the everyday ones I described in chapter 3: denial of victim and denial of harm.

For instance, in the Bush administration's rendering, victims of torture were "unlawful, enemy combatants," "the worst of the worst," or, simply, "terrorists."[41] They were frequently described as resisting traditional—that is, nontorturous—interrogation techniques. And the US public was told that these detainees had information about imminent terrorist attacks. Through these descriptions of detainees, the Bush administration denied the victim status of those who suffered torture, cast survivors of torture as deserving of their treatment, and construed torture as a necessary, life-saving practice.[42]

The Obama administration used implicatory denial to justify the linchpin of its national security policies: drone strikes. To an unprecedented extent, the Obama administration employed unmanned aerial vehicles, or drones, to conduct surveillance of, and, in many cases, missile strikes against, apparent terrorists, supposed threats to US security. In a May 2013 speech, Obama described the program's efficacy, doubling down on many of the same justifications that Bush had used when addressing CIA torture.

> To begin with, our actions are effective. Don't take my word for it. In the intelligence gathered at bin Laden's compound, we found that he wrote, "We could lose the reserves to enemy's air strikes. We cannot fight air strikes with explosives." Other communications from al Qaeda operatives confirm this as well. Dozens of highly skilled al Qaeda commanders, trainers, bomb makers and operatives have been taken off the battlefield. Plots have been disrupted that would have targeted international aviation, U.S. transit systems, European cities and our troops in Afghanistan. Simply put, these strikes have saved lives.[43]

And yet the *New York Times'* Scott Shane reported in 2015 that "every independent investigation of the strikes has found far more civilian casualties than administration officials admit. Gradually, it has become clear that when operators in Nevada fire missiles into remote tribal territories on the other side of the world, they often do not know who they are killing, but are making an imperfect best guess."[44]

The Obama administration's rhetorical management of force-feeding at Guantánamo also included both interpretive and implicatory forms of denial. In 2013, approximately 100 detainees at Guantánamo participated in a prolonged hunger strike. About forty, or one-quarter of all detainees, were eventually force-fed. Military personnel strapped detainees to a restraint chair, inserted feeding tubes through their noses into their stomachs, and pumped fluids—such as the meal supplement Ensure—through those tubes. Legal, medical, and human-rights experts referred to the practice as torture. Detainees described the act as extraordinarily painful and humiliating. In an April 2013 op-ed in the *New York Times*, Samir Naji al Hasan Moqbel, then a detainee at Guantánamo, evocatively described the horror of force-feeding.

> I will never forget the first time they passed the feeding tube up my nose. I can't describe how painful it is to be force-fed this way. As it was thrust in, it made me feel like throwing up. I wanted to vomit, but I couldn't. There was agony in my chest, throat and stomach. I had never experienced such pain before. I would not wish this cruel punishment upon anyone.[45]

As the number of detainees on hunger strike rose, and as more and more of those hunger strikers were force-fed, the Obama administration faced a brewing scandal. Press coverage of Guantánamo increased dramatically with the spread of the hunger strike. And even members of Obama's party, such as Senator Dianne Feinstein, spoke against force-feeding.[46]

Military spokespeople responded by denying that force-feeding constituted torture. In fact, they denied that force-feeding constituted force-feeding, referring to it with a medicalized term, "enteral feeding." This use of interpretive

denial downplayed the act's coercive qualities; like euphemisms and jargon more generally, it names the act without
calling up a picture of it.[47] The Obama administration, meanwhile, used the discourse of care to justify force-feeding, calling the practice a necessary, life-saving measure.[48] "I don't
want these individuals to die," Obama told reporters in April
2013, at the onset of the hunger strike.[49]

Changing the Topic

By using literal, interpretive, and implicatory denial, those
caught in scandal try to extricate themselves. By literal
denial, they attempt to void allegations of wrongdoing. By
interpretive denial, they attempt to downplay allegations by
draining them of their seriousness. And through implicatory
denial, they admit so much—the allegation is true—but then
they explain it away.

Still other rhetorical strategies are less direct, aiming not
at the allegations but at public attention to the allegations. In
this, I have in mind the rhetorical strategies of redirection,
which are meant to keep public attention from focusing on a
scandal in the first place. Or, if that attention is already there,
the rhetorical strategies of redirection aim at relocating it.

Robert McNamara, in his interviews with the documentary filmmaker Errol Morris, described how he, as secretary
of defense during the Vietnam War, learned to "never answer
the question that is asked of you. Answer the question that
you wished that was asked of you and quite frankly I follow
that rule, it's a really good rule."[50]

Pivot, in other words. Politicians, commentator after commentator after commentator has pointed out, rely on pivoting to subtly change a topic from a losing one to a winning one. A 2012 NPR article illustrates the strategy.

> During the 2004 debates between President Bush and his challenger, Democrat John Kerry, the moderator, Bob Schieffer of CBS News, asked President Bush about job loss. What, Schieffer wondered, would Bush say to someone who has lost his job? Bush began by promising to "continue to grow our economy" and then, subtly, changed course. Suddenly, Bush was talking about education, specifically his signature No Child Left Behind legislation. "I went to Washington to solve problems," he explained. "And I saw a problem in the public education system."[51]

Redirecting to education is, apparently, an instinct of politicians. Former president Bill Clinton did just this when, in late January 1998, he issued a defiant denial of his sexual relationship with Lewinsky. Introduced by Vice President Al Gore as "America's true education President," Clinton spoke for six minutes on education and child care, even as he addressed the investigation into his relationship with Lewinsky. According to the *New York Times*, "White House aides claimed to be delighted with the coverage of the event, arguing that Mr. Clinton's initiatives had received more attention than they would have otherwise."[52]

Later in the year, when Clinton would admit to a relationship with Lewinsky, he would employ another strategy

of redirection, declaring that the scandal—or the surrounding "blame game"—was itself a distraction from more "important work."[53] After apologizing for misleading his wife,
Congress, and the US people about his relationship with
Lewinsky, Clinton closed his August 17, 1998, speech with
this strategy:

> Our country has been distracted by this matter for too long,
> and I take my responsibility for my part in all of this. That is
> all I can do. Now it is time—in fact, it is past time to move
> on. We have important work to do—real opportunities to
> seize, real problems to solve, real security matters to face.
> And so tonight, I ask you to turn away from the spectacle
> of the past seven months, to repair the fabric of our national
> discourse, and to return our attention to all the challenges
> and all the promise of the next American century.[54]

Donald Trump used a similar strategy in his videotaped
apology for his statements to Billy Bush, redirecting attention
back to what he calls the "real world": "Let's be honest—we're
living in the real world. This is nothing more than a distraction from the important issues we're facing today. We are losing our jobs, we're less safe than we were eight years ago, and
Washington is totally broken. Hillary Clinton and her kind
have run our country into the ground."[55] There are still other
forms of redirection to be found in Trump's statement. In it,
Trump uses two well-worn strategies of denial: condemning the condemners and advantageous comparisons. Using
the former strategy, Trump calls out Hillary Clinton—the

person most likely to politically gain from the scandal in which Trump put himself. Then, after this condemnation, Trump used an advantageous comparison, contrasting his "foolish" words with the worse actions of the Clintons: "I've said some foolish things but there's a big difference between the words and actions of other people. Bill Clinton has actually abused women, and Hillary has bullied, attacked, shamed, and intimidated his victims."[56] The comparison is meant to diminish the significance of Trump's behavior by drawing attention to other, allegedly worse behaviors. The Trump campaign tried to add a performative dimension to this rhetorical denial by attempting to seat accusers of Bill Clinton in the VIP Box during the second presidential debate.[57]

Corporations build advantageous comparisons into their public relations strategies. In a study of corporate malfeasance, Jenny White, Albert Bandura, and Lisa A. Bero show how the tobacco and lead industries relied on this technique to downplay concerns about their products. Philip Morris, for instance, produced an "environmental tobacco smoke" strategy that involved a "risk assessment methodology" to contrast the harms of cigarettes with the equivalent or worse, "commonly found environmental agents such as those found in indoor air (volatile organic chemicals), foods (pesticides), and water (lead, fluorine)."[58] These claims may trickle down to users. Years ago, standing at a busy intersection at Boston, I reactively flinched when a pungent puff of a nearby smoker's cigarette drifted into my face. At my response, the smoker muttered, "There's more toxins in a cup of water."

Stanley Cohen, meanwhile, documents the use of advantageous comparisons by governments accused of human-rights violations. "By contrasting your own harmful acts," Cohen writes, "with the more reprehensible inhumanities committed by your adversary, your record looks good. . . . So: whatever we do is nothing compared with what they do. Indeed, under the circumstances, we behave with great restraint and according to the rule of law."[59] Consider President George W. Bush's 2004 statement to mark the UN's International Day in Support of Victims of Torture. The day, June 26, was not two months after the release of photographs showing US soldiers "abusing" detainees at Abu Ghraib.[60] Bush acknowledged this: "The American people were horrified by the abuse of detainees at Abu Ghraib prison in Iraq. These acts were wrong. They were inconsistent with our policies and our values as a Nation. I have directed a full accounting for the abuse of the Abu Ghraib detainees, and investigations are underway to review detention operations in Iraq and elsewhere."[61] But then, Bush pivoted to advantageous comparisons with the atrocities of Saddam Hussein:

A little over a year ago, American service members and our coalition partners freed the Iraqi people from a dictatorship that routinely tortured and executed innocent citizens because of what they believed in or what ethnic or religious group they came from. In torture chambers, innocent Iraqis were brutalized and the bodies of the dead left in mass graves. Throughout the past year, Americans have assisted the Iraqi people in establishing institutions to ensure accountability so that such acts do not occur again and to help victims recover.[62]

A century prior, the *New York Times'* editors used an appalling advantageous comparison to downplay and redirect from the United States' use of water-torture techniques—then euphemistically referred to as the "water cure"—in the country's colonial war in the Philippines. In an editorial entitled "Tortures and Tortures," the *Times'* editors denied the seriousness of the water cure by comparing it to the lynching of Black Americans. Addressing one of their own correspondents, who the day prior wrote, "the torture . . . could not with impunity be employed . . . on the Continent of North America," the editors respond, "[We] commend to our correspondent the stories of roasting to death, in North America, of persons accused of crimes, and to point out to him that these human holocausts are avowedly made for mere revenge, whereas the water cure, in every instance in which the employment of it has been charged, was employed as a practical measure of prevention and self-protection, and not vindictively, nor as punishment at all."[63]

The *Times'* editors go further by claiming that members of Congress most concerned with the water cure represent communities most "rife" with lynching. Here, an advantageous comparison does several things at once. It issues a condemnation of the condemners—by suggesting the hypocrisy of apparently antitorture members of Congress, who are (allegedly) indifferent to lynching in the United States. It denies the harms of the water cure, by contrasting it to death at the hands of the white American lynch mob. And it involves implicatory denial, offering the "legitimate" justification of water torture: it is a "practical measure of prevention" and, according to the *Times'* editors, therefore justifiable for not being "mere revenge." From the tone of the editorial, however, it's not clear whether the *Times'* editors believe the average reader should be more outraged at lynching than they are or merely less outraged at the "water cure."[64]

Sorry, Not Sorry

Yet another strategy of scandal management, the apology, is the frontier between denial and acknowledgment. The ideal apology neither excuses nor justifies the transgression. Rather, the ideal apology includes several things: recognition of the harmfulness of an act; an acceptance, by the apology giver, of responsibility; and an expression of remorse, preferably the words "I'm sorry," for the act and its harms. Often, the ideal apology includes a promise that the apology giver will not repeat the behavior. This apology is a magical combination of words. Through the sheer language of genuine remorse and responsibility, a deep, meaningful, and enduring transformation may occur. The wrong is righted. The social norm, injured by the transgression, is healed. And the transgressor's identity, broken by the offense, may be repaired.[65]

But such apologies are rare. More common are nonapologies. One apologizes not for the transgression, but for how others responded to it. "I'm sorry if I offended you," this apology goes. Here, the apology giver excuses their behavior, implying that they had no intent to harm or offend. Worse, the apology giver insinuates that the wrong, in fact, is on the side of the aggrieved, whose response is the problem, rather than the act itself.[66]

Nonapologies often include forms of bolstering. The communications scholar William L. Benoit identified bolstering in the "image-repair" strategies that politicians and corporations use in the face of scandal. Those who use it emphasize their own positive qualities, even in the face of allegations of wrongdoing. Bolstering redirects from first-order and second-order transgressions by putting attention on qualities that those ensnared in scandal hope may redeem them yet.

On October 5, 2017, the *New York Times* published an investigation, written by Jodi Kantor and Megan Twohey, of Harvey Weinstein's serial sexual harassment and abuse of women. The same day, Weinstein gave a brief, written statement to the *Times*, staking his reputation and career on 400 or so words. His response, which superficially resembles an apology, contains a dizzying mix of common rhetorical denials, those described in chapter 3, deployed with neither skill nor precision. Weinstein opens the statement with an excuse, a denial of responsibility for his behavior: "I came of age in the 60's and 70's, when all the rules about behavior and workplaces were different." Then he denies that the very excuse that he's offered is an excuse at all, implying lack of intent in his treatment of others: "I have since learned it's not an excuse, in the office—or out of it." Then, an apology: "I appreciate the way I've behaved with colleagues in the past has caused a lot of pain, and I sincerely apologize for it." Nowhere in the statement does Weinstein name that behavior. Instead, he disguises his sexual violence with vague words, more excuses, and euphemisms. Weinstein calls the allegations "a wake-up call." He writes of being on a "journey" and, along the way, encountering "demons."[67]

Having appeared to submit to the judgment of the reader, Weinstein closes by reasserting himself through bolstering. His final words are aimed at the potentially sympathetic and, presumably, liberal readers who regularly read the *Times*. These are the very readers who may be most outraged by Weinstein's crimes against women, committed, as they were, by a fellow Democrat and apparent advocate of women's rights. (Weinstein was a major donor to the Democratic Party and a fundraiser for Hillary Clinton during her 2016 presidential run. He also participated in the January 2017 Women's March.) In an attempt to rebuild himself, Weinstein's final few paragraphs promise the reader that he's going to "channel" the "anger" that fuels his assaults on women. How? By challenging the National Rifle Association (NRA) and raising funds for a scholarship for female directors. Much of this is nonsensical. "I hope Wayne LaPierre [the executive vice president of the NRA] will enjoy his retirement party. I'm going to do it at the same place I had my Bar Mitzvah," Weinstein writes. All of it is beside the point.[68]

Predictably, Weinstein's statement did none of the face work he intended for it. The accusations were too serious, too credible, and too criminal for any statement, let alone the three-quarters of a page of lousy words that Weinstein assembled. Ultimately, he was convicted for rape and sexual assault, receiving a twenty-three-year sentence. (At the time of writing, Weinstein was appealing the conviction to the New York State Supreme Court, while also facing further prosecution in California.[69]) Even so, the playbook from which Weinstein drew isn't unusual. Public figures accused of sexual harassment, abuse, or assault often reassert their credentials and, especially, their respect for women through bolstering.[70]

Bolstering tries to turn attention from the offending self to the better angels of the transgressor, the supposed "authentic" or true self, in an effort to isolate the latter from the former. If successful, others may view those transgressions as incidental or irrelevant to who the transgressor "really is." But bolstering can backfire. Bolster too much or too hard, and one gives the impression of not taking one's own offending actions seriously. This was the case with the public response to Facebook and its chief executive Mark Zuckerberg's use of bolstering to answer accusations about violating the privacy of Facebook's users. Appearing before Congress in April 2018, Zuckerberg apologized for Facebook's failures, but only after 100 words of (transparent) bolstering.

> Facebook is an idealistic and optimistic company. For most of our existence, we focused on all of the good that connecting people can do. And, as Facebook has grown, people everywhere have gotten a powerful new tool for staying connected to the people they love, for making their voices heard and for building communities and businesses.
>
> Just recently, we've seen the "Me Too" movement and the March for our Lives organized, at least in part, on Facebook.

After Hurricane Harvey, people came together to raise more than $20 million for relief. And more than 70 million businesses—small business use Facebook to create jobs and grow.

But it's clear now that we didn't do enough to prevent these tools from being used for harm, as well. And that goes for fake news, for foreign interference in elections, and hate speech, as well as developers and data privacy.

We didn't take a broad enough view of our responsibility, and that was a big mistake. And it was my mistake. And I'm sorry. I started Facebook, I run it, and I'm responsible for what happens here.[71]

Later in the month, Facebook released a commercial, too sweetly titled ("Here Together"), that repeated Zuckerberg's story: "We came here for friends . . . we felt a little less alone . . . but then something happened."[72] Facebook's critics answered by scrutinizing the social media company's use of bolstering. Of Facebook's "Here Together," *Slate*'s Aaron Mak wrote, "Stripped of its saccharine score and tear-jerking snapshots, the ad is essentially a defense of Facebook's underlying model that glosses over [the] platform's endemic flaws and its missteps while seeking relentless growth."[73] The *New York Times*, in turn, referred to the ad as "gauzy."[74]

Public apologies are also riddled with euphemisms. This is particularly so of public apologies in the United States, where those giving public apologies often believe that any admission of engaging in specific behavior or causing harm to others opens them to legal liability.[75] Weinstein apologized for "the way he behaved with colleagues," rather than any specific incident described in the *Times'* initial investigation. Robert Kraft, the owner of the New England Patriots, avoided even euphemism in his March 2019 apology after being arrested for soliciting sex at a massage parlor in Florida. Though saying he was "truly sorry" and admitting having "hurt and disappointed my family, close friends, my co-workers, our fans and many others who rightfully hold me to a higher standard," Kraft never identified what he'd done that had hurt and disappointed others.[76] That Kraft's apology could be read alongside his lawyers' denials that Kraft had engaged in any illegal activity further confounded readers. Unlike Weinstein's apology, Kraft's did not have to contend with a mass of accusations or a trial. The State of Florida dropped Kraft's prosecution after losing a legal ruling that barred them from using surveillance footage from cameras that the state had secretly installed in the massage parlor Kraft allegedly frequented.[77]

An earnest apology risks the self. It is an admission that one is the type of person who has done harm, sometimes profound harm, knowingly and intentionally, to another. The partial apology is something else. It shifts the burden of a wrong from the apologist to those whom the apologist harmed. Victims are pressured to accept that the hurt wasn't so hurtful or the person responsible wasn't so responsible. It is hardly an apology. It does not seek to repair social relationships, but to salvage the self of the offender. This apology, then, is just another rhetorical move, just another denial, only better dressed.

* * *

In 2008, while surveying the human and political wreckage of the George W. Bush administration, the journalist Mark Danner called scandal "our growth industry." He continued,

> Revelation of wrongdoing leads not to definitive investigation, punishment, and expiation but to more scandal. Permanent scandal. Frozen scandal. . . . [F]rozen scandals metastasize, ramify, self-replicate, clogging the cable news shows and the blogosphere and the bookstores. The titillating story that never ends, the pundit gabfest that never ceases, the gift that never stops giving: what is indestructible, irresolvable, unexpiatable is too valuable not to be made into a source of profit. Scandal, unpurged and unresolved, transcends political reality to become commercial fact.78

I thought, while writing this chapter in early 2020, that the scandal of Trump's impeachment would be the foundation of my analysis. But Danner's writing proved prophecy. That impeachment merely became Trump's *first* impeachment. A second followed Trump's incitement of a siege of the US Capitol by spreading the lie that the 2020 election had been stolen from him and using violent, though plausibly deniable, language when addressing supporters.[79]

Between these two impeachments and after them still: the scandal of the federal and state responses to the COVID-19 virus. The Trump administration knowingly misled the US public about the severity and risks of the pandemic; they undercut scientists working with the federal government; they spread junk science; and they mocked the most basic of precautions that an unvaccinated public could take—social distancing and mask wearing, especially.[80]

Many US states hardly comported themselves better. Some local and state governments flaunted those basic precautions. Others dissembled. Most notably, Andrew Cuomo performed authoritatively in public performances, pushing science and definitive action. Meanwhile, Cuomo's aides allegedly rewrote studies by the state's health officials to minimize, by about 50 percent, the number of New Yorkers who had died in nursing homes. That this effort seemed tethered, through the involvement of aides and timing, to Cuomo's writing of a book on the state's response to COVID-19 doubled the scandal.[81]

Scandals come and go, talking of the transgressions of the powerful. Each one, replaced by newer news, leaves an open question: will this transgression be remembered? Will this momentary disruption to the status quo leave a legacy?

A final time, denial. This time as collective amnesia. This time as silence. Denial remakes the public into an image of itself—so that when we finally gather round the open secrets, we avert our eyes, avoid the topic, and speak, instead, of easier things.

6

HOW TO HIDE IN PLAIN SIGHT

Denying Racism

I N the spring and summer of 2020, protests of anti-Black racism in the United States changed the ways that many Americans understand racial inequality in the country. Politicians, the media, and even corporations began speaking about "systemic racism." This social scientific concept refocuses attention from the racist behavior of individuals to the ways that "discriminatory practices and racialized institutions" in the United States have been "engineered to produce the long term domination" of people of color.[1] It seemed like the nation and its major institutions were finally ready to acknowledge how the past—particularly slavery, but also segregation and the white terrorism that followed Emancipation—produced living legacies of racial violence, inequality, and oppression.

I remember my surprise, back then, at finding a prominent display of books on racism in a local big-box store's media section. On one endcap, new releases in popular music. On the next, Robin DiAngelo's *White Fragility*, Richard Rothstein's *The Color of Law*, and Ibram X. Kendi's tome *Stamped from the Beginning*. Public discourse, it seemed, had shifted.

Antiracist writing and ideas now had a home in dominant culture.

A year later, public discourse, it seemed, had shifted again. Conservative politicians, editorial boards, media members, scholars, and parents argued for bans of the teaching of critical race theory, the *New York Times*' Pulitzer-winning 1619 Project, and equity in public schools and universities.

In March 2021, in the very same county where that big-box store sold antiracist books, the local school district canceled a planned equity program after facing vehement opposition from parents and community members. In written comments to the district's school board, some claimed that equity programs are racist against white students. Others invoked the threat of critical race theory. One wrote that the district, in a predominantly white county, should concern itself with serving the majority. Another conjured Martin Luther King Jr.'s "I Have a Dream" speech to describe equity work as a contrasting nightmare. Still another denied, wholesale, need for the training, expressing skepticism that racism and prejudice even existed in the district. Undiscussed were the experiences of overt and implicit racism that Black students had bravely shared with local media just a month prior.[2]

"Denial of racism is the heartbeat of racism," Kendi wrote in a 2018 op-ed in the *New York Times*.[3] Kendi's claim was proven right in 2020, by the power of acknowledgment to surface long-denied truths about US racism. But the next year proved it righter still, with the effort to rebury those truths. This chapter follows the denial of racism further. Building on scholarship on color-blind racism and white ignorance, I show the multiple ways that denial is implicated in systemic racism. I also show how Americans adapt the forms of denial described in earlier chapters to maintain racism and protect white racial domination.

But, first, two disclaimers. Most of the social scientific scholarship on which I draw addresses white Americans' denials of systemic racism. This chapter, in turn, focuses on white Americans' uses of denial. But these denials circulate more widely in US culture, and white Americans are not the only people who engage in the denial of racism. In other words, despite the focus of this chapter, I do not mean to suggest that *only* white Americans deny systemic racism. Even still, we are innovators in the denial of systemic racism. We also gain the most from this denial. This leads to my second disclaimer: throughout this chapter, I write of "white people" and "white Americans." I do not exclude myself from either whiteness or its privileges. However, except in a few strategic moments, I've elected not to use the pronoun "we" when referring to white people, so as to not inscribe the reader into this category.

Historical Denial and the Hidden Curriculum

Denial's first move is to keep people from knowing in the first place. Recall the efforts of organizations to hide their transgressions: the avoidance of paper trails and the redactions. But once found, the corruptions and crimes of social groups, organizations, and political elites can again be lost. Buried deep in learned and taught histories are long-overlooked facts that, if recognized, would challenge the political and social status quo.

Historical remembering and forgetting happen through a range of rituals and cultural artifacts. Public holidays, memorials, and museums, for instance, are implicated in collective memory. But because I was a student for the better part of three decades and because I am now an educator, I'll focus on one way historical facts are denied: through formal education and its hidden curriculum. In a study of the hidden curriculum in sociology, Eric Margolis and Mary Romero show how educators' decisions about what will and will not be included in curricula produce gaps in knowledge and reproduce inequality.[4] Frequently, this happens through the exclusion of teaching and learning about domination and oppression.

People cannot acknowledge what they do not know. They cannot act on knowledge that they do not possess. And they will struggle to fill gaps in their understanding of history and society when they are unaware of those very gaps. Here, I'd like to co-opt Donald Rumsfeld's notorious quote about the Iraq War, if only in hopes of inverting it so it serves not power but scrutiny of power: "As we know, there are known knowns; there are things we know we know. We also know there are known unknowns; that is to say we know there are some things we do not know. But there are also unknown unknowns—the ones we don't know we don't know."[5] Through historical omissions, the hidden curriculum produces unknown unknowns. There are histories that many people do not know that they do not know. These are histories that complicate, if not directly challenge, dominant national histories. In the United States, these are histories that would complicate, if not directly challenge, the prevailing notions of American exceptionalism, meritocracy, and equality.

James W. Loewen, in his influential book *Lies My Teacher Told Me*, documents historical omissions in a dozen leading US history textbooks. The violence of Christopher Columbus's incursions into Haiti, for instance, have historically been omitted from US textbooks.[6] (A more recent study found this omission endemic in children's literature books on Columbus.[7]) Textbooks hardly do better with twentieth-century incursions. The US occupation of Haiti, which began under President Woodrow Wilson in 1915, was omitted from half of the twelve textbooks Loewen reviewed in his initial study.[8] Meanwhile, the segregation of the federal government, which also occurred during the Wilson administration, is mentioned in only four.[9]

Loewen is especially critical of history textbooks' erasure of Wilson's racist politics. Wilson's presidency spanned the release of D. W. Griffith's white supremacist—and genre-defining—film *Birth of a Nation*. The film, which valorizes the Ku Klux Klan (KKK) and depicts African American men as rapists, was shown at the White House. Despite protests by the National Association for the Advancement of Colored People (NAACP) and the reluctance of censorship boards, Wilson's approval of the film helped ensure a widespread screening throughout the country.[10] For Loewen, "omitting or absolving Wilson's racism goes beyond concealing a character blemish. It is overtly racist. . . . Textbooks that present him as a hero are written from a white perspective.

The cover-up denies all students the chance to learn something important about the interrelationship between the leader and the led. White Americans engaged in a new burst of racial violence during and immediately after Wilson's presidency."[11] Indeed, during Wilson's presidency, white Americans massacred Black Americans in East St. Louis, Illinois (1917); Valdosta, Georgia (1918); Elaine, Arkansas (1918); and Ocoee, Florida (1920).[12] The latter massacre occurred on the day of the 1920 election, leaving at least three dozen Black Americans dead.[13] "Americans need to learn from the Wilson era," Loewen writes, "that there is a connection between racist presidential leadership and like-minded public response."[14] But this learning would require the genuine teaching of that connection.

Textbook publishers and education boards continue to efface historical inequality and violence through omissions. In January 2020, the *New York Times* compared history textbooks adopted by market-setter states California and Texas. Specifically, they compared textbooks that both states had adopted but which were, at the behest of state educational boards, "customized" for each state's use. As described by Dana Goldstein, the author of the *Times* article, the gulf between these panels is substantial. "All the members of the California panel were educators selected by the State Board of Education, whose members were appointed by former Gov. Jerry Brown, a Democrat. The Texas panel, appointed by the Republican-dominated State Board of Education, was made up of educators, parents, business representatives and a Christian pastor and politician."[15] Goldstein further notes that "recent textbooks have come a long way from what was published in past decades. Both Texas and California volumes deal more bluntly with the cruelty of the slave trade. . . . The books also devote more space to the women's movement and balance the narrative of European immigration with stories of Latino and Asian immigrants." Still, in Texas's version, references to housing discrimination against US citizens of color, redlining, and white flight were absent. All appeared in the California version.[16] Without teaching and learning on these issues, students will be unable to understand contemporary America, with its high levels of segregation and the inequalities that these create. The efforts by conservative politicians, media members, and parents to ban antiracist teaching are meant to ensure that these gaps in understanding endure.

Omissions are not just a problem of secondary school textbooks. Kathleen J. Fitzgerald, a sociologist of race, analyzed the four leading undergraduate textbooks in the sociology of race and race relations. Fitzgerald did so to assess the adequacy of the books' coverage of the race "riots" of the late nineteenth and early twentieth centuries, such as those in Tulsa, Oklahoma; Wilmington, North Carolina; and East St. Louis. Fitzgerald found that only one of the four textbooks she analyzed provided discussion of these massacres. The "other three," she writes, "completely ignore the nationwide pattern of violence directed at African Americans."[17] Meanwhile, criminologists K. B. Turner, David Giacopassi, and Margaret Vandiver analyzed twenty-one criminology and criminal justice textbooks published after 2000 to see how these books presented slavery and slave patrols. They found that most either neglected or offered only superficial analysis of the role of slavery and slave patrols, despite the fact that contemporary US policing is rooted in slavery.[18]

Hidden in Plain Sight

There are other ways to keep history's reality at bay. What textbooks and educators teach must be framed—that is, portrayed in ways that make some understandings more salient than others. Framings can produce a different sort of denial—not the outright forms of collective amnesia toward violence and trauma, but interpretive denial of the ways that violence and its enduring legacies operate.

Keffrelyn D. Brown and Anthony L. Brown have analyzed portrayals of racial violence in nineteen textbooks adopted by the state of Texas. Like Goldstein's report for the *New York Times*, Brown and Brown's research finds that contemporary textbooks indeed address racial violence. As an example, they cite a passage in *History Alive*, a textbook for fifth graders, on the slave trade: "But losing slaves meant losing money, so the ships' captains tried to keep them alive. They whipped slaves who refused to eat and forced their jaws open or burned their lips with coals."[19] Historical denial, in this case, is not shaped through forgetting and historical omissions. Rather, its shape takes the form of the textbook's frame of history. Brown and Brown find that the textbooks adopted by Texas treat racialized violence as the result of a "few bad men," such as slave-ship captains, slave traders, slave overseers, and members of the KKK.[20] Even as it individualizes racist violence, passages, like the one above, also offer excuses and justifications. The cruelty and the violence of slave-ship captains itself seem almost necessary (if they are not to lose money) and forced by economic powers out of the control of these few bad men. Meanwhile, the politics of slaves' hunger strikes are stripped away; they are mere human obstacles to the captains' pursuit of money, rather than agentic human beings actively resisting their captors. This framing also produces absences. Gone are discussions that would link discrete episodes of violence to political power, legal institutions, social groups, and social structure. Gone, too, is historical analysis that reveals how the violence of white Americans "operated systematically to oppress," as Brown and Brown put it, and terrorize African Americans.[21]

A popular textbook in my discipline, sociology, offers its own limited, inadequate framing in its half-paragraph on the 1917 East St. Louis "riots" (the textbook's word). The "riots," the reader learns, left "nine whites and hundreds of African Americans dead." It resulted from "racialized competition for housing and employment." And it caused an "estimated 6,000 black citizens, fearing for their lives," to flee East St. Louis, "another stark example of [racial] withdrawal."[22]

How we tell history shapes how we think about the past and the present. Here, this telling leaves out crucial details that would encourage an adequate sociological understanding of the massacre and displacement of Black Americans in East St. Louis. A reader does not learn that, in 1917, specific labor disputes between the (white-owned) Aluminum Ore

Company and striking white workers contributed to the massacre. The company, like many northern companies at the start of the twentieth century, replaced striking white workers with Black workers, knowingly and intentionally stoking divisions among laborers.[23] Members of the white workers' union, the East St. Louis Central Trades and Labor Union, responded by assaulting Black men throughout the spring and summer of 1917, events that precipitated the massacre in early July.[24]

The telling also omits the involvement of local and state institutional actors in the massacre. In the *St. Louis Republic,* inaccurate and racist newspaper coverage of a confrontation between plainclothes white officers and armed Black men, which ultimately left two officers dead, stoked the rage of white residents of East St. Louis. So, too, did the public display of the car, scarred with bullet holes and the officers' blood, in which those officers had been killed.[25] Local white police officers and members of the Illinois National Guard contributed to the massacre through inaction and, in some cases, direct participation in the massacre.[26]

Finally, there are two euphemisms in this book's coverage: "withdrawal" and "riot." "Withdrawal" suggests a voluntary departure from East St. Louis. The flight of Black Americans from the violence of whites in the city is more accurately described as forced displacement—among the intended purposes of white violence against Black Americans. Accordingly, Harper Barnes, in his 2008 account of the massacre, refers to those who fled East St. Louis as refugees. We must ask, in what sense does one withdraw from one's home, when it is already burning? In what sense does one withdraw from mobs of armed white men, women, boys, and girls who have already shot, hanged, beaten (with fists, broomsticks, clubs, guns, pick-axes), maimed, stoned, and burned alive others?[27]

The use of the second euphemism, "riot," is not unique to this textbook. Historically, white massacres of Black Americans have been remembered by white Americans, if at all, as riots. This form of interpretive denial frames white violence as spontaneous explosions of violence, perhaps random and disorderly, and maybe even defensive. Instead, white massacres were sometimes premeditated, as the 1898 massacre in Wilmington, North Carolina, was.[28] It was rarely random and disorderly; rather, it targeted Black communities and, often, specific Black leaders. And its defensiveness was a lie, built on racist propaganda and rumors of planned uprisings by Black Americans. For these reasons, the historian H. Leon Prather Sr. writes, in his 1984 history of the Wilmington coup d'état and racial massacre, that "social scientists need a new term for what has been called a race riot. The traumatic episode in Wilmington, like many others, was largely one-sided: a white massacre of defenseless blacks with a macabre mixture of carnage and carnival."[29] Similarly, Carlos F. Hurd, a journalist who witnessed the 1917 massacre in East St. Louis, used the word "massacre," not "riot," in his first-person account, published the day after the massacre ended. Of the perpetrators of the massacre, Hurd wrote,

A mob is passionate; a mob follows one man or a few men blindly; a mob sometimes takes chances. The East St. Louis

affair, as I saw it, was a manhunt, conducted on a sporting basis, though with anything but the fair play which is the principle of sport. The [white] East St. Louis men took no chances,
except the chance from stray shots, which every spectator of
their acts took. They went in small groups, there was little
leadership, and there was a horribly cool deliberateness and a
spirit of fun about it. I cannot allow even the doubtful excuse
of drink. No man whom I saw showed the effect of liquor.[30]

How texts frame historical events contributes to readers'
understanding of the past. It also contributes to how readers
understand the relevance of the past to the present. When the
continuities between the former and the latter are obscured
or erased, readers may believe that the past returns merely
as curious or tragic episodes, rather than as an explanation
of or, more radically, a demand on the present. This contributes to a form of denial that Stanley Cohen refers to as "temporal containment."[31] Temporal containment voids calls for
acknowledgment by claiming that historical wrongs are too
far gone to the past for the pursuit of accountability, justice,
and reparation.

In the United States, temporal containment frequently appears in debates about reparations for slavery, Jim Crow laws,
and institutional racism.[32] For instance, Mitch McConnell,
a white senator from Kentucky, used temporal containment,
with denial of responsibility, to reject calls to study restitu-
tion and reparations for slavery: "I don't think reparations for
something that happened 150 years ago for whom none of us
currently living are responsible is a good idea."[33] Testifying

to Congress, Ta-Nehisi Coates deconstructed McConnell's denial, explaining how the violence and economics of slavery have persisted in US institutions, policies, and social practices throughout the country's history.[34] But temporal containment is not only for politicians. Many white Americans, when asked about slavery and reparations, similarly combine temporal containment and denial of responsibility.[35]

There are many reasons that textbooks promote incomplete, even misleading, versions of history. I've alluded to one reason already. Textbook adoption committees make ideological demands on publishers, and those in market-setting states wield significant influence. Loewen lists a range of other potential explanations: "pressure from the 'ruling class[,]' . . . the wish to avoid ambiguities, a desire to shield children from harm or conflict, the perceived need to control children and avoid classroom disharmony, [and] pressure to provide answers."[36] There are consequences to this erasure of history. Educators, and especially white educators, may struggle to teach the history of white racial domination beyond the textbook, as they, too, simply don't know the history well enough to teach it, if they're aware of that history at all. They may be immobilized by fear—of losing control, of making mistakes, and of being seen as biased.[37] And they may also be untrained, unpracticed, and inexperienced in teaching on these topics. But these limitations in historical knowledge and competency in teaching on race are not accidental; they are both a product and a protector of systemic racism.

Ignorance of the past is often willful, expressing a mix of genuine ignorance, curated ignorance, and outright denial of what one indeed knows or could know. This ignorance, in turn, produces a misapprehension of the present. "The mystification of the past," the philosopher Charles Mills writes, "underwrites a mystification of the present. The erasure of the history of Jim Crow makes it possible to represent the playing field as historically level, so that current black poverty just proves blacks' unwillingness to work. As individual memory is assisted through a larger social memory, so individual amnesia is then assisted by a larger collective amnesia."[38]

Color-Blind Racism

Collective amnesia about racism is not only a product of schooling and its hidden curriculum. Denial—now in the form of the interactional strategies of chapter 1 and the rhetorical ones of chapter 3—keeps white privilege and racism behind the façade of color-blindness.

To many white Americans, the civil rights movements revealed the violence and injustice of US racism. It also succeeded at transforming law and, even, the sentiments of many white people. Today, social scientists find that public attitudes about race are far less explicitly, outwardly, and directly racist than they were in the past. But this does not signal the end of racism. On institutional and structural levels, racism endures in myriad forms: residential segregation, now allegedly accidental or voluntary rather than enforced, as through Jim Crow; the enduring wage and wealth gaps between white people and people of color; unequal access to social opportunities and resources, as well as to occupational and political ones; and the disproportionate policing and punishment of people of color.

Ideologically, a set of color-blind beliefs effaces ethnic and racial inequalities.[39] Sociologists Tyrone A. Forman and Amanda E. Lewis succinctly describe the ideological underpinnings of what they call the "new racism":

> The central beliefs of color-blind racism are that (1) most people do not even notice race anymore; (2) racial parity has for the most part been achieved; (3) any persistent patterns of racial inequality are the result of individual and/or group-level shortcomings rather than structural ones; (4) most people do not care about racial differences; and (5) therefore, there is no need for institutional remedies (such as affirmative action) to redress persistent racialized outcomes.[40]

Strategies of denial support color-blind ideology. Attention-management strategies keep race and racism out of the "front stages" of social life. In this way, denial supports color-blind racism by allowing white people to feign "an oblivion to race," as Zeus Leonardo and Ronald K. Porter put it.[41] Rhetorical strategies, meanwhile, neutralize claims that race is salient in the lives of Americans and that racism privileges white Americans and harms Americans of color. These strategies also permit people accused of racist speech or behavior to (try to) fend off those accusations. The denial of racism is, then, the paradoxical sounds of silence and noise. It is the silence of withdrawal and avoidance of public talk about race; it is the noise of white people's furies, which abruptly end conversations about racism; and it is the public talk that explicitly denies race and its relevance.

Denying Racism in Social Interactions

I argued earlier that interactional, everyday strategies of denial like avoidance have certain pro-social uses. Now, I want to qualify that statement: everyday, interactional forms of denial have pro-social uses when they help us overcome the myriad accidents, blunders, and mistakes of social life. The damage is done when we use them to efface enduring public issues, keeping these out of our conversations, out of our interactions, and perhaps even out of awareness.

Interactional forms of denial are perhaps nowhere more essential, nowhere more dependable, than in the everyday erasures of white privilege and racism. White people use behavioral and rhetorical techniques alike to take conversations about "racism off the table," as Robin DiAngelo puts it in *White Fragility*.[42] Behaviorally, white people use a range of attention-management strategies—silence, withdrawal and avoidance, and emotional outbursts—to foreclose discussions of white privilege, racism, and, especially, their own racist acts or speech.

SILENCE AND SILENCING STRATEGIES
Many white witnesses to others' racist behaviors act like the passive bystanders discussed earlier.[43] Those who do intervene, meanwhile, find that perpetrators and collaborators consistently excuse racist behavior. The latter may claim lack

of intent, attempting to neutralize racist speech as jokes.[44] Or they may claim fatalistic forces, citing alcohol use as an excuse.[45] In the face of this repeated resistance, many who once elected to intervene eventually give up.[46]

But silencing strategies need not be passive. White people use emotional outbursts to stifle conversations about race and, especially, considerations of their own behaviors. They may dissolve into tears or rage when asked to grapple with their own racist behaviors or even white privilege. DiAngelo recounts how one participant in a training told others at her office that she was suffering cardiac distress after receiving what DiAngelo describes as "sensitive and diplomatic feedback on how some of her statements had impacted several people of color in the room."[47] The result of the display was that "all attention was immediately focused back onto her and away from engagement with the impact she had had on the people of color."[48]

White peoples' outbursts disrupt conversations and considerations about race, racism, and white privilege. They lead people to spend a disproportionate amount of resources—emotional energy, attention, and time—on the volatile white person. For this, these outbursts are an explicit reassertion of white privilege. They silence conversations about how racism structures workplace interactions and opportunities. They also siphon resources from antiracist activities. In the case of displays of anger, this reassertion is more explicit. Such displays, particularly by white men, mix the institutional power (usually held by those very same or still other white men) with threats, implicit or explicit, of both institutional retribution and physical force. Moreover, the effect of all these strategies is to silence conversations about race through the very mobilization of white privilege—for the right to engage in an emotional outburst in professional or public settings without sanction is itself a privilege afforded primarily to white people.[49]

White people may also use a discourse of safety to silence conversations about race. White participants in diversity trainings may claim that people of color are "slamming" them, "throwing" things (like the white person's own words) "in their face," or, more generally, making them (the white participants) feel unsafe.[50] This rhetorical move denies the actual history of white violence targeting people of color. In this way, it also erases the contemporary uses to which collective power, disciplinary practices, and violence are often put: to maintain white privilege. And it fuels white people's demand for "safety" in discussions of race and racism. But "safety" is a misnomer, Leonardo and Porter argue in an analysis of race talk, because "it often means that white individuals can be made to feel safe" and because it denies "that race dialogue is almost never safe for people of color in mixed-racial company." Instead of "safety," the demand instead establishes "a space of oppressive color-blindness."[51]

AVOIDANCE

Avoidance strategies are used to dodge knowledge—particularly guilty knowledge—of racism. Forman and Lewis, through interviews with white suburbanites in a Midwestern city, show that avoidance of thinking and talking about racism underlies apathy. "When asked about race relations today," they write, "many respondents said that they did not have much to say and offered the following kinds of statements: 'I'm not a real political person.'"[52]

White people also use avoidance strategies to dodge social interactions in which race and racism may become salient. For instance, Jennifer Mueller, a sociologist of race, asked students in two of her courses to interview family members about "intergenerational wealth transmission," linking their findings from the interview to course readings.[53] Specifically, this paper challenged students to think about how structural racism and, in the case of white students, racial privilege shaped life outcomes and wealth transmission. Mueller found, however, that some white students simply avoided asking family members about race and racial privilege, despite it being an "explicit guideline" of the assignment.[54]

WITHDRAWAL

White people, meanwhile, use withdrawal strategies to disassociate themselves from ongoing conversations about race and, especially, their own racist behavior. For instance, white professors report that some white students will leave classrooms during difficult discussions of race.[55] White participants in diversity trainings often remain silent throughout conversations, resisting opportunities, even invitations, to participate. When asked why, they'll excuse or justify their silence. For instance, they may claim that their "personality"—that they're introverts, for instance—keeps them from engaging.[56] (This is the claim of fatalistic forces, as described in chapter 3.) There are a litany of other explanations, but a few are of particular note. White participants may use credentialing, claiming that they "already know" about white privilege and racism, insinuating a training is redundant and that they are obviously not racist.[57] Conversely, other participants may hedge, claiming they "don't know much about race" and, so, have nothing to add to the discussion.[58] By hedging, white participants claim a racial naiveté that implies innocence (of participating in racism and gaining from white privilege). Withdrawal, like apathy more generally, "serves to deny, distort, and minimize race and racism in society, because if one does not have *feelings* about racism, then racism must not be important."[59]

Color-Blind Discourses and the Rhetoric of Denial

Attention-management strategies may keep race and racism out of public conversations. Color-blind rhetoric, meanwhile, supports more direct denials of racism. Disclaimers, especially, are common techniques, allowing those who engage in racist speech or behavior to (attempt to) deny allegations that they indeed engaged in that racist speech or behavior.

HEDGING

The use of the rhetoric of denial to downplay racism is extensively documented by the sociologist Eduardo Bonilla-Silva, a leading theorist and researcher of color-blind racism. Through interview research, Bonilla-Silva has documented the ways that white Americans use hedging to deny racism.

For instance, white interviewees told Bonilla-Silva that they couldn't really be sure of or understand discrimination because they aren't a person of color. When Bonilla-Silva asked Liz, a college student, a direct question about racial discrimination, Liz offered, "Um, just because I'm not black, I'm not Hispanic, I don't really, don't understand." Another student, Brian, offered, "But I can't speak for like a black person who says they're being harassed or being uh, prejudice or uh, discriminated against."[60] (Similarly, white respondents to surveys increasingly respond with "don't know" to questions about race and racism.[61]) Despite their initial expressions of uncertainty, both students then expressed positions, as Bonilla-Silva puts it, "betraying a strong stance on the matter in question." Those stances, in fact, minimized the reality of racism.[62] Liz packaged her disclaimers with statements about "reverse racism" against whites. Brian, meanwhile, expressed doubt about the severity of contemporary forms of racism and discrimination. But the initial hedge provides cover, leaving the respondent enough conversational space to walk back their remarks if challenged by another. This use of hedging also allows white Americans to deny responsibility for having to talk about race and racism.

A different form of hedging appears in white people's discussions of race: the devil's advocate. By beginning a statement by saying one is simply "playing devil's advocate," one attempts to build a wall between one's "true" motives in making a remark and the consequences of those remarks on others. If the "devil's advocate" is called to account for their speech, they can both hedge and excuse themselves by claiming they did not intend to offend. In a 2017 essay, Maya Rupert deftly analyzed this disclaimer's use in racist discourse.

> Most often, the devil's advocate is really saying there is something at the core of the argument that they are (perhaps ashamedly) compelled by, and so they employ a rhetorical trick allowing themselves to argue a position without ever having to hold it. This allows exploration of deep-seated racism under the guise of putting forth someone else's argument. The irony is that it could invite a deeper discussion of race than may otherwise happen, since it inherently reveals what white people really think and struggle with around race. But because of the charade, no one is able to benefit from it—the person being vulnerable is essentially able to call "take back" and act as though the conversation never really happened.[63]

CREDENTIALING

Credentialing, or the claiming of a special privilege to make an offensive remark, may be the most familiar and most notorious type of disclaimer. A few simple words—"I'm not racist, but . . ." or "Some of my best friends are Black . . ."—typically signal the arrival of a racist remark.[64] Users of the former statement signal their awareness of the potentially racist nature of their remarks; they hope that their audience will accept that someone who is aware of how racism works cannot behave in racist ways. Users of the latter statement try to inoculate themselves against accusations of racism; they hope that the fact of associations with people of color will signal to others that they cannot harbor racist beliefs.

Credentialing disclaimers are often used retrospectively, to downplay past remarks and actions. For instance, Donald J. Trump, as both candidate and president, has used hyperbolic, implausible forms of credentialing to deny accusations of racism and sexism. He asserts that he is "the least racist person" around. This was, for instance, his response to allegations that he had described countries in Africa as "shithole countries."[65] He claims, too, to having done more for the "Black community than any other president . . . with the possible exception of Abraham Lincoln."[66] Likewise, Trump frequently answers accusations of sexism with "Nobody has more respect for women than I do."[67] Trump used this disclaimer in the first presidential debate of 2016, soon after the release of the *Access Hollywood* videotape in which he brags about sexually assaulting women and in response to a question about accusations of sexual assault against him. The audience to that debate refused him, mockingly laughing at his answer.

Credentialing, in other words, has its limits. Critics quickly deconstruct the claim that one cannot be racist because one has friends, family, or employees of color. The claim, in other words, rarely does the necessary face work. Today, those making it are often met not with absolution but with further accusations and scrutiny.

We saw this, dramatically, during a February 2019 House Committee on Oversight and Reform hearing. At the hearing, Michael Cohen, a former attorney and alleged "fixer" for President Trump, described the president as racist (among many other things). In response, Mark Meadows, a white Republican representative in Congress, asked Lynne Patton, a Black woman and an official in the Department of Housing and Urban Development, to stand. "There is no way she would work for an individual who is racist," Meadows proclaimed.[68]

The backlash was immediate. Representative Rashida Tlaib, a Democrat on the committee, explained to Meadows, "Just because a person has a person of color, a black person, working for them does not mean they aren't racist. . . . And it is insensitive, and some would even say the fact that someone would actually use a prop, a black woman, in this chamber, in this committee, is alone racist in itself."[69] Unable or unwilling to understand Tlaib's remarks, Meadows defended himself with even more credentialing. As evidence that he could not engage in a racist act, he cited his own friendship with Representative Elijah Cummings and the fact of having "nieces and nephews [who] are people of color."[70] Meadows also attempted to silence the debate through an emotional display of anger, shouting back at Tlaib that her accusation was itself racist. But the response only begged for more scrutiny, leading to the resurfacing of a 2012 video in which Meadows vowed to send President Obama "back home to Kenya or wherever it is."[71] The renewed scrutiny compelled Meadows to disavow the 2012 remark and claim that "anyone who knows me knows that there is not a racial bone in my body."

COLOR-BLIND DISCLAIMERS

Because credentialing is hackneyed and transparent, those making controversial remarks about race often rely on other disclaimers. They try hedging, as noted above. But they may also try using color-blind disclaimers, to suggest that their remarks are about "anything but race," as Bonilla-Silva puts it.[72] For instance, one of Bonilla-Silva's white interviewees explained her position against interracial marriage as being motivated by a concern for the hypothetical children of that marriage, who would likely face difficulties due to others' racism. In so doing, she framed her position so that it wouldn't appear to be about her views on race per se.[73]

Collectively, a coded political discourse, commonly referred to as dog-whistle politics, permits Americans—white Americans especially, though not exclusively—to invoke racist ideas without mentioning race. In his study of dog-whistle politics, the legal scholar Ian Haney López shows how this coded discourse emerged in US politics in the mid-1960s, was refined by the Nixon and Reagan administrations, was picked up by Democrats during Bill Clinton's presidential campaign, and persists today. Nixon's calls for "law and order" and Reagan's invocations of "welfare queens" included no explicit mention of race; López argues, though, that white voters hear the message *"politician W is with us and against those minorities."*[74] But this is the point. The coded message provides cover, allowing those who blow the dog whistle to deny having made racist statements and to attack their critics for playing the so-called race card.[75]

DISCLAIMERS OF DIFFERENCE

Paradoxically, white Americans also invoke disclaimers of difference, mobilizing ethnic ancestry to deny the relevance of race and racism today. Charles A. Gallagher, a sociologist who studies race and inequality, interviewed white Americans about their ethnic heritage and its contemporary meaning. He found that few described ethnicity as an important part of their identity. Still, many of Gallagher's interviewees invoked a selective history of ethnic heritage to negate the racism and discrimination that Americans of color experience today. The invocation of ethnicity involves a three-part claim: (1) one's own white ancestors once faced discrimination in the United States because of their ethnicity, (2) but, through hard work and perseverance, those ancestors overcame discrimination and, the story usually goes, assimilated into (white, though this is usually left unstated) American society. For those who invoke this claim, it follows, then, that (3) contemporary inequality cannot be explained by racism; rather, individual failures to work hard and persevere explain inequality. In this way, the invocation of difference supports the ideology of color-blind racism, as it conveys that difference, in fact, does not matter.

A quote from one of Gallagher's interviewees—"Tom, a twenty-two-year-old from New Jersey," who self-identified as Italian and Irish American—is illustrative.

I wouldn't be surprised if people just said [about blacks], "get off your butt, get an education, go to work." These people

[Asians] came into this country not having anything. They worked hard, that's how they got here. *There's no difference between what they did not and what my grandparents did eighty, ninety, hundred years ago when they came to this country.* They didn't know anything. They worked hard and survived. They didn't even think of looking at the government or turning to the government and saying this isn't fair because I'm Italian that you are not giving me a job.[76]

The invocation of ethnicity mobilizes a selective history of whiteness to negate contemporary claims about racism. The power of this claim is that it's partly true: many European immigrants to the States did indeed face xenophobia, discrimination, and violence from "native" white Americans. However, "the problem," as Bonilla-Silva, writing with Amanda Lewis and David G. Embrick, notes, "is that this story line equates the experiences of immigrant groups with those of involuntary 'immigrants' (enslaved Africans, etc.)."[77] The invocation of ethnicity also erases the ways that white privilege is accrued and transmitted over generations.[78]

* * *

White ignorance of privilege and racial domination, Elizabeth V. Spelman writes, is "an appalling achievement; managing to create and preserve it can take grotesquely prodigious effort."[79] Those final few words are apt and startling. They suggest the depth, the active coordination, the passive acquiescence, and the energy and resources spent to keep histories unlearned and the façade of color-blindness in place.

This effort can be measured by the perpetual shock many white people feel when reality insists that we are not who we believe we are: a presidential candidate dog-whistles his way to the White House, as if for the first time; chants of "All Lives Matter" answer calls for racial justice in law enforcement; and grotesquely prodigious levels of state violence are deployed against those who protest police violence against Black Americans.

But this effort can be measured by even less, the white despair or rage when another person suggests that we grapple with our words and our actions. And it can be measured by mere absence, the retreat into stubborn lives of illusion, at the mere mention of reality.

CONCLUSION

ENIAL is endemic to human life. It appears in the most banal of interactions between people and strangers. Then it wanders into workplaces, showing up in slogans, paperwork, and trainings. Politicians and members of the media are experts in it, using it to erase the problems and inequalities that structure social life. But many of us are experts in denial, too, using it in the same ways to keep ourselves and others from reckoning with those problems.

We will, then, inevitably encounter denial. This, in turn, forces a decision: accept it, feigning obliviousness to our problems and speaking those we can't ignore out of existence, or reject it, trading it for acknowledgment. We've seen much of the former. But what of the latter?

Because denial is multiple, acknowledgment is, too. It takes different forms and requires different things of us in interactional, organizational, and collective contexts. It also means something different, has a different urgency, and certainly has different consequences, depending on what denied fact it surfaces. For instance, I remain unconvinced of the necessity and benefit of calling attention to the minor disturbances that inevitably appear in social interaction, though I know of others who might argue that there is nothing more disruptive to those interactions than *not* acknowledging those blunders. I'm unprepared, in other words, to argue that the foregrounding of distressing information is always to our benefit. The consequences of acknowledgment, like those of denial, are always an empirical question. And beyond the empirical question, there are the permanently unsettled questions of politics and values, of *whether* we should work toward acknowledgment of any particular denied fact.

There's even a case to be made for some amount of collective forgetting. This, according to both Susan Sontag and Lewis Hyde, is a prerequisite of collective reconciliation.[1] Historical traumas can be grounds for social conflict and spur calls for vengeance. Eventually, these must be surrendered to time. And yet neither Sontag nor Hyde really equates forgetting with denial; forgetting is what both hope follows after harms have been acknowledged, wrongs righted, and breaches in social life repaired. Their hoped-for forgetting comes after acknowledgment; it is not a replacement for it. Denial is different; it is a forced forgetting so as to dodge the reckoning with harms, wrongs, and breaches.

Another qualifier: because neither denial nor acknowledgment is a *state*, the former does not simply give way to the latter. Those engaging in the work of acknowledgment must continually contend with those engaging in the work of denial. Acknowledgment, after all, disrupts social relationships and assumptions. Those responsible for such disruptions are rarely thanked, rewarded, or recognized for that work, at least not initially. History may redeem protesters and whistleblowers, but the present usually isn't so generous. Those who dare speak of others' transgressions are often targeted and harassed. They suffer the vindictiveness of the powerful, who lash out, ostracize, bully, and threaten. Harvey Weinstein, for instance, allegedly sicced intelligence operatives and former spies on those who he suspected would reveal his sexual harassment and assaults of women.[2] Others lose jobs, standing, friends, even family. Yesenia Guitron, a banker with Wells Fargo, raised concerns about the bank's fraudulent practices for nearly two years.[3] For her good work, she was fired. Joseph Darby, the soldier who passed photographs of torture at Abu Ghraib to military investigators, was still stationed in Iraq when his identity as the whistleblower was revealed by former secretary of defense Donald Rumsfeld during a public congressional hearing. Darby returned home to find that many of his neighbors and even some family members viewed him as a traitor.[4] Meanwhile, General Antonio Taguba, who conducted an honest and vigorous investigation of Abu Ghraib, was sent into retirement.[5]

These are cautionary examples. And yet, as examples, they exceed the caution. Those who confront denial, those who testify to what others won't, can change the flow of social and political action. They can mobilize help for others or directly provide it themselves. They can stop offensive speech in its tracks. They can, if the world be ready, even chip away at the ideologies that denial sustains. And they often remain secure in their knowledge that their actions were right.[6]

Toward Acknowledgment

The forms of acknowledgment that I have in mind involve both cognitive and social demands. Commonly, we associate acknowledgment simply with the cognitive—the awareness and acceptance of information. But even a passive bystander can be in this state. The social demand takes us further down the path of acknowledgment, toward individual and collective action that may produce consequential social change.[7] Without this, even those who cognitively acknowledge a problem are liable to backtrack to denial. This is the case for the climate change believers, described in the introduction, whom Kari Marie Norgaard interviewed. Norgaard's interviewees *knew* climate change was a problem. Yet they were frozen by their helplessness, their sense that they could not "do something." Lacking the path between cognitive acknowledgment and collective action, they resigned themselves to inaction and avoidance. So as we walk the path of acknowledgment, the strategies become ever more collective and direct. And they take us beyond simple recognition of denied facts toward reform, justice, remedy, and reparation.

Naming Denial

Acknowledgment contains ironies. One irony is this: simply knowing of denial, speaking its names, describing how it does its work, is to disrupt it. Those using denial need it to go unnoticed; they need their denials to seem natural and true. But by spotting and then naming another's use of denial, one can jam their messages, revealing these to be contrived, artificial, and self-serving.[8]

When left unmarked and unnamed, violence, domination, and oppression go unnoticed by many, but do their damage still. The same is true of denial, but doubled. For denial does the hiding; it is the social process that keeps violence, domination, and oppression unmarked and unnamed. And denial is also what is hidden, the social process that remains unmarked and unnamed.

To mark a social problem, one must name it, lifting it out of the shadows that denial casts.[9] Naming, meanwhile, has long been a technique of those involved in social change. Indeed, human-rights organizations often use "name and shame" strategies to stigmatize human-rights offenders and their international supporters.[10] The scholarship of critical race scholars, meanwhile, named systemic racism and, so, made it visible.[11]

Naming denial, we foreground it. Foregrounding it, we denaturalize it, by which I mean we reveal its strategic use by people to explain away their transgressions. The denier no longer appears spontaneous and authentic in their efforts at defending themselves and protecting allies. Rather, their use of denial appears scripted, rehearsed, intentional, and self-serving, as the use of denial usually is; the denier is acting and speaking in ways that most anyone in their position, accused of the similar offenses, acts and speaks.

Drawing attention to denial, one can reveal it to be so much artifice. This is what Representative Rashida Tlaib accomplished when she criticized, as racist, Representative

Mark Meadows's protection of Donald Trump. Tlaib saw Meadows's protective use of credentialing for what it was: a boilerplate denial of color-blind racism. Describing Meadows's speech in this way, she effectively jammed his messaging, forcing him to stumble his way to an unsatisfying account for himself and leading the media to take notice.

Tlaib used naming as a political intervention. Importantly, she has a platform to transform naming, which is largely a descriptive act, into an intervention. However, for many of us, naming is less an intervention as it is an act of witnessing. Like those whom Stanley Cohen calls "moral witnesses," those who speak denial's proper names search "for the quiet but certain knowledge of what the powerful deny and would rather not have witnessed." The witnesses, like those who name denial, are "*active* bystanders—powerless to intervene, but a reminder to perpetrators that not everyone approves or colludes."[12] Active, because those who name denial speak of reality. But bystanders still, because naming describes, but does not necessarily remedy, that reality.

Jeremiah Bey Ellison, a member of the Minneapolis City Council, made this point in a *New York Times* editorial on the city and its pervasive inequalities, the latter made worse by coronavirus. Ellison writes,

> During every crisis, well-meaning white people here make a ritual of acknowledging the city's steep inequities, but we've been hearing the same "woe is you" sentiment for a long time. It's as if people think the mere acknowledgment is the work. But as North Minneapolis prepares to brace ourselves

for the grim future Detroit and Milwaukee have shown us,
the death tolls suggest that acknowledgments don't mean a
thing. I want to take us back to this notion of remedy.[13]

Remedy treks further than naming. It treks further, even,
than the conventional meaning of acknowledgment, as the
cognitive recognition of truth, takes us. The remedies Ellison
has in mind are deeply social and structural. These are the
most advanced forms of acknowledgment, far on its path.
First, though, more modest responses.

Redirection

Acknowledgment contains another irony. One of its strategies is, in fact, a form of denial. We can effectively harness
redirection to indirectly disrupt uncomfortable and even
dangerous social encounters.

In 2012, a fight broke out on the No. 6 train in New York
City between a woman and a man whom she accused of following her. Writing of the fight, the *New York Times* invoked a
familiar urban scene: "The most enduring and useful custom
of New York subway riders is that they don masks of stone at
the turnstile, and keep them on until they've gotten where
they are going. The origins of this sound practice are beyond
the memory of any living New Yorker, but . . . its value continues to be proved every day."[14] Indeed, the video of the
fight shows textbook bystander behavior. Those nearest the
fight look around nervously but take no action. But then, a
third person, Charles Sonder, steps between the woman and

man. Sonder deescalates the conflict through his sheer physical presence and his distracting performance of normalcy. Between the two strangers, Sonder casually eats a pile of potato chips he'd brought with him. It would be laughable if it wasn't so effective.

Redirection is the least one can do, and the least one can do is sometimes enough to disrupt the everyday harassments and threats that people encounter. Bystander intervention programs, such as Bringing in the Bystander at the University of New Hampshire (UNH), train college students to use redirection when they observe risk markers of sexual assault. Jane Stapleton, co-director of the UNH's Prevention Innovations Research Center, describes how she "tells students they'll need to be creative about outmaneuvering aggressors. Among the diversions she discusses: suddenly turning on the lights at a party or turning off the music [or] accidentally spilling a drink on the guy."[15]

Likewise, a 2016 *New York Times* article on disrupting offensive speech highlights the power of changing the topic or causing a distraction. According to Gail Stern, who trains college students and members of the military in sexual violence prevention techniques, one might try, for instance, reframing another's offensive speech as "satire." According to Stern, "one deft approach might be to assume that the speaker is being outrageous on purpose, and to respond with something like this: 'I love satire. It's so weird that people believe that for real and it's so cool you called that out.'"[16]

Redirection can change the course of social events. It can move offensive conversations away from their offensiveness.

It can deescalate conflicts and, even, potentially violent encounters. Still, it is a relatively weak intervention. There is a reason, after all, that it's a form of denial. While it may alter a discrete incident (e.g., the offensive speech), it often leaves the underlying causes of that incident (e.g., norms that tolerate sexist or racist speech) untouched, as well as the enduring harms on those subjected to the speech. Indeed, by turning attention, redirection may, ultimately, conceal what it interrupts.

Disruption

Disruption is more powerful than redirection. By telling another that their speech or behavior is offensive, one directly interrupts the incident and calls out the underlying norms expressed in it. Disruptions don't need to be elaborate. One study of college men's anti–sexual violence efforts shows how men use "short, brief and immediate statements" to disrupt offensive talk or abusive behavior. Men report using phrases like "that's not cool," "you know that's not appropriate," or even, a disapproving "yo, dude" to get other men to stop engaging in offensive talk. (Admittedly, "you might have to do it five times before they'll stop saying it around you," one man reported.)[17]

Disruption risks the ire of those at whom it's directed. Still, disruption has great potential. The disruptor often finds allies, as their interventions empower other disruptors. Silence often keeps would-be helpers immobilized by uncertainty or fear. They're likely to remain bystanders until another person speaks or acts. In a study of white college students' participation in racist incidents, Leslie Houts Picca and Joe R. Feagin document this. For instance, "Don" reported telling a pair of friends to stop making racist jokes. He did so after another witness to the joking, a white female student, "groaned" at the jokes "in a disapproving way." Don reports, "It was only after this grumble that I felt like any verbal objections I made would be supported, and only then did I speak up." "Tina," a white sociology major, condemned another's stereotyping of African Americans after she noticed that others in her group (of white students) were "appalled." Indeed another in the group explicitly asked Tina to "say something."[18] In both cases, the initial displays of disapproval are weaker than Don's and Tina's interventions. And yet the initial interventions give way to the stronger disruptions. This is at least in part because the initial moves weaken pluralistic ignorance, the belief that the group is unconcerned by or even approving of some of its members' racist speech.

Disruption is particularly important in organizational settings, especially workplaces. There, and in ways that both bystander experiments (chapter 2) and Asch's experiment (chapter 4) foreshadow, people often experience pressure toward consensus and silence. Of this "organizational silence," Elizabeth Wolfe Morrison and Frances J. Milliken, professors of management in New York University's Stern School of Business, write,

> There are many different types of issues that people in orga-
> nizations are silent about and many reasons why people may

elect to be silent. An employee may keep quiet about unethical practices that he or she has observed, for example, out of
fear of being punished. Members of a group may choose to
not express dissenting opinions in the interest of maintaining consensus and cohesiveness in the group. Thus, silence
can be caused by fear, by the desire to avoid conveying bad
news or unwelcome ideas, and also by normative and social
pressures that exist in groups.[19]

According to Morrison and Milliken, organizational silences
are not likely to be corrected by individual employees or even
individual managers. Instead, "revolutionary change" to the
system may be required to rebuild trust, protect employees
who speak up, and create processes that can transform dissenting opinions and inconvenient facts into change.[20] Still,
some contexts may be more favorable to the surfacing of dis-
sent and problems. When employees perceive their superiors
as willing to listen and do not fear reprisal, they're more likely
to raise difficult issues.[21]

But Morrison and Milliken's research into organizational silences raises something even more basic to social
life. Workers who remain silent about difficult issues report
doing so because they fear negative social reactions, such as
being labeled a tattletale. They also fear damaging a relationship with a co-worker. Fear of retaliation—losing a job, for
instance—actually ranked fourth among reasons that forty
interviewees gave to Morrison and Milliken for staying silent at work. Just as a class of students overlooks a professor's
mistakes for fear of embarrassing themselves or the professor,

co-workers may tolerate offensive behavior or organizational problems because of the common stresses, worries, and fears of social interaction. Pluralistic ignorance, an employee's sense that others do not share their concerns, also contributes to organizational silence over problems. Disruption—even those as weak as the "groan" that empowered Don or as informal as a sidebar or private conversation—can help undo these states, suggesting to would-be disruptors that their concerns are real, legitimate, and shared.

Documentation

Redirection and disruption support acknowledgment in everyday encounters with others. Like the everyday forms of denial, these forms are particularly well suited to emergent troubles and difficulties within the encounter themselves. Still other strategies are needed to support acknowledgment of more complex, enduring, and organizational forms of denial.

Literal denial, the outright denial of a problem, struggles to endure a paper trail. Documentation not only provides evidence of those first-order transgressions I discussed in chapter 5. It also can provide evidence of guilty knowledge—that supervisors, human resources officers, an organization's lawyers, or watchdogs knew of those transgressions, yet tolerated them.

Ideally, paper trails will be official. They will be sent to the appropriate authority, using organizational documents and conventions. Accounts of transgressions that are localized, describing witnessed or known events in detail, are especially disruptive. They approach the limits of literal denial, in that particularly descriptive and even-handed documentation can sometimes secure the previously denied reality.

Second-order paper trails are also important. The position of would-be whistleblowers is strengthened if they have documentation of their documentation. Archived emails, copies of letters, and receipts for the latter's mailing help. For instance, in December 2005, Dennis Hambek, a Wells Fargo employee,

> sent a letter via certified mail to Carrie Tolstedt, who had become the head of regional banking at Wells Fargo in 2002. In the letter, which would have been passed on to the bank's legal department, he described the gaming he'd witnessed, and told her that employees were leaving. "It would behoove someone to survey these employees as to the true reason they left the company." He added, "Upper management is also aware of this, as is the ethics line, yet no action has been taken."[22]

That Hambek sent his letter via certified mail and that he kept a copy of it gave him and Bethany McLean, an editor with *Vanity Fair*, leverage when reporting on Hambek's allegations.

There are good reasons one may not wish to share a paper trail, either internally or externally. Disrupting through documentation can open one to retaliation. Supervisors may not be trustworthy, or may not appreciate bad news, or may be the subject of those paper trails. Indeed, one study of whistleblowers found that those who make disclosures internally tend to be fired more quickly than those who make their disclosures externally. Their disclosures, meanwhile, tend not to produce as much change as externally directed whistleblowers. But the latter were subject to prolonged, extensive periods of retaliation. At the same time, protections of whistleblowers are complex and uneven. Some US states protect whistleblowers who report internally to their organizations. Some protect whistleblowers who report externally. Other states make no distinction.[23]

Despite these reservations, I expect that the push for documentation will become ever greater. Today, most of us expect that our lives will be documented in the forms of photographs, texts, and emails. This is a double-edged sword. Textual records are more permanent, for being digitally stored, and more easily and discreetly created than ever before. But that recognition means that others are likely to treat what isn't well documented as unreal, for the expectation now is that all of life will inevitably be captured. Sontag wrote this of photographs nearly two decades ago, and it is even truer of all types of communication today.[24]

Lacking a paper trail, investigative journalists often seek contemporaneous accounts of allegations. That is, they investigate whether the person making an allegation shared it with others at the time the alleged wrongdoing occurred. To explain the *New York Times'* slow and ambivalent reporting on Tara Reade's accusations that Joe Biden had sexually assaulted her, Dean Baquet, executive editor of the *Times*, offered, "We did what we always do. One thing we have tried to do, going all the way back to the Bill O'Reilly story, is to find out whether people talk to people contemporaneously, whether they describe their stories to people before they became public. And in fact, she had talked to a couple of people who confirm that to us." Contemporaneous accounts (weakly) mimic a paper trail, in that they suggest that an allegation has history and was not invented for the political or personal needs of the present. Still, they're not the "ultimate test," as Baquet puts it later in his account of the *Times*' reporting. Nor do they guarantee that others will perceive an allegation as credible. And they remain vulnerable to the outright denials of the accused.[25]

* * *

Doubts lurks at the edges of these pages. One of those doubts is that denial, and the people and groups invested in it, will surrender so easily. Perhaps one can effectively intervene at the edges of social life—the public emergency among anonymous strangers, the muttered offense by a co-worker. But as denial scales up, into workplaces, organizations, and politics, it demands a more complex, more powerful response. Even the whistleblowers, staring down power armed only with an allegation and piles of documents, require outlets and allies ready to defend their claims.

Truth, a paper trail to support it, and a person to speak it are necessary but insufficient conditions of collective acknowledgment. Writing of photographs, the supposedly undeniable form of evidence, Sontag argues that a "context of feeling and attitude" must be present for a photograph to move public opinion.[26] I agree with this but seek to extend it.

A context of feeling and attitude must sustain any revelation. This context must prepare the public to listen to those who speak of hidden truths; it must ready them to remain steadfast in the face of the accused's predictable denials. More than this is needed, though. The message must be carried and amplified—and this is how we, as social actors, indeed build a resilient context of feeling and attitude. The messenger, in turn, needs to be defended from the inevitable attacks by the well-paid lawyers, the mercenary private investigators, and the better-resourced rhetoricians.

To match collective denial, acknowledgment must be leveled up into a collective form. This transformation mobilizes those harmed by problems, organizes activists and advocates, activates bystanders, and, eventually, may even compel the powerful to take notice. It pushes toward new policies, words, and ideas. In support of this, it generates new data and evidence, to secure the reality of what some would prefer to ignore. And it designs actions and solutions, helping people shed their bystander states by making paths of change visible.

There is no fact, there is no truth, so undeniable as to be undeniable. But collective acknowledgment can remake society. Curricula are redesigned and textbooks revised, so as to hide ever less. New memorials are erected and signage posted, to bring history out of the forgotten. Old ones, their mistruths now recognized, are altered or removed. Sites of historical traumas and denials are recovered and marked. We cut new paths of acknowledgment through our world. Along the way, we find our way to thoughts, selves, and communities remade, though never fully.

ACKNOWLEDGMENTS

THIS book has been my companion, for the past decade or so, as I've studied and taught on the denial of torture. For the past five years, I've followed denial past this topic, teaching a course on it for the Department of Sociology and Criminology at the University of Denver (DU). The ever-curious people who've enrolled in this course have taught me much, particularly around the denial of inequality, sexism, and racism. By doing so, they have changed my teaching and this book. I owe much of this book to the learners I've met in this course. I hope I have represented them well.

I'm also grateful to two former DU undergraduates, one of whom never took my course on denial and one of whom did: Kira Pratt and Richie Snooks. Pratt's and Snooks's undergraduate theses on Confederate memorials and men's responses to sexual assault allegations, respectively, shed light on the ways that denial operates today in public discourse. In similar ways, I learned much from the members of the Office of Teaching and Learning's *White Fragility* reading group, during our Fall 2019 bimonthly meetings. I owe special thanks to my former colleague Valentina Iturbe-LaGrave, who led the group and who, during her time at DU, was generous with her expertise on social theory and critical pedagogy.

Still others have been generous with their time and skills, providing feedback on drafts of this book. Ilene R. Kalish and New York University Press's anonymous reviewers provided invaluable feedback on drafts of this book, challenging me to more clearly define and describe denial. Snooks, Dustin Weilbach, and Matthew Cort, all former students in my course on denial, provided feedback on the first few chapters. Geoff Stacks helped me keep my writing writerly. Casey Stockstill, Diane Pike, Lisa Martinez, Hava Gordon, Amie Levesque, and Jeffrey Lin helped me keep my writing sociological.

I'm especially grateful to Stockstill, Gordon, and Martinez, who have kept a writing group with me for the past several years. Our meetings and time together helped me sustain progress on this book. Meanwhile, a series of writing workshops and retreats at the University of Denver, organized by Alison Staudinger and facilitated by Helen Sword, energized the final month of work on revisions to this book.

I owe less to, but would still like to acknowledge, Steve Altman and Andrew Del Rosso, who provided several dozen recommendations of things for me to write about, none of which I took. I'm sorry but I'm not going to apologize for that.

As with all things, I owe the most to Jennifer J. Esala, always my first reader.

APPENDIX

Toward Sociologies of Denial

THE study of denial has been at the edges of sociological theory and empirical work for a long time. For the past five decades, sociologists of social problems have examined the claims and counterclaims of those promoting and contesting the reality of social problems, producing what could be considered prototypes for the study of collective denial.[1] Before that, Erving Goffman's studies of interaction, Gresham Sykes and David Matza's theory of neutralizations, and Marvin B. Scott and Stanford M. Lyman's theory of accounts prefigured contemporary social theories of interpersonal denial.[2] But we can push further into the history of sociology and still find denial. In US sociology, the study of ignorance, the state of not knowing, dates to at least 1949, with the publication of Wilbert Moore and M. Tumin's article "Some Social Functions of Ignorance."[3] W. E. B. Du Bois's concluding chapter, "The Propaganda of History," in his 1935 book *Black Reconstruction in America: 1860–1880*, offers an early analysis of the hidden curriculum, collective memory, and the erasure of knowledge—and especially white knowledge—of systemic racism in the United States.[4]

Obviously, Eviatar Zerubavel and Stanley Cohen were not the first sociologists to write of denial or denial-like processes. But their works in the late 1990s and early 2000s, particularly Zerubavel's *The Elephant in the Room* and Cohen's *States of Denial*, have given a more formal structure and analytic vocabulary to the sociological study of denial. Zerubavel's theory of "socially organized denial," for instance, reveals how silence about problems is maintained through socialization, interactions, social sanctions, and social norms like taboos. Cohen, meanwhile, identified three forms of human-rights denial in the discourse of governments—literal, interpretive, and implicatory— that have proven remarkably generalizable across time and social problems. Social scientists, myself included, have documented how these forms of denial appeared in public discourse of US torture.[5] Kari Marie Norgaard, meanwhile, synthesizes Zerubavel's and Cohen's frameworks for the study of climate change denial.

Despite the inroads that Zerubavel and Cohen made, there remains no single framework for the sociology of denial. Norgaard's *Living in Denial* offers us the closest thing, a robust and sophisticated theory of denial that addresses the role of the micro, through the study of emotions, and the macro, through the study of cultural narratives and national identity, in both interpersonal and collective denial. In this regard, *Living in Denial* simultaneously synthesizes Zerubavel's and Cohen's works, while also advancing the sociology of denial by connecting it to other dimensions of social life. For these reasons, Norgaard's scholarship should be, in my view, the departure point for scholars interested in building a social theory of denial.[6]

I have tried to do something different in this book. Rather than build an overarching theory of denial, I've identified and described the myriad forms that denial takes, continuing to develop the analytic vocabulary that Cohen first began arranging. I've done this with two different category of readers in mind. Some, like the people who take my undergraduate course on denial, want to perceive social life more clearly, understand it more deeply, and describe it with greater precision than they could before taking a course or reading a book. Others, mainly other professional sociologists, share much with that first category of reader. They, too, want to perceive social life more clearly, understand it more deeply, and describe it with greater precision than they could before reading an article or book. But they're also interested in building formal, theoretical descriptions or explanations of social life and designing empirical studies to test those explanations.

To the former category of reader, I've tried, through this book, to be a guide to the use of denial in social life. I've pointed out the moments when and contexts in which this reader will likely observe specific forms of denial. I've offered names to those forms, and I've tried to define those forms and illustrate them with multiple examples. This, in a sense, is the pedagogical purpose of this book, which largely tracks with my course on denial.

To the latter category of reader, I hope I've offered a set of threshold concepts for the study of denial. These concepts can be employed in studies of denial; they can also be adapted for the study of various social issues and problems more generally. There are other forms to be found, named, and described. Some may already be available in the vast literature relevant to the study of denial. Still others may yet be invented by some particularly innovative and masterful denier.

To this reader, I've also tried to demonstrate just how diffuse denial is in social life. Denial, I believe, is a key that unlocks so much of social life—the interactional processes of face work, neutralizations, and account making; organizational misconduct and white-collar crime; scandal management; and collective memory and the hidden curriculum. So rather than explain denial, I've tried to explain how denial is implicated in these other social processes.

Denial's diffusion, in turn, partly explains the underdevelopment of the sociology of denial, despite the discipline's appreciation of Zerubavel's, Cohen's, and Norgaard's works. Denial has and perhaps always will have too many disciplinary and subdisciplinary homes. In everyday interaction, people use strategies of denial to background or minimize distressing information; symbolic interactionists, ethnomethodologists, and social psychologists have made the most important contributions to our understanding of these strategies. Scholarship on accounts, excuses, disclaimers, and apologies—the rhetoric of denial—spans criminology, communications, philosophy, and political science. Denial is central to organizational misconduct and white-collar crime; organizational sociology, organizational and management studies, and critical criminology have the most to offer here. Political communication is replete with strategies to background or minimize distressing information; communications scholars, political scientists and sociologists, and cultural sociologists offer us vocabularies for describing denial in politics. Meanwhile, sociologists of ignorance, themselves navigating a fairly new disciplinary terrain, cross paths with those of us studying denial, even as our reference lists diverge. And because one of the central tasks of social scientists is to make the previously invisible—that is, the previously denied—visible, many subfields have theories and empirical studies relevant to the study of denial. For instance, Eduardo Bonilla-Silva's studies of color-blind racism and Ian Haney López's studies of dog-whistle politics should be as foundational to the study of denial as they are to the study of contemporary racism.

Because denial is diffuse, it also suffers from definitional issues. The reviewers of a draft of this book pointed this out to me, and I have struggled with finding a path forward through their (constructive) critiques. Definitional issues ultimately frustrate efforts to build a theoretical framework for denial, as it's not yet clear that we know the composition, size, or shape of the thing we're trying to frame. This appendix explores some of these definitional issues. I suspect, though, that it does not resolve these issues, for they have long appeared in the study of other, related phenomena—social problems and moral panics, to name two. Still, by foregrounding these issues, I hope to show my own circuitous way through these definitional challenges. I also hope to add texture to this book, moving beyond description of forms of denial to description of the sociological project of studying denial.

Defining Denial

Over the course of this book, I describe denial as two sets of strategies—those that people and organizations use to keep potentially discrediting or distressing information in the background of social life and rhetorical or discursive ones that people use to minimize that information when it surfaces. This description dovetails with Norgaard's definition of denial "as the process by which individuals collectively distance themselves from information because of norms of emotions, conversation, and attention and by which they use an existing cultural repertoire of strategies in the process."[7] Both of our definitions emphasize processes and strategies; they emphasize, in other words, that denial is something that people *do* rather than a state.

My definition lacks Norgaard's explanation—what follows the "because . . ." (of norms of emotions, conversation, and attention). There are two reasons that I forgo the built-in explanation. The first is because I'm hesitant to ascribe motives to social action. Motives, as C. Wright Mills showed and as neutralization theory emphasizes, are part and parcel of the intersubjective construction of reality. People invoke motives to account for themselves, and motives themselves are socially organized into cultural repertoires.[8] Norms of attention, emotions, and conversation are as much part of our shared cultural vocabularies as are strategies of denial. The second reason I avoid the "because . . ." is because it is simultaneously too narrow and too general. Narrow, because if we are to ascribe motivating factors to denial, the list of underlying reasons people minimize information is likely longer than those any definition can include. For instance, if I were to develop a list of underlying motives to denial, I'd add norms of identity performance to Norgaard's definition. I'd also add norms protecting social and political power to it. General, because "norms"—and on this I agree with Howard Becker, and John Darley and Bibb Latané—are often so vague and conflicting as to offer only weak explanations of social action.[9] I recognize, though, that not all social scientists share these positions on norms and, indeed, explanations of behavior. I don't intend to reject Norgaard's definition, but only to describe some of the differences here.

My definition also differs from Norgaard's in identifying two distinct sets of strategies of denial—those used to background information and those used to minimize information. These fall under Norgaard's umbrella term of "cultural repertoire of strategies." By identifying and describing two distinct sets of strategies, I hope this book helps advance the study of denial by organizing the strategies to which Norgaard alludes. I'd add, too, that I don't see these strategies as exclusively cultural, in the sense that Norgaard means. Citing Ann Swidler's work, Norgaard describes the cultural resources underlying denial as "symbols, stories, rituals and world-views which people may use in varying configurations to solve different kinds of problems."[10] The strategies of denial also include interactional rituals, culturally mediated rhetorical forms like disclaimers and accounts, and organizational strategies of knowledge building and knowledge effacement. These strategies, too, include the material and textual activities that give enduring form to denial, such as curating archives, editing textbooks, or designing historical markers to efface problems. I expect that others will identify sets of strategies deployed to background and minimize information.

Beyond Strategies of Denial

While more work needs to be done to uncover the strategies of denial, sociologies of denial should not be limited to the description of those strategies. On one hand, these strategies are likely endless. A single strategy can be parsed into multiple substrategies, and new strategies are discoverable still. There are diminishing returns in the building of a typology of techniques or strategies of denial. We see this, for instance, in the studies of accounts, neutralizations, and image-restoration techniques. William L. Benoit dedicates about ten pages of his book *Accounts, Excuses, and Apologies* to listing the various typologies associated with particular social scientists and, even, particular social scientists' different studies.[11] The typologies themselves are helpful, insofar as they generate material for empirical studies of *how* people use accounts. But their diversity, their lengths, and their different levels of analysis mean that they are poorer guides to accounts than a typology should be. For this reason, I decided to be rather selective in presenting the rhetorical forms of denial, foregrounding those forms that I view as most important to everyday and collective denial.

There is another risk in the focus on types, strategies, techniques, or forms of denial. This focus can obscure the core differences in expressions or enactments of those forms. A reviewer of this book, for instance, helpfully pointed out that processes of attention management are different when confronting the plainly visible "spinach in the teeth" of a speaker and the far less immediately visible and intelligible problem of climate change. In both cases, people may attempt to "feign ignorance" of the problems. But the leaf of spinach is simply there, unadorned in the tooth. (I'd add, though, that even the "spinach in the teeth" is part of public discourse, within popular writing on manners and as a bit of physical comedy in television and movies. In a sense, these contribute to the act of noticing the leafy green by shaping how we respond to them.) By contrast, underlying the act of *noticing* climate change is the knowledge that is built by experts, climate change organizations, activists, journalists, and politicians to make climate change visible to others.

Denial's form and behavior will depend on the sociological niches in which it's used. (The same is true of many living things within ecological niches, but I don't want to push that metaphor too far.) Its purpose or the consequences of its uses will differ, too, depending on how it's used and who uses it. (The same is true of many tools in the hands of differently skilled and resourced builders, but I don't want to push that metaphor too far either.) There's a reason that Zerubavel invokes interactionist theories to develop a theory of silence in everyday life, while Cohen invokes neutralization theory to develop his categories of official discourse. Some analytical tools are better suited to examining some forms of denial than are others.

I don't think the study of denial is unique in this, as I suspect this is the case with nearly all social phenomena that appear across social settings of differing complexity. The study of collective memory, for instance, has to account for the fact that individuals carry understandings of history that are socially structured, while those understandings are produced, invoked, and also contested at institutional and collective levels. This has left the study of collective memory, a seemingly unified and coherent social thing, fragmented and, according to one leading theorist, nonparadigmatic, transdisciplinary, and centerless.[12] Why should the sociological study of denial be different?

Rather than try to remedy the nonparadigmatic, transdisciplinary, and centerless enterprise of studying denial, we might instead be adaptable, nimble, even omnivorous in our definition and theorizing of denial. We need, after all, to track denial across an expansive social terrain. In other words, I believe that the definitional troubles we face when examining social problems, collective memory, and perhaps, too, denial follow from the sociological impulse to purify social phenomena, seeking something singular and internally consistent. My preference is for sociologies of denial that enable us to describe the heterogeneity of forms of denial; the interactional, communicative, and organizational strategies that make up those forms; the sociocultural resources that

support those strategies; and the material and symbolic vehicles that allow socially constructed forms of denial to tra-
verse the social.

In my earlier works on the denial of torture, I bor-
rowed from the constructionist sociologies of knowledge
of James A. Holstein, Dorothy Smith, and Bruno Latour.[13]
In Holstein's constructionist analytic approach, I find a
method of describing the relationship between micro-
interactions implicated in the construction of problems and
the collective representations that add structure to those
micro-interactions. In Smith's institutional ethnography
and Latour's actor-network theory, I find vocabularies and
theoretical concepts for describing the symbolic, textual,
and material vehicles that allow those collective representations to "travel" from the meso and macro levels where
they're produced to microsettings where they can be invoked in interactions and where they structure interactions.
In all three approaches, I find an impulse toward examining how social constructions of problems extend their reach
through the social, knitting together sites at the micro,
meso, and macro levels. And, in all three, I find a recognition of the diversities of things out of which people build
or deny social problems. I did not write this book to adapt
this sociology of knowledge approach to the study of denial.
Still, by documenting the myriad forms that denial takes,
the contexts in which those forms appear, and by hinting at
the materials—such as textbooks—that allow those forms
to circulate across those contexts, this book is largely consistent with this approach.

Objectivity, Values, and the Sociology of Denial

There are other challenges—narrower ones, but still deep—in defining denial. One follows from the sociologist's need to assess others' claims about problems as true or false. Should studies of denial be limited to the denial of *true* accusations and *real* social problems? Commonly, we use the word "denial" to indeed describe the denial of real things. But, sociologically, this question is more difficult to answer than common sense would lead us to believe.

For instance, the dictionary definition of denial does not presume that the allegation is indeed true or that the denial is false, though that is how we commonly think of denial as working. Rather, the person engaging in denial can be on the side of the truth. For instance, the *Oxford English Dictionary* offers one definition of denial as "the asserting (of anything) to be untrue or untenable; contradiction of a statement or allegation as untrue or invalid; also, the denying of the existence or reality of a thing."[14] A denial can be true or false, just as the allegation or information it aims at can be.

When examining individual statements in response to an allegation, I sometimes tread closely to the dictionary definition; statements that deny an allegation (as opposed to a social problem), the harm of the alleged behavior, or the speaker's responsibility for that behavior—whether a seemingly accurate or not statement—appear in my research of the denial of torture and in this book.[15] For instance, in an article and in my book on torture, I analyze General Ricardo Sanchez's denial of responsibility for the torture of detainees at Abu Ghraib. Specifically, Sanchez denied that he had permitted any techniques depicted in the photographs taken at Abu Ghraib. As far as I know, this statement is true. But this doesn't make it uninteresting or unimportant as a denial. Though literally true, Sanchez's denial remains sociologically interesting, at least to those interested in organizational misconduct and social problems. It offers an example of how a relatively powerful institutional actor constructs his responsibility for the behavior of subordinates while on the relatively high-profile stage of a congressional hearing. For instance, Sanchez and those who defended him invoked specific texts, which described permitted and prohibited interrogation techniques; this suggests the textual mediation of claims about organizational accountability.[16]

There's another way of thinking about Sanchez's denial. It frames organizational accountability in rather narrow terms, as what a superordinate literally and directly permits. Another framing of responsibility appeared in a Department of Defense investigation of Abu Ghraib, which argued that General Sanchez set the conditions for torture by continually changing interrogation policies; this confused his subordinates and introduced torturous practice into military guidelines in Iraq.[17] Sociologically and criminologically, an even more robust understanding of organizational misconduct and responsibility for it is available in the notion of "strain," as developed in the work of Robert K. Merton and Diane Vaughan and briefly described in chapter 4 here. Similarly, social psychologists emphasize the role of superordinates in creating environments that make violence like torture likely.

These theories provide further leverage for understanding Sanchez's truthful statement about not directly authorizing the use of torture at Abu Ghraib as a denial of responsibility.

Admittedly, I tend to be drawn to moments when people deny allegations that are, to the best of our knowledge, true. But the issue for a sociologist studying denial is not, primarily, to establish the truth of allegations or the lie of a specific denial. This can sometimes be impossible to do and rarely will a sociologist be positioned to accomplish this. Rather, sociologies of denial consider how statements work as denials, in the broadest sense. What's being denied—the harm of the alleged behavior, responsibility for it, or something else entirely? How does social context, as well as the positions of those making allegations and denials, influence the effectiveness of the denial? What symbolic, textual, and material resources does the person making the denial bring to bear to make their denial seem credible? What performative strategies do they use? How do audiences respond to the denial? How does the denial circulate through public arenas and social contexts? And how does the denial relate, or not, to available evidence supporting both the denial and the allegation?

This final question is especially relevant to the treatment of the veracity of allegations and denials, though it works on a different register. By detecting whether there are differences in how people construct denials in relation to different forms, amounts, and social perceptions of evidence, we can do two things at once. We can sidestep the issue of whether any specific denial is true or false, by focusing on what the claims makers caught up in denials and the counterclaims makers define as providing proof of the truth or falsehood of claims. We can also understand how different constructions of allegations and evidence shape the ways people use denial and how audiences receive those denials.

Denial and the Reality of Collective Problems

At the collective level, when addressing social problems, the study of denial transforms, just as denial itself does. Zerubavel, Cohen, and Norgaard all seem to reserve the word "denial" for occasions when people are denying *real* social problems. I, too, am inclined to reserve denial for these uses. This helps distinguish the study of denial from the study of related phenomena, particularly social problems and moral panics.

Sociologists of social problems examine all claims about problems—those drawing attention to problems and those downplaying them—while backgrounding whether those claims are true.[18] This act of backgrounding the validity of claims allows sociologists of social problems to study all claims with a single theoretical vocabulary. Doing so, they explain the rise and fall of public attention and constructions of problems by reference to subjective concern for, rather than the objective conditions of, problems. Critical examinations of the sociology of social problems have shown that this effort at backgrounding those objective conditions is never fully realized; in most studies of social problems, the researcher takes a stance on whether a problem is real and claims about it true.[19] Still, in its insistence that claims about problems be studied with a single vocabulary, the study of social problems remains distinct from the study of denial and its polar opposite, moral panics.

Sociologists who have studied "moral panics" examine people's efforts to build awareness, outrage, and action toward problems that, evidence suggests, are not nearly as widespread and/or harmful as those people say. In this way, the study of moral panics differs from the study of social problems more generally because scholars concerned with the former tend to foreground the misalignment between subjective concern for and objective harms of a problem. With moral panics, subjective concern for a problem is high, even as the objective basis for that concern is relatively low. This concern can usually be observed across the media, politics, institutions, and even everyday life: there is an abundance of talk about and work on moral panics. In a sense, there is an abundance of acknowledgment, perhaps even too much relative to other problems or to the very reality of the problem itself.[20]

Sociologists tend to describe two types of moral panics. Some problems are said to rise to the level of a moral panic when public concern, attention, and work on them is disproportionate to the documented harms and risks of the problem. Crimes against children are some of the most common examples. Kidnapping by strangers and cyberbullying, for instance, are two problems that have, at times, provoked substantial public concern, even as social science research and crime data suggested that these problems were not nearly as widespread and common as many believed. There can be no impartial standard for how much concern any problems rightly deserve;

this complicates analysis of the first type of moral panics, ensuring that work on them is always value-laden. But usually the standard is a comparative one. If Problem X has similar harms and effects on a similar number of people as Problem Y, but receives substantially more concern than Problem Y, Problem X may be viewed as a moral panic. Or if Problem X is not occurring more frequently, or is as limited in scope, or is harming no more people than it was in the past but public concern spikes, it may be viewed as a moral panic.

Other problems rise to the level of moral panic because there is simply no evidence that the problem even exists. For instance, from the late 1970s through the early 1990s, there was widespread concern among the public, politicians, law enforcement, and the media about sadistic Satanic cults that were said to be kidnapping and killing tens of thousands of people a year in the United States.[21] They weren't, but this subjective concern for cult activity shaped media coverage, investigations, and prosecutions of some violent crimes.

Denial is the mirror image of moral panics. (Not surprisingly, Cohen, whose career spanned the development of scholarship on both moral panics and denial, was at the vanguard of theory and research of both.) Sociologists interested in collective denial of social problems are generally concerned with problems about which two things are true. Those problems have, to the best of our knowledge, a demonstrated, objective reality and harms. Even so, significant segments of the public, the media, or elites demonstrate little subjective concern for that problem and/or make claims that aim to depress concern for those problems.

There are analytical challenges to this approach to denial, just as there are analytic challenges to the study of moral panics.[22] There is no impartial, objective standard to invoke to establish that public concern for a problem is so out of alignment with that problem's reality as to qualify as denial. (For instance, one can claim that so long as one person is harmed by a problem it deserves attention and ought not be denied.)[23] The descriptive approach, focused on *strategies* of denial, I've taken in this book only partially dodges this issue. This approach asks us to identify and investigate those activities through which people avoid, depress, or collectively suppress knowledge of and concern for a problem. This can be done without reference to a standard for determining how much knowledge and concern to a problem is appropriate; any interactional, organizational, or rhetorical move that avoids, depresses, or suppresses concern for a problem can be considered relevant to the study of denial.

Still, this book is predicated on a value-laden position that there ought to be more belief in or recognition of certain problems. This distinguishes this book and the study of denial from the more general study of social problems. It also leads to the use of the phrase "denial of problems," as opposed, say, to the more neutral phrase of "backgrounding problems." I'm comfortable with the latter but clearly prefer the former.

This position leads to other problems. As a prerequisite for research into the denial of social problems, we must rely on the expertise of others, including scientists outside our own discipline, to establish which allegations and problems are real, in order to label some people's responses to those allegations and problems as "denial." In some cases, knowledge about information and allegations may be in flux or ambiguous. Or knowledge may itself be implicated in the back-and-forth between those acknowledging problems and those denying those same problems. Because information about the problems being denied is itself implicated in the denial and acknowledgment of problems, the sociological study of denial cannot shed politics. To study the denial of climate change, as Norgaard has, or torture, as Cohen and I have, is to assert that, to the best of our knowledge, climate change is happening and specific instances of torture occurred, even though some people—and usually powerful people invested in these problems not being recognized—contest these facts.

There is an enduring tradition of value-free sociology that has legitimate critiques of value-laden work. From this perspective, the study of denial is on precarious terrain, for it is, at its very foundation, an intervention into the topics we're studying, rather than a disinterested look at those topics. But there is an equally enduring tradition of public sociology that argues for the absolute necessity of work that takes value-laden positions.[24] Most professional sociology programs socialize graduate students into the former, which is its own study in denial (already written by sociologists like Eric Margolis and Mary Romero).[25] By contrast, I think that most studies of the denial of social problems require an act of public sociology. They will involve a judgment about the validity of claims. They will also involve work, through the act of research and writing, to compose a world in which specific problems may be recognized.

I have no unmovable intellectual foundation on which to ground the study of denial. Instead, I have the recognition of the value-laden nature of my work. I'm comfortable with this; it's a tentative position, one that's ever-evolving, likely to lead toward mistakes, and, so, one that's always in need of revision. I suspect that any sociologist interested in studying collective denial will also need to be comfortable with this.

Politics and Denial

Though we cannot lift the study of denial out of politics, it does not mean that the *politics* of denial are straightforward. Denial crosses political lines, simply because it is the tool of people who wield social, political, and economic power. When facing allegations of sexual harassment, abuse, and assault, men associated with the Democratic Party have used similar excuses and justifications as those associated with the Republican Party; they have also relied on similar legal and media strategies, such as nondisclosure agreements and "catch and kill" arrangements, to silence accusers. To defend the use of drones, President Barack Obama employed nearly identical rhetorical arguments as President George W. Bush did when defending torture: both presidents argued that the violence of these acts was lawful, restrained, necessary, and effective.

This does not mean that political liberals and conservatives deploy denial in the exact same ways, on the same issues, or in equal parts. (Indeed, this book is not designed to establish whether these claims are so.) But it does mean that denial is a generic social tool, which confounds common partisan political divides. Any person with social, political, or economic power to defend will likely use denial when they see an allegation or social problem threatening that power. Certainly, effective deniers will adapt their denials to the commonsensical modes of reasoning shared by the audiences they most want to convince. But denial remains a socially and culturally mediated activity; to effectively deny something, one must align one's efforts with commonsensical modes of reasoning about the behavior, event, or problem in question, as the introduction and chapter 3 suggest.

And though we cannot lift the study of denial out of politics, it also does not mean that politics is all there is to denial. Chapter 1, for instance, addresses the ways that some forms of denial may serve as basic interactional strategies in the face of everyday mistakes and blunders, the sort that are as close to apolitical as any in social life can be. In these cases, denial appears as an interactional ritual that allows people to smooth over minor disruptions in social life. These uses of denial are baked into interaction; people need to background irrelevant and disruptive information to maintain functioning human relationships and social settings.

Similarly, some uses of excuses and justifications—what I refer to as the rhetoric of denial—may be an inevitable and, in some cases, even functional ritual of social life. People deploy the rhetoric of denial to account for their violations of others' expectations. Their uses of excuses and justifications often have the effect of preserving both underlying social expectations and their own identities; in other words, some uses of the rhetoric of denial may *restore* social life in the face of disruptions. In a sense, they can be rituals of restoration, countervailing rituals to the ceremonies of degradation that Harold Garfinkel theorized.[26] Shadd Maruna and Heith Copes's 2005 review of five decades of neutralization research in criminology makes a parallel point, positing that neutralizations may signal a "weak attachment" to the behavior being neutralized and "a willingness to change."[27]

I'm suggesting that some forms of denial can have prosocial effects, insofar as they permit people to maintain the flow of social life, mend social relationships, and restore discredited identities.

But this recognition raises a question: how do we distinguish between "functional" and "dysfunctional" forms of denial—those that restore social life and those that entrench problems? Here, I can offer no firm analytic distinction, for the harms of denial are always an empirical question that needs to be considered within the contexts in which denial occurs. They are also very much part of the claims-making processes in which denial occurs, as those who want others to acknowledge a problem will likely invoke the harms of denial. (The study of the social construction of denial awaits, as most of us working on denial treat it as an objective social phenomenon.) My working position is based on the well-known distinction that C. Wright Mills makes between personal troubles and public issues.[28] The former are the inevitable, but unstructured, "blips" of imperfect social beings—the genuine accidents, isolated mistakes, and the like. The latter are the structured problems of societies—the inequalities and inequities, systems of dominance, and forms of social suffering. In this book and my teaching, I tend to describe the use of denial to gloss over personal troubles as benign, perhaps functional, even pro-social, though this may not inevitably be so. Conversely, I emphasize the social harms of uses of denial to efface public issues. These uses of denial tend to serve the interests of those implicated in and benefiting from social problems; they also obscure the harms of those problems, thereby becoming one contributing factor in the persistence of those harms.

This is not an absolute position. Many of the things that seem like "blips" of social life indeed relate to social structures, hierarchies, and inequalities, as a reviewer of this book pointed out to me.[29] And many of the things that seem like "blips" in one era are revealed as collective problems to the next. Qualifications also apply to public issues. Recall my brief discussion, in the conclusion, of Sontag's and Hyde's position that collective forgetting may be a prerequisite of reconciliation. I'd also distinguish between a momentary denial of a social problem by an individual and the systemic, collective denials of communities, groups, institutions, and cultures. For instance, a social scientist may need to background climate change in order to research and teach on other social problems, even though they know that most problems tend to overlap and intersect. This is different, though, from an entire social science department, professional organization, subdiscipline, or discipline neglecting climate change in their research and teaching. The former, I think, is a necessary act of backgrounding of one topic to meaningfully foreground another, akin to Zerubavel's rules of relevance, which I describe in the introduction. The latter is a collective enactment of rules of relevance that produces a denial of certain problems. This distinction, in the end, is meant as an invitation, not a conclusion, to conversations about the consequences of denial.

* * *

Denial is an old theme, appearing in fables and morality plays centuries, even thousands of years, old. Yet there's a sense that, today, denial has been remade. Politics and people are more polarized, facts less factual, and disinformation ever more viral. We're said to live in impervious social media bubbles, which filter, refract, even reject reality. If this is true, and I'm not convinced that it is, it is all the more important that sociologies of denial keep pace with our objects of study. Denial is multiple, nimble, and adaptable. So, too, must be our theoretical and empirical tools.

Still, I recognize that it is unusual to close a book with the ambivalence, hesitancies, and revisable positions underlying one's sociological approach. (And I recognize the irony of hedging here, in a book meant to reveal how hedging functions.) Social science is supposed to be definitive. Confident, even. If we are neither definitive nor confident, then surely we lean on our writing, effacing our doubt with definitive-enough prose.

But I've closed this book not with that, but with recognition of my uncertainty at defining and theorizing denial. As an educator and a sociologist, I've found that revelatory and truly generative conversations often happen when we accept that we are lost amid the complexity of social life. And I've learned, again and again, that there are others whose aid I need to find my way out of that complexity.

NOTES

PREFACE

1   Ballhaus, "Trump Declines to Condemn White Supremacist."
2   *Wall Street Journal*, "Trump Stokes the Transition Panic."
3   Hughes and Rubin, "Republican Lawmakers Air Unease over Donald Trump"; Stephens, "Staring at the Conservative Gutter."
4   Commission on Presidential Debates, "October 19, 2016 Debate Transcript."
5   *Washington Post*, "13 Times Trump Said the Coronavirus Would Go Away."
6   Weiland et al., "Trump Was Sicker Than Acknowledged with Covid-19."
7   Kolata and Rabin, "'Don't Be Afraid of Covid,' Trump Says."
8   Del Rosso, *Talking about Torture*.
9   Cohen, *States of Denial*.
10 Weiser, "Swastikas, Slurs and Torment in Town's Schools."
11 Liu, "Pine Bush and the Pledge"; Izadi, "Pledge of Allegiance Reading in Arabic Sparks Controversy."
12 Izadi, "Pledge of Allegiance Reading in Arabic Sparks Controversy."
13 Weiser and Schweber, "Swastika on a Bathroom Stall."
14 Isacsson, "The Rumor at Pine Bush."
15 Associated Press, "KKK Unit Head Won't Resign"; John Brown Anti-Klan Committee, "Smash the Klan"; Klemsrud, "Women in Ku Klux Klan."
16 Evangelist and Nani, "Pine Bush Residents Rally to Dispute Bias Accusations."
17 CBS New York, "Pine Bush Residents Rally After Anti-Semitic Bullying Claims."
18 Lemert, *Social Things*, 32–33.
19 Solnit, *Call Them by Their True Names*, 5.

INTRODUCTION

1   This is a common claim of linguistic, anthropology, and psychology textbooks about the languages spoken by the indigenous people of the Arctic region; however, it appears to be a mix of linguistic misunderstanding, willful ignorance, exaggeration, and the sloppiness of textbook writers. See Martin, "'Eskimo Words for Snow.'"

2   In truth, ostriches bury their eggs in the sand to protect them from the heat of their habitats; they drop their heads into these holes in order to rotate their eggs. Corney, "Do Ostriches Really Bury Their Head in the Sand?"

3   This paragraph was helped along by posts made to an English-language forum on the website *StackExchange*. *StackExchange*, "Is There Any Idiom or Proverb Discouraging Knowledge?"; *StackExchange*, "What Is an Alternative Phrase to 'Swept under the Rug?'"

4   In fact, Ajit Varki and Danny Brower argue that denial is fundamental to the evolution of humans. Their suggestion is, in other words, that denial is embedded in our very DNA. See Varki and Brower, *Denial*.

5   Durkheim, *The Rules of Sociological Method*, 62.

6   Baumeister, Dale, and Sommer, "Freudian Defense Mechanisms and Empirical Findings in Modern Social Psychology."

7   Zerubavel, *Hidden in Plain Sight*, 63–64.

8   Zerubavel, *The Elephant in the Room*, 21.

9   Norgaard, *Living in Denial*, 9; Zerubavel, "The Social Sound of Silence," 32.

10   Norgaard, *Living in Denial*, 81–83, 188–189.

11   Norgaard, 191; Eliasoph, *Avoiding Politics*.

12   Norgaard, *Living in Denial*, 191.

13   Eliasoph, *Avoiding Politics*.

14   Orbuch, "People's Accounts Count," 458.

15   Hewitt and Stokes, "Disclaimers."

16   Scott and Lyman, "Accounts."

17   C. Wright Mills, "Situated Actions and Vocabularies of Motive," 906–907.

18   Scott and Lyman, "Accounts," 54.

19 Alexander, "Cultural Pragmatics."

20 See, for instance, Mark Danner's analysis of the George W. Bush administration's method of defusing the scandal that followed the release of photographs of torture taken at Abu Ghraib prison in Iraq. Danner, "Abu Ghraib."

21 Del Rosso, "The Textual Mediation of Denial"; Del Rosso and Esala, "Constructionism and the Textuality of Sociology Problems"; Del Rosso, "From Claims to Chains."

22 Cohen, *States of Denial*; Goodwin, "Professional Vision."

23 Alexander and Smith, "The Discourse of American Civil Society"; Del Rosso, "The Toxicity of Torture."

24 Colorado Public Radio Staff, "Colorado Civil War Soldier Statue Torn Down at the Capitol"; McKinley, "Sand Creek Massacre Statue."

25 By positing an interplay between forms of denial, I'm invoking the works of James H. Holstein, with Jaber F. Gubrium and Gale Miller, on constructionist analytics and social problems work, respectively. Holstein theorizes that collective meaning structures shape everyday interpretations of social problems; they do so by providing interpretive resources that everyday actors can creatively deploy to recognize and interpret social problems in their lives. In a sense, I'm suggesting, then, that institutional or collective denial provides everyday actors with templates for themselves denying problems in everyday life. See Holstein and Gubrium, "A Constructionist Analytics for Social Problems"; and Holstein and Miller, "Social Constructionism and Social Problems Work."

26 Sutton and Norgaard, "Cultures of Denial."

27 Monahan and Best, "Clocks, Calendars, and Claims."

28 Zerubavel, *The Elephant in the Room*, 14.

29 Cohen, *States of Denial*.

CHAPTER 1. HOW NOT TO NOTICE

1 Rafalovich, "Making Sociology Relevant."

2 Sharp and Kordsmeier, "The 'Shirt-Weenie.'"

3 Villano, "The Scent of a Co-worker"; Echlin, "Is There Something in My Teeth?"; Christensen, "Etiquette"; McKee, "How to Handle the Three Most Common Embarrassing Situations!"

4 Goffman, "On Face-Work"; Goffman, "Embarrassment and Social Organization"; Goffman, *The Presentation of Self in Everyday Life*.

5 This biographical information comes from interviews conducted by Dmitri N. Shalin and generously made available on the Digital Scholarship@UNLV website. See also Shalin, "Interfacing Biography, Theory and History."

6 Irwin, "Goffman Was by Far the Smartest."

7 Irwin, "Goffman Was by Far the Smartest"; Zerubavel, "Dmitri Shalin Interview"; Best, "Goffman Told Me."

8 Irwin, "Goffman Was by Far the Smartest"; Cavan, "Having Been Goffman's Student"; Gamson, "A Stranger Determined to Remain One"; Scheff, *Goffman Unbound!*

9 Best, "Goffman Told Me"; Schelling, "If There Were a Nobel Prize for Sociology."

10 Harold Bershady tells a similar story, though he recounts it as an apocryphal joke about Goffman. Bershady, "Erving Turned to Me and Said . . . ."

11 Goffman himself wrote that "the familiar theme of conspicuous consumption describes how husbands in modern society have the job of acquiring socio-economic status, and wives the jobs of displaying this acquisition." Of course, to describe such a "theme" is not to endorse it. Goffman, *The Presentation of Self in Everyday Life*, 103.

12 J. Lofland, "Erving Goffman's Sociological Legacies," 27–30.

13 Goffman, *Stigma*, 128.

14 Shalin, "Interfacing Biography, Theory and History," 13.

15 Shalin, 14.

16 That Goffman so often undermined his graduate students betrays this commitment, and most of these stories, read today, speak of someone who regularly abused his significant disciplinary and departmental power.

17 Nir, "Frances Bay."

18 Goffman, *The Presentation of Self in Everyday Life*, 72.

19 Goffman, 106–134.

20 Goffman, 24.

21 Goffman actually referred to the front and back regions, but I prefer the more familiar phrases of front and back stages. Goffman, 107.

22 Goffman, 252.

23 Goffman, 216.

24 Goffman, 242.

25 Sharp and Kordsmeier, "The 'Shirt-Weenie'"; Goffman, "Embarrassment and Social Organization," 268.

26 Modigliani, "Embarrassment and Embarrassability," 314.

27 Breaching experiments bear out this rather extreme claim. See, for instance, Sadri and Sadri, "Doppelganger"; and Garfinkel, "Studies of the Routine Grounds of Everyday Activities."

28 Goffman, "On Face-Work," 5; Gardner, "Passing By."

29 Albas and Albas, "Aces and Bombers."

30 Blair and Roese, "Balancing the Basket"; Karp, "Hiding in Pornographic Bookstores."

31 Justin Peters, "The Slate Guide to Crime."

32 Karp, "Hiding in Pornographic Bookstores."

33 King, "Neutralizing Marginally Deviant Behavior," 45.

34 Goffman, *The Presentation of Self in Everyday Life*, 229–233.

35 Turkle, *Alone Together*; Marche, "Is Facebook Making Us Lonely?"

36 J. Lee, "Escaping Embarrassment," 314.

37 Rezvani, "Four Ways to Stop Saying 'Um.'"

38 J. Lee, "Escaping Embarrassment," 316–319.

39 Goffman, "Embarrassment and Social Organization," 266–267.

40 Cavan, "Having Been Goffman's Student."

41 Goffman's term for this is "tactful blindness." I'm employing obliviousness to avoid the ableism in the original concept and to expand our sense of how tactful nonnoticing operates. Noticing is not simply a visual act. Tactful obliviousness can involve strategies to pretend one hasn't heard embarrassing behavior as well.

42 Goffman, "On Face-Work."

43 David Karp, in his 1973 study of men's behaviors at pornographic bookstores in New York City, describes this behavior. Many men who entered adult bookstores leisurely and seemingly aimlessly "window shopped" at the storefront before entering, as if mere curiosity or simple, undirected consumer behavior led them in, rather than a prurient interest. See Karp, "Hiding in Pornographic Bookstores."

44 Goffman poetically referred to this sort of bodily response as "body gloss," by which he means that the actor, upon realizing a mistake, manages the surface of the body so as to signal the (apparent) unseriousness of the act. See Goffman, *Relations in Public Microstudies of the Public Order*, 122–137.

45 I'm grateful to Kayli Short and H. F., two students in my 2019 Sociology of Denial course, for providing these examples.

46 Goffman, *The Presentation of Self in Everyday Life*, 53; A. Thompson, "'Sometimes, I Think I Might Say Too Much.'"

47 Cahill et al., "Meanwhile Backstage," 44.

48 Cahill and Eggleston, "Managing Emotions in Public," 303.

49 Cahill and Eggleston, 303.

50 Goffman, "On Face-Work," 34; Villano, "The Scent of a Co-worker." See also Solnit, "All the Rage."

51 Snow, Robinson, and McCall, "'Cooling Out' Men in Singles Bars and Nightclubs," 435.

52 Here, I'm generalizing Clinton R. Sanders's notion of "demonstrative disciplining," which dog owners use to indicate to audiences that they are working on the bad behavior of their dogs. Sanders, "Excusing Tactics," 86.

53 Cahill et al., "Meanwhile Backstage," 44.

54 Goffman, *Interaction Ritual*, 111.

55 Cahill et al., "Meanwhile Backstage," 44.

56 Cahill, "Children and Civility," 316; Sanders, "Excusing Tactics," 86.

57 Goffman, *Relations in Public Microstudies of the Public Order*, 124–125.

CHAPTER 2. HOW TO BE A BYSTANDER

1 *New York Times*, "Queens Woman Is Stabbed to Death in Front of Home."

2 Cook, *Kitty Genovese*, 75–78.

3 There is an irony in A. M. Rosenthal's account of his indifference toward Genovese's death. The book, *Thirty-Eight Witnesses*, offers a lament on the indifference of New York City residents to the suffering of others. Amid this lament, Rosenthal withholds an apology for neither acting nor caring when he first learned of Genovese's death, failing to note the parallels among his behavior, the *Times*' bland coverage of violent murders, and the apparent behavior of those who directly witnessed the attack. Rosenthal, *Thirty-Eight Witnesses*, 5; Gallo, *No One Helped*, 94–95.

4 Rosenthal, *Thirty-Eight Witnesses*, 6–7.

5 Rosenthal, 13.

6 Rosenthal, 14.

7 There is no explanation of the discrepancy between the "37" in the headline and Murphy's "thirty-eight." The latter number is referenced in the text of the story.

8 *New York Times*, "37 Who Saw Murder Didn't Call the Police."

9 Rosenthal, *Thirty-Eight Witnesses*, 38.

10 Simmel, *The Sociology of Georg Simmel*, 415.

11 Simmel, 415.

12 Between Simmel's and Becker's interventions, Louis Wirth published a foundational analysis in urban sociology; Wirth, too, built on Simmel's analysis of the blasé, reserved attitude of urban dwellers. See Wirth, "Urbanism as a Way of Life."

13 Becker, *Outsiders*, 123.

14 Becker, 124.

15 This position is most associated with the disorganization theory of crime, which held, among other things, that the demographic diversity of cities brought diversity of norms and values that, in turn, undercut dominant norms and social control. See, for instance, Kobrin, "The Conflict of Values in Delinquency Areas"; and Shaw and McKay, *Juvenile Delinquency and Urban Areas*, 319.

16 Becker, *Outsiders*, 122–123.

17 Becker, 124.

18 Goffman, *Behavior in Public Places*, 84.

19 Goffman, 83–84.

20 Lankenau, "Stronger Than Dirt"; Lankenau, "Panhandling Repertoires and Routines."

21 Blumer, "Social Problems as Collective Behavior."

22 Best, *Threatened Children*; J. Johnson, "Horror Stories and the Construction of Child Abuse."

23 Rasenberger, "Kitty, 40 Years Later"; Manning, Levine, and Collins, "The Kitty Genovese Murder"; Cook, *Kitty Genovese*; Roberts, "Sophia Farrar Dies at 92."

24 Manning, Levine, and Collins, "The Kitty Genovese Murder."

25 Zerubavel, *Hidden in Plain Sight*; Milgram, "The Experience of Living in Cities."

26 Latané and Darley, *The Unresponsive Bystander*, 72–73.

27 Latané and Darley, 41.

28 Piliavin et al., *Emergency Intervention*, 59–72; Fischer et al., "The Bystander-Effect"; Fischer et al., "The Unresponsive Bystander"; Harari, Harari, and White, "The Reaction to Rape by American Male Bystanders"; Shotland and Stebbins, "Bystander Response to Rape."

29 Latané and Darley, *The Unresponsive Bystander*, 87–91.

30 Darley and Latané, "Bystander Intervention in Emergencies."

31 Fischer et al., "The Bystander-Effect."

32 Piliavin et al., *Emergency Intervention*; Fischer et al., "The Bystander-Effect."

33 TV Tropes, "Bystander Syndrome."

34 Wikipedia, "Bystander Effect."

35 Manning, Levine, and Collins, "The Kitty Genovese Murder"; Rebecca A. Clay, "Trend Report"; Gurung et al., "Strengthening Introductory Psychology."

36 Beaman et al., "Increasing Helping Rates through Information Dissemination."

37 Cahill and Eggleston, "Managing Emotions in Public," 308–309.

38 Gardner, "Passing By"; L. Lofland, "Self-Management in Public Settings"; G. Smith, "Incivil Attention and Everyday Intolerance"; Stop Street Harassment, "Unsafe and Harassed in Public Spaces."

39 Gardner, "Passing By"; L. Lofland, "Self-Management in Public Settings"; G. Smith, "Incivil Attention and Everyday Intolerance."

40 Finley, "Existing while Black."

41 Oeur, "Recognizing Dignity."

42 Gaertner and Dovidio, "The Subtlety of White Racism"; Gaertner, Dovidio, and Johnson, "Race of Victim."

43 Latané and Nida, "Ten Years of Research on Group Size and Helping," 317.

44 Latané and Darley, *The Unresponsive Bystander*, 12.

45 Zerubavel, *The Elephant in the Room*, 20–25.

46 Latané and Darley, *The Unresponsive Bystander*, 21.

47 Piliavin et al., *Emergency Intervention*, 150–159.

48 Only six of the fifty-three articles included in Fischer et al.'s 2011 meta-analysis reported on experiments involving a perpetrator of antagonistic or criminal behavior. Fischer et al., "The Bystander-Effect."

49 My colleague Casey Stockstill alerted me to a 2010 episode of ABC's show *What Would You Do?*, which staged bike thefts with one white "thief" and one Black "thief." In the aired episode, the white "thief" is occasionally aided by (mostly white) passersby when he explains his use of a saw on a bike lock by saying that he's lost his key to the lock. Meanwhile, the Black "thief," who offers the same explanation, is aggressively questioned and photographed by (again, mostly white) passersby; several clearly make their intention of alerting the police known. All deny that the race of the apparent thief mattered to them. Burton, "Double Standard."

50 B. Payne, "Prejudice and Perception"; Eberhardt et al., "Seeing Black"; Duncan, "Differential Social Perception"; Correll et al., "The Police Officer's Dilemma."

51 Hart and Rennison, "Reporting Crime to the Police, 1992–2000."

52 Bass, "Policing Space, Policing Race."

53 Sanger, "Callers Support Subway Gunman"; Fein, "Angry Citizens in Many Cities Supporting Goetz"; *New York Times*, "Why Surrender on the Subway?"; Purnick, "Ward Declares Goetz Didn't Shoot in Self-Defense."

54 Rosenthal, *Thirty-Eight Witnesses*, 34.

CHAPTER 3. HOW TO AVOID BLAME

1 Scott and Lyman, "Accounts."

2 Caron, Whitbourne, and Halgin, "Fraudulent Excuse Making"; Roig and Caso, "Lying and Cheating."

3 Goffman, *Relations in Public Microstudies of the Public Order*, 112.

4 Hewitt and Stokes, "Disclaimers."

5 Pollner, *Mundane Reason*.

6 Galloway, "Guillermo del Toro on Seeing a UFO."

7 Hewitt and Stokes, "Disclaimers," 5.

8 Paugh, "Making Sense of 'Conflicting Observations,'" 25.

9 Hewitt and Stokes, "Disclaimers," 6.

10 Whitesides and Sullivan, "Biden Comes Out Swinging at Debate."

11 Here, I'm paraphrasing sports journalist and radio host Dan Le Batard, who observed that you cannot start a sentence with "no offense" and then say "that's stupid." Le Batard made these remarks to Jay Bilas, an ESPN commentator on NCAA basketball, after Bilas, claiming to intend "no offense," called Le Batard's questions about race and NCAA basketball players "stupid." Powell, "Radio Fight!"

12 Appelo, "Ditch the Praise Sandwich."

13 This strategy is so overused as to be both transparent and annoying to some students. See Del Rosso and Nordstrom-Wehner, "Team Grade Anarchy."

14 Hewitt and Stokes, "Disclaimers," 4.

15 Hewitt and Stokes, 4.

16 Greg Cote offered his initial criticisms of Smokey Robinson in his March 13, 2017, entry to his *Random Evidence* blog for the *Miami Herald*. He defended his criticisms on ESPN's *Dan Le Batard Show with Stugotz*; however, the archive of the show is no longer available online. Presumably, Cote offered his defense, which I quote here, on March 14, as he normally appears on the *Le Batard Show* on Tuesdays. See Cote, "Latest Hot Button Top 10."

17 Pérez, "Learning to Make Racism Funny."

18 Caron, Whitbourne, and Halgin, "Fraudulent Excuse Making"; Roig and Caso, "Lying and Cheating."

19 Kalab, "Student Vocabularies of Motive."

20 Or do they? One reviewer of this book helpfully pointed me to the work of Joseph Gusfield, whose research on car "accidents" shows that even the events that we call accidents are socially constructed as such. While accidents seem like random events caused by chance, it's often because our understanding of them is socially organized so that they seem like random events caused by chance. Often, this results from data-collection practices and collective claims-making practices that *individualize* the events; causes are identified only in the most local of factors or human error, while systemic patterns remain unstudied and, so, invisible. See chapter 2 in Gusfield, *The Culture of Public Problems*.

21 Scott and Lyman, "Accounts," 47–48.

22 Goffman, *Relations in Public Microstudies of the Public Order*, 111.

23 Hegedus, "Man Could Get Life for Hoax."

24 Kilgannon, "Anthrax Joke 'Not Funny.'"

25 Lerer, "Joe Biden Jokes about Hugging in a Speech."

26 *New York Times*, "Louis C.K. Responds to Accusations."

27 Scott and Lyman, "Accounts."

28 Both car and computer troubles can also include claims about accidents. If we claim that we dropped and broke our laptop, spilled liquid on it, or accidentally deleted a file, we're claiming that an accident accounts for our failures.

29 Caron, Whitbourne, and Halgin, "Fraudulent Excuse Making"; Roig and Caso, "Lying and Cheating."

30 McCaghy, "Drinking and Deviance Disavowal"; Scully and Marolla, "Convicted Rapists' Vocabulary of Motive."

31 Goffman, *Interaction Ritual*, 17.

32 Sykes and Matza, "Techniques of Neutralization," 668.

33 Esala, "Communities of Denial," 104–105.

34 See, for instance, Temkin, Gray, and Barrett, "Different Functions of Rape Myth Use"; Zaveri, "Judge Who Asked Woman in Sexual Assault Case If She Closed Her Legs Faces Suspension."

35 C. Lee, "Race and Self-Defense."

36 C. Lee.

37 K. Johnson, "Goetz Is Cleared in Subway Attack."

38 Campo-Flores and Waddell, "Jury Acquits Zimmerman of All Charges"; Jonsson, "Zimmerman Jury of Peers."

39 Sykes and Matza, "Techniques of Neutralization," 667.

40 Cromwell and Thurman, "The Devil Made Me Do It."

41 Indeed, the word "bully" has a long and mostly endearing entomology. See "Bully, n.1."

42 Esala, "Communities of Denial."

43 Cavanagh et al., "'Remedial Work,'" 705–706.

44 Del Rosso, "'Its Own Kind of Torture.'"

45 Saletan, "Death Is Good"; Mague, "College Coaching Scandals Raid Nation"; Connolly, "There's Only One Way to Respond."

46 Heinonen, "Neutralizing Disciplinary Violence," 284–285.

CHAPTER 4. HOW TO CONCEAL MISCONDUCT

1 Asch, "Studies of Independence and Conformity," 3.

2 Asch; Friend, Rafferty, and Bramel, "A Puzzling Misinterpretation."

3 Gourevitch and Morris, *The Ballad of Abu Ghraib*, 87–88.

4 Gourevitch and Morris, "Exposure."

5 Gourevitch and Morris, *The Ballad of Abu Ghraib*, 101–104.

6 Gourevitch and Morris, 104.

7 Gibson and Haritos-Fatouros, "The Education of a Torturer"; Huggins, Haritos-Fatouros, and Zimbardo, *Violence Workers*.

8 Stoddard, "Informal Code of Police Deviancy."

9 Skolnick, "Corruption and the Blue Code of Silence."

10 Ashforth and Anand, "The Normalization of Corruption in Organizations," 13–14; Ashforth and Kreiner, "Normalizing Emotion in Organizations."

11 Vaughan, *The Challenger Launch Decision*, 65.

12 Stoddard, "Informal Code of Police Deviancy," 209.

13 Whearley, "Exposé of Police Burglaries"; *New York Times*, "Denver Police Scandal Widens."

14 Stoddard, "Informal Code of Police Deviancy."

15 Stern, "What Makes a Policeman Go Wrong?"; Stoddard, "Informal Code of Police Deviancy."

16 Stern, "What Makes a Policeman Go Wrong?," 99.

17 Stern, 101.

18 Whearley, "Exposé of Police Burglaries."

19 Simpson, "Denver Cop and Robber Reconciles His Troubled Past."

20 Eligon and Levin, "In Minneapolis, Looking for Police Recruits"; R. Johnson, "Whistleblowing and the Police," 76; Mastrofski, "Controlling Street-Level Police Discretion."

21 Eligon and Levin, "In Minneapolis, Looking for Police Recruits."

22 Chanen, "Fear-Based Training for Police Officers"; Schatz, "'Are You Prepared to Kill Somebody?'"; Reaves, "State and Local Law Enforcement Training Academies, 2013."

23 Skolnick, "Corruption and the Blue Code of Silence."

24 Skolnick, 10.

25 Orwell, "Politics and the English Language."

26 Bandura, "Moral Disengagement in the Perpetration of Inhumanities."

27 Like the word "bully," "mooching" also has its own, mostly endearing etymology. See "Mooch, v."

28 Stoddard, "Informal Code of Police Deviancy," 205.

29 Cressey, "The Criminal Violation of Financial Trust."

30 Skolnick, "Corruption and the Blue Code of Silence," 11.

31 Skolnick, 17.

32 Skolnick, 17.

33 Rejali, *Torture and Democracy*, 55–60.

34 Cohen, *States of Denial*, 83.

35 Chandler, *Voices from S-21*, 88, 129; Hinton, *Man or Monster*.

36 Panh, *S21*.

37 Rejali, *Torture and Democracy*, 58.

38 Bear, "American Indian Boarding Schools Haunt Many."

39 Bear, "American Indian Boarding Schools Haunt Many."

40 Taguba, "AR 15-6 Investigation of the 800th Military Police Brigade."

41 Taguba, 8, emphasis added.

42 Del Rosso, *Talking about Torture*, 80.

43 Jones and Fay, "Fay Report," 75.

44 Bauman, *Modernity and the Holocaust*, 163.

45 Luban, "Liberalism, Torture, and the Ticking Bomb Essay."

46 Vaughan, "Regulating Risk."

47 Heffernan, *Willful Blindness*.

48 McLean, "How Wells Fargo's Cutthroat Corporate Culture Allegedly Drove Bankers to Fraud."

49 McLean.

50 Cowley and Goldstein, "Accusations of Fraud"; Morgenson, "Wells Fargo Forced Unwanted Auto Insurance on Borrowers."

51 Flitter, "The Price of Wells Fargo's Fake Account Scandal Grows by $3 Billion."

52 On strain and innovation, see Merton, "Social Structure and Anomie"; and Vaughan, *Controlling Unlawful Organizational Behavior*, 55–62.

53 Levin, "6 Ways Wells Fargo Made Its Employees' Lives a Living Hell."

54 Egan, "Workers Tell Wells Fargo Horror Stories."

55 Levin, "6 Ways Wells Fargo Made Its Employees' Lives a Living Hell."

56 Here, I'm borrowing Alberto Mora's use of the phrase "wink and a nod." Mora, a former Navy lawyer, described a note that former secretary of defense Donald Rumsfeld made on a memorandum authorizing abusive interrogation practices at Guantánamo as offering a "wink and a nod" to go beyond the memo. The note asked why detainees were limited to two to four hours of continuous force-standing when Rumsfeld (working at a standing desk) stood six to eight hours a day. Mora suggested that military interrogators would likely interpret that note as "a wink and a nod . . . to the interrogator that, never mind what might be the words of limitation or the constraints of this memorandum. What you were truly signaling to the interrogators was, 'Do what it takes to get the information, we don't care how.'" Task Force on Detainee Treatment, "Transcript of Interview with Alberto Mora."

57   Heffernan, *Willful Blindness*; McGoey, "The Logic of Strategic Ignorance."

58   Katz, "Concerted Ignorance," 298.

59   Flitter, "The Price of Wells Fargo's Fake Account Scandal Grows by $3 Billion."

60   Zerubavel, *The Elephant in the Room*, 34–35.

61   Vaughan, *The Challenger Launch Decision*, 250.

62   Forsyth, "Status of the Independent Special Counsel's Investigation."

63   Vaughan, *Controlling Unlawful Organizational Behavior*.

64   Taguba, "Taguba Report"; Jones and Fay, "Fay Report."

65   Rejali, *Torture and Democracy*; Huggins et al., *Violence Workers*.

66   I'm grateful to Jennifer J. Esala for bringing this overlooked passage to my attention. Goffman, *The Presentation of Self in Everyday Life*, 45.

67   Rabin, "New York Sues Sackler Family Members and Drug Distributors."

68   Rabin.

69   Hilts, "Scientists Say Cigarette Company Suppressed Findings on Nicotine."

70   Franta, "Shell and Exxon's Secret 1980s Climate Change Warnings"; Hiltzik, "A New Study Shows How Exxon Mobil Downplayed Climate Change"; Schwartz, "New York Sues Exxon Mobil"; Schwartz, "Exxon Misled the Public on Climate Change."

71   Hilts, "Scientists Say Cigarette Company Suppressed Findings on Nicotine."

72   Twohey et al., "Weinstein's Complicity Machine."

73   Prasad, "If Anyone Is Listening, #MeToo"; Steel, "Employers Who Talk Up Gender Equity"; Rutenberg, "A Long-Delayed

Reckoning"; Dean, "Contracts of Silence"; Zerubavel, *The El-ephant in the Room*, 42.

74 CIA Inspector General, "Counterterrorism Detention and Inter-rogation Activities," 45.

75 CIA Inspector General, 85.

76 Associated Press, "Ex-Spy."

77 Del Rosso, "The Toxicity of Torture."

78 Lerer and Ember, "Democratic Frustration Mounts."

79 Twohey et al., "Weinstein's Complicity Machine"; Palazzolo, Rothfield, and Alpert, "*National Enquirer* Shielded Donald Trump."

80 Cohen, *States of Denial*, 224.

81 Cohen, 225.

CHAPTER 5. HOW TO AVOID SCANDAL

1 J. Thompson, "Scandal and Social Theory."

2 J. Thompson, 57.

3 In fact, the photographer was likely Sabrina Harman, a guard at Abu Ghraib. The detainee, Manadel al-Jamadi, was killed while in CIA custody at Abu Ghraib. A CIA interrogator and Arabic-speaking contractor hanged al-Jamadi by his wrists to a prison window. This is an extremely painful and stressful form of tor-ture, causing excruciating pain to the shoulders, back, and arm; it also makes it difficult for the victim of torture to breathe. This position, combined with earlier beatings and episodes of torture, likely committed by Navy SEALs and another CIA interrogator, contributed to al-Jamadi's death. See Mayer, "A Deadly Interroga-tion"; and Gourevitch and Morris, *The Ballad of Abu Ghraib*.

4 Rumsfeld, "Allegations of Mistreatment of Iraqi Prisoners," 5.

5 Sontag, "Regarding the Torture of Others."

6 Farrow, "How an Élite University Research Center Concealed Its Relationship with Jeffrey Epstein"; Farrow, "From Aggressive Overtures to Sexual Assault."

7 J. B. Thompson, *Political Scandal*, 16–17.

8 Markovitz and Silverstein, "Introduction," 6; Alexander and Smith, "The Discourse of American Civil Society."

9 Mitchell, "Clinton Impeached."

10 Bennet, "Clinton Emphatically Denies an Affair"; Kramer and Olson, "The Strategic Potential of Sequencing Apologia Stases"; Clinton, "Transcript"; Stewart, "Consider the Sources."

11 *New York Times*, "Brett Kavanaugh's Opening Statement"; Stolberg and Fandos, "Brett Kavanaugh and Christine Blasey Ford Duel with Tears and Fury."

12 Kavanaugh also benefited from the privilege of white masculinity, which authorizes white men's displays of anger, even violence, while denying white women and people of color the same right. See Solnit, *Whose Story Is This?*

13 J. B. Thompson, *Political Scandal*, 67–71; Del Rosso, "Textuality and the Social Organization of Denial"; Del Rosso, "The Textual Mediation of Denial"; Del Rosso, "From Claims to Chains"; D. Smith, *Texts, Facts and Femininity*; D. Smith, "Texts and the Ontology of Organizations and Institutions"; Del Rosso and Esala, "Constructionism and the Textuality of Sociology Problems."

14 As quoted in Del Rosso, "The Textual Mediation of Denial," 174.

15 Rove denies that he ever invoked the "reality-based community"; the anonymous quote, however, remains a peculiar cultural artifact of the George W. Bush administration. See Schonfeld, "The Curious Case."

16 D. Smith, *Texts, Facts and Femininity*, 175.

17 Blinder, "Michael Slager."

18 Romo, "NYPD Judge Recommends."

19 Barthes, *Camera Lucida*, 76.

20 J. B. Thompson, *Political Scandal*, 69.

21 CNN, "Read and Search."

22 Rejali, *Torture and Democracy*.

23 Cohen, "Government Responses to Human Rights Reports," 524.

24 L. Payne, *Unsettling Accounts*.

25 Del Rosso, "Textuality and the Social Organization of Denial"; Del Rosso, *Talking about Torture*.

26 Quoted in Goldenberg, "Memos Show FBI Agents Complained about Abuses at Guantánamo Bay."

27 Federal Bureau of Investigation, "Emails between Valerie Caproni and Others."

28 Zagorin and Duffy, "Inside the Interrogation of Detainee 063."

29 Loseke, *Thinking about Social Problems*; Best, "Rhetoric in Claims-Making"; Best, "Constructionist Social Problems Theory."

30 Cohen, *States of Denial*; Seu, "'Doing Denial.'"

31 Tracy, "Joe Paterno Knew of Sandusky Abuse in 1976"; Twohey et al., "Weinstein's Complicity Machine."

32 Eliasoph, *Avoiding Politics*; Norgaard, *Living in Denial*.

33 *New York Times*, "Transcript."

34 Cohen, *States of Denial*, 105.

35 Disis, "Donald Trump Won't Say Vulgar Remarks Reference 'Sexual Assault.'"

36 Bennett, Lawrence, and Livingston, "None Dare Call It Torture."

37 Leung, "Abuse at Abu Ghraib."

38 Department of Defense, "Transcript."

39 Del Rosso, "The Toxicity of Torture"; Del Rosso, *Talking about Torture*.

40 Cohen, *States of Denial*, 109.

41 Jackson, "Language, Policy and the Construction of a Torture Culture"; Jackson, "Constructing Enemies."

42 Del Rosso, "The Toxicity of Torture."

43 Obama, "Remarks by the President at the National Defense University."

44 Shane, "Drone Strikes Reveal Uncomfortable Truth."

45 Moqbel, "Hunger Striking at Guantánamo Bay."

46 Feinstein, "Letter to Secretary of Defense Chuck Hegel."

47 Del Rosso, "'Its Own Kind of Torture.'"

48 More recently, Trump used an especially callous variant of the discourse of "care" to justify his withdrawal of US support of Kurdish fighters in northern Syria. Following the withdrawal, the Turkish military attacked Kurdish forces in Syria. In response, Trump took credit, likening the withdrawal to "tough love": "Like two kids in a lot, you've got to let them fight and then you pull them apart." See Rucker and Johnson, "Trump on Turks and Kurds."

49 Savage, "Amid Hunger Strike, Obama Renews Push to Close Cuba Prison."

50 Morris, *The Fog of War*.

51 Spiegel, "How Politicians Get Away with Dodging the Question."

52 Bennet, "The President under Fire."

53 Zerubavel, *The Elephant in the Room*, 71.

54 Clinton made this argument in later speeches, too, as impeachment bore down on him. Clinton, "Transcript"; Kramer and Olson, "The Strategic Potential of Sequencing Apologia Stases," 362–364.

55 Craggs, "Trump: 'I Said It, I Was Wrong, and I Apologize.'"

56 Craggs.

57 Jeremy W. Peters, "Trump Campaign Tried to Seat Bill Clinton's Accusers in V.I.P. Box."

58 White, Bandura, and Bero, "Moral Disengagement in the Corporate World," 51.

59 Cohen, *States of Denial*, 111.

60 The 2004 statement contrasts sharply with Bush's 2003 statement. The 2004 statement is restrained; it also invokes the threat of terror in its conclusion and the need to "question terrorists." The 2003 statement, meanwhile, is clear-throated and evocative. It conjures the terror of torture: "No people, no matter where they reside, should have to live in fear of their own government. Nowhere should the midnight knock foreshadow a nightmare of state-commissioned crime." See Bush, "President's Statement on the U.N. International Day" (2003).

61 Bush, "President's Statement on the U.N. International Day" (2004).

62 Bush; Bush, "President's Statement on the U.N. International Day" (2003).

63 *New York Times*, "Tortures and Tortures."

64 *New York Times*.

65 Tavuchis, *Mea Culpa*.

66 Pierre, "'I'm Sorry If I Caused Offense.'"

67 Weinstein, "Statement from Harvey Weinstein."

68 Weinstein.

69 *BBC News*, "Harvey Weinstein Appeals against Conviction for Sex Crimes."

70 Snook, "Facing the Consequences."

71 *Washington Post*, "Transcript of Mark Zuckerberg's Senate Hearing."

72 Mak, "Facebook's New TV Ad."

73 Mak.

74 Frenkel et al., "Delay, Deny and Deflect."

75 Patel and Reinsch, "Companies Can Apologize."

76 NBC Sports Boston, "Kraft Apologizes for Allegations in Statement."

77 Winter, "Robert Kraft Prostitution Charges."

78 Danner, "Frozen Scandal."

79 Landay, Holland, and Landay, "Trump Summoned Supporters."

80 Abutaleb, Parker, Dawsey, and Rucker, "The Inside Story"; Costa and Rucker, "Woodward Book."

81 Goodman, McKinley, and Hakim, "Cuomo Aides Spent Months Hiding Nursing Home Death Toll"; McKinley, Hakim, and Alter, "As Cuomo Sought $4 Million Book Deal."

CHAPTER 6. HOW TO HIDE IN PLAIN SIGHT

1 Feagin and Barnett, "Success and Failure," 1103.

2 I've decided against using direct quotes, with references, from local media coverage of this school district, as it's not clear to me that those involved in these discussions were aware that their written comments would be published.

3 Kendi, "The Heartbeat of Racism Is Denial."

4 Margolis and Romero, "'The Department Is Very Male . . . ,'" 3–4.

5 Rumsfeld, as cited in Graham, "Rumsfeld's Knowns and Unknowns."

6 Loewen, *Lies My Teacher Told Me*, 56.

7 Bickford, "Examining Historical (Mis) Representations of Christopher Columbus."

8 Loewen, *Lies My Teacher Told Me*, 18.

9 Loewen, 20.

10 Franklin, "'Birth of a Nation.'"

11 Loewen, *Lies My Teacher Told Me*, 21.

12 Ghoshal, "Transforming Collective Memory."

13 Hoffmann and Strom, "A Perfect Storm."

14 Loewen, *Lies My Teacher Told Me*, 21.

15 Goldstein, "Two States. Eight Textbooks. Two American Stories."

16 Goldstein.

17 Fitzgerald, "A Sociology of Race/Ethnicity Textbooks," 351.

18 Turner, Giacopassi, and Vandiver, "Ignoring the Past."

19 Brown and Brown, "Silenced Memories," 144.

20 Brown and Brown, 147.

21 Brown and Brown, 150.

22 Conley, *You May Ask Yourself*, 360.

23 More generally, though, the book notes that "African Americans found . . . exploitation by factory owners looking for cheap black labor [and] increasing hostility from white workers" as they moved northward in the first two decades of the twentieth century.

24 Bachelier, "Hidden History," 18; Barnes, *Never Been a Time*.

25 Barnes, *Never Been a Time*, 120–122.

26 Barnes.

27 W. E. B. Du Bois documented this violence in an early investigation of the East St. Louis Massacre, conducted with the National Association of Colored People. It's of note that this investigation isn't mentioned in the textbook, despite Du Bois's foundational work in sociology at the turn of the twentieth century. This oversight has two effects. It prevents the introductory sociology student from learning of Du Bois's full influence on US sociology and politics; it also effaces the legacies of public sociology in the United States. National Association for the Advancement of Colored People, "The Massacre of East St. Louis."

28 Cecelski and Tyson, *Democracy Betrayed*.

29 Prather and Davis, *We Have Taken a City*.

30 Hurd, "'Post-Dispatch Man.'"

31 Cohen, *States of Denial*, 114.

32 Forman and Lewis, "Racial Apathy and Hurricane Katrina."

33 Barrett, "Mitch McConnell Says He Opposes Paying Reparations for Slavery."

34 Paschal and Carlisle, "Read Ta-Nehisi Coates's Testimony on Reparations."

35 Forman and Lewis, "Racial Apathy and Hurricane Katrina," 193.

36 Loewen, *Lies My Teacher Told Me*, 28.

37 Sue et al., "How White Faculty Perceive and React to Difficult Dialogues on Race."

38 Charles Mills, "White Ignorance," 31.

39 Bonilla-Silva, "The Linguistics of Color Blind Racism"; Bonilla-Silva, Lewis, and Embrick, "'I Did Not Get That Job Because of a Black Man . . .'"; Bonilla-Silva and Dietrich, "The Sweet Enchantment of Color-Blind Racism in Obamerica."

40 Forman and Lewis, "Racial Apathy and Hurricane Katrina," 176–177.

41 Leonardo and Porter, "Pedagogy of Fear," 150.
42 DiAngelo, *White Fragility*, 152.
43 Picca and Feagin, *Two-Faced Racism*, 115–116.
44 Eliasoph, *Avoiding Politics*, 102; Picca and Feagin, *Two-Faced Racism*, 69.
45 Picca and Feagin, *Two-Faced Racism*, 79.
46 Case and Hemmings, "Distancing Strategies," 610–613.
47 DiAngelo, *White Fragility*, 111.
48 DiAngelo, 111.
49 Wingfield, "The Modern Mammy and the Angry Black Man"; Wingfield, "Are Some Emotions Marked 'Whites Only'?"; Lorde, "The Uses of Anger"; Solnit, "All the Rage."
50 DiAngelo and Sensoy, "Getting Slammed."
51 Leonardo and Porter, "Pedagogy of Fear," 147.
52 Forman and Lewis, "Racial Apathy and Hurricane Katrina," 187.
53 Mueller, "Producing Colorblindness," 223.
54 Mueller, 223.
55 Sue et al., "How White Faculty Perceive and React to Difficult Dialogues on Race," 1100.
56 DiAngelo, "Nothing to Add," 6.
57 DiAngelo, 10.
58 DiAngelo, 9.
59 Spanierman and Cabrera, "The Emotions of White Racism and Antiracism," 11.
60 Bonilla-Silva, "The Linguistics of Color Blind Racism," 49.
61 Forman, "Color-Blind Racism and Racial Indifference," 55.
62 Bonilla-Silva, "The Linguistics of Color Blind Racism," 49.
63 Rupert, "I'm Done Debating Racism with the Devil."
64 Hewitt and Stokes, "Disclaimers," 3.
65 Shear, "'I'm Not a Racist.'"
66 Yahoo! News, "Trump: 'I've Done More for the Black Community Than Any Other President.'"
67 Krieg, "12 Times Donald Trump Declared His 'Respect' for Women."
68 Cauley, "Mark Meadows and the Victim Card."
69 Cauley.
70 *Washington Post*, "Tlaib Calls Meadows Use of HUD Official 'Racist Act.'"

71 Cummings, "After Denying Racism."

72 Bonilla-Silva, "The Linguistics of Color Blind Racism," 52–54; Mueller, "Producing Colorblindness."

73 Bonilla-Silva, "The Linguistics of Color Blind Racism," 53.

74 López, *Dog Whistle Politics*, 5, emphasis in the original.

75 López, 3–5.

76 Gallagher, "Playing the White Ethnic Card," 149, emphasis in the original.

77 Bonilla-Silva, Lewis, and Embrick, "'I Did Not Get That Job Because of a Black Man . . . ,'" 566.

78 For instance, a study conducted by Brandeis University's Institute on Assets and Social Policy found that the number of years of homeownership accounts for 27 percent of the approximately $152,000 increase in the wealth gap between white and Black Americans over the past three decades. Homeownership and home values, however, are both a product of racism—formal and de facto practices of segregation and discrimination that allowed white Americans, including Irish and Italian Americans like those in Tom's (and the author's) families, to gain access to lines of credit, mortgages, and communities that Black Americans could not access. See Shapiro, Meschede, and Osoro, "The Roots of the Widening Racial Wealth Gap"; Coates, "The Case for Reparations"; and Mueller, "Producing Colorblindness."

79 Spelman, "Managing Ignorance," 120.

CONCLUSION

1 Sontag, *Regarding the Pain of Others*; Hyde, *A Primer for Forgetting*.

2 Farrow, "Harvey Weinstein's Army of Spies."

3 McLean, "How Wells Fargo's Cutthroat Corporate Culture Allegedly Drove Bankers to Fraud."

4 Hylton, "Prisoner of Conscience."

5 Cloud, "General Says Prison Inquiry Led to His Forced Retirement."

6 Hylton, "Prisoner of Conscience"; Stanger, *Whistleblowers*.

7 Stanley Cohen's writing on acknowledgment, crossed with work on hope, underlies my claims here. Cohen, *States of Denial*;

Solnit, *Hope in the Dark*; Standish, "Learning How to Hope"; Wright, "Real Utopias."

8   The sociologist Jeffrey C. Alexander offers the concept of "defusion" to describe states in which critics reveal another's performance and message to be contrived and artificial. It's this sense that I refer to when I write of "jamming" a message. Alexander, "Cultural Pragmatics."

9   Best, "Rhetoric in Claims-Making."

10 Hafner-Burton, "Sticks and Stones"; Kumar, "Confronting the Shameless."

11 Bonilla-Silva, "The Invisible Weight of Whiteness."

12 Cohen, *States of Denial*, 256.

13 Ellison, "'Woe Is You,' White People Say."

14 Dwyer, "When Fists and Kicks Fly on the Subway."

15 Winerip, "Stepping Up to Stop Sexual Assault."

16 Carey and Hoffman, "Lessons in the Delicate Art of Confronting Offensive Speech."

17 Casey and Ohler, "Being a Positive Bystander," 70.

18 Picca and Feagin, *Two-Faced Racism*, 120–121.

19 Morrison and Milliken, "Speaking Up, Remaining Silent," 1353.

20 Morrison and Milliken, "Organizational Silence," 722.

21 Milliken, Morrison, and Hewlin, "An Exploratory Study of Employee Silence," 1455.

22 McLean, "How Wells Fargo's Cutthroat Corporate Culture Allegedly Drove Bankers to Fraud."

23 Dworkin and Baucus, "Internal vs. External Whistleblowers."

24 Sontag, *Regarding the Pain of Others*.

25 Baquet's explanation of the *New York Times*' coverage appears in B. Smith, "The *Times* Took 19 Days."

26 Sontag, *Regarding the Pain of Others*, 17.

APPENDIX

1   Spector and Kitsuse, *Constructing Social Problems*; Best, *Social Problems*.

2   Goffman, "Embarrassment and Social Organization"; Goffman, *The Presentation of Self in Everyday Life*; Sykes and Matza, "Techniques of Neutralization"; Scott and Lyman, "Accounts."

3 Moore and Tumin, "Some Social Functions of Ignorance"; see also McGoey, "The Logic of Strategic Ignorance."

4 Du Bois, *Black Reconstruction in America, 1860–1880*.

5 Del Rosso, *Talking about Torture*; Del Rosso, "'Its Own Kind of Torture'"; Sutton and Norgaard, "Cultures of Denial."

6 Norgaard, *Living in Denial*.

7 Norgaard, 9.

8 C. Wright Mills, "Situated Actions and Vocabularies of Motive"; Scott and Lyman, "Accounts"; Orbuch, "People's Accounts Count."

9 Becker, *Outsiders*; Latané and Darley, *The Unresponsive Bystander*.

10 Swidler, "Culture in Action," 273.

11 Benoit, *Accounts, Excuses, and Apologies*, 51–61.

12 Olick and Robbins, "Social Memory Studies."

13 See Del Rosso, "The Textual Mediation of Denial"; Del Rosso and Esala, "Constructionism and the Textuality of Sociology Problems"; and Del Rosso, "From Claims to Chains."

14 See "Denial, n."

15 Del Rosso, *Talking about Torture*.

16 Del Rosso, "Textuality and the Social Organization of Denial."

17 Gourevitch and Morris, *The Ballad of Abu Ghraib*; Del Rosso, *Talking about Torture*.

18 Best, *Social Problems*; Loseke, *Thinking about Social Problems*; Spector and Kitsuse, *Constructing Social Problems*.

19 Woolgar and Pawluch, "Ontological Gerrymandering"; Best, "But Seriously Folks"; Ibarra and Kitsuse, "Vernacular Constituents of Moral Discourse."

20 Goode and Ben-Yehuda, "Moral Panics."

21 Best, "But Seriously Folks."

22 Goode and Ben-Yehuda, "Moral Panics."

23 Best, "Rhetoric in Claims-Making."

24 Romero, "Sociology Engaged in Social Justice."

25 Margolis and Romero, "'The Department Is Very Male . . . .'"

26 Garfinkel, "Conditions of Successful Degradation Ceremonies."

27 Maruna and Copes, "What Have We Learned from Five Decades of Neutralization Research?," 272.

28 C. Wright Mills, *The Sociological Imagination*.

29 Gusfield, *The Culture of Public Problems*.

REFERENCES

Abutaleb, Yasmeen, Ashley Parker, Josh Dawsey, and Philip Rucker.
"The Inside Story of How Trump's Denial, Mismanagement and
Magical Thinking Led to the Pandemic's Dark Winter." *Washington
Post*, December 19, 2020. www.washingtonpost.com.

Albas, Daniel, and Cheryl Albas. "Aces and Bombers: The Post-Exam
Impression Management Strategies of Students." *Symbolic Interaction*
11, no. 2 (1988): 289–302. https://doi.org/10.1525/si.1988.11.2.289.

Alexander, Jeffrey C. "Cultural Pragmatics: Social Performance between
Ritual and Strategy." *Sociological Theory* 22, no. 4 (2004): 527–573.
https://doi.org/10.1111/j.0735-2751.2004.00233.x.

Alexander, Jeffrey C., and Philip Smith. "The Discourse of American
Civil Society: A New Proposal for Cultural Studies." *Theory and
Society* 22, no. 2 (1993): 151–207. https://doi.org/10.1007/BF00993497.

Appelo, Jurgen. "Ditch the Praise Sandwich, Make Feedback Wraps."
Forbes, August 17, 2015. www.forbes.com.

Asch, Solomon E. "Studies of Independence and Conformity: I. A
Minority of One against a Unanimous Majority." *Psychological
Monographs: General and Applied* 70, no. 9 (1956): 1–70. https://doi.
org/10.1037/h0093718.

Ashforth, Blake E., and Vikas Anand. "The Normalization of Corruption
in Organizations." *Research in Organizational Behavior* 25 (2003): 1–
52. https://doi.org/10.1016/S0191-3085(03)25001-2.

Ashforth, Blake E., and Glen E. Kreiner. "Normalizing Emotion in
Organizations: Making the Extraordinary Seem Ordinary." *Human
Resource Management Review* 12, no. 2 (June 1, 2002): 215–235. https://
doi.org/10.1016/S1053-4822(02)00047-5.

Associated Press. "Ex-Spy: Destroying CIA Tapes Purged 'Ugly
Visuals.'" *Fox News*, March 25, 2015. www.foxnews.com.

———. "KKK Unit Head Won't Resign from Pine Bush School Board." *Press and Sun-Bulletin* (Binghamton, NY), January 21, 1975.

Bachelier, Samanthé. "Hidden History: The Whitewashing of the 1917 East St. Louis Riot." *Confluence*, Fall 2017 / Winter 2018. www.lindenwood.edu/academics/beyond-the-classroom/publications/the-confluence/all-issues/fall-winter-2017-2018/hidden-history-the-whitewashing-of-the-1917-east-st-louis-riot/.

Ballhaus, Rebecca. "Trump Declines to Condemn White Supremacist." *Wall Street Journal*, September 29, 2020. www.wsj.com.

Bandura, Albert. "Moral Disengagement in the Perpetration of Inhumanities." *Personality and Social Psychology Review* 3, no. 3 (August 1, 1999): 193–209. https://doi.org/10.1207/s15327957pspr0303_3.

Barnes, Harper. *Never Been a Time: The 1917 Race Riot That Sparked the Civil Rights Movement*. New York: Walker Books, 2008.

Barrett, Ted. "Mitch McConnell Says He Opposes Paying Reparations for Slavery." CNN, June 19, 2019. www.cnn.com.

Barthes, Roland. *Camera Lucida: Reflections on Photography*. New York: Hill and Wang, 1981.

Bass, Sandra. "Policing Space, Policing Race: Social Control Imperatives and Police Discretionary Decisions." *Social Justice* 28, no. 1 (83) (2001): 156–176.

Bauman, Zygmunt. *Modernity and the Holocaust*. Ithaca, NY: Cornell University Press, 2000.

Baumeister, Roy F., Karen Dale, and Kristin L. Sommer. "Freudian Defense Mechanisms and Empirical Findings in Modern Social Psychology: Reaction Formation, Projection, Displacement, Undoing, Isolation, Sublimation, and Denial." *Journal of Personality* 66, no. 6 (1998): 1081–1124. https://doi.org/10.1111/1467-6494.00043.

BBC News. "Harvey Weinstein Appeals against Conviction for Sex Crimes." April 5, 2021, sec. US & Canada. www.bbc.com.

Beaman, Arthur L., P. Jo Barnes, Bonnel Klentz, and Betty McQuirk. "Increasing Helping Rates through Information Dissemination: Teaching Pays." *Personality and Social Psychology Bulletin* 4, no. 3 (July 1, 1978): 406–411. https://doi.org/10.1177/014616727800400309.

Bear, Charla. "American Indian Boarding Schools Haunt Many." NPR.org, May 12, 2008. www.npr.org.

Becker, Howard S. *Outsiders*. New York: Free Press, 1963.

Bennet, James. "Clinton Emphatically Denies an Affair with Ex-Intern: Lawyers Say He Is Distracted by Events." *New York Times*, January 27, 1998, sec. US. www.nytimes.com.

Bennett, W. Lance, Regina G. Lawrence, and Steven Livingston. "None Dare Call It Torture: Indexing and the Limits of Press Independence in the Abu Ghraib Scandal." *Journal of Communication* 56, no. 3 (September 1, 2006): 467–485. https://doi.org/10.1111/j.1460-2466.2006.00296.x.

Benoit, William L. *Accounts, Excuses, and Apologies, Second Edition: Image Repair Theory and Research*. Albany: State University of New York Press, 2014.

Bershady, Harold. "Erving Turned to Me and Said, 'You Know, Elijah Anderson Is Really a Professional Sociologist, He Is Not a Professional Black.'" Bios Sociologicus: The Erving Goffman Archives, May 8, 2009. https://digitalscholarship.unlv.edu/goffman_archives/5.

Best, Joel. "But Seriously Folks: The Limitations of the Strict Constructionist Interpretation of Social Problems." In *Constructionist Controversies: Issues in Social Problems Theory*, edited by Gale Miller and James A. Holstein, 109–130. New York: Routledge, 1993.

———. "Constructionist Social Problems Theory." *Annals of the International Communication Association* 36, no. 1 (January 1, 2013): 237–269. https://doi.org/10.1080/23808985.2013.11679134.

———. "Goffman Told Me, 'It Is Really Hard to Do That Kind of Thing Well,' and That Was about All the Advice I Ever Got from Him." Bios Sociologicus: The Erving Goffman Archives, July 23, 2008, 1–6.

———. "Rhetoric in Claims-Making: Constructing the Missing Children Problem." *Social Problems* 34, no. 2 (1987): 101–121. https://doi.org/10.2307/800710.

———. *Social Problems*. New York: W. W. Norton, 2016.

———. *Threatened Children: Rhetoric and Concern about Child-Victims*. Chicago: University of Chicago Press, 1993.

Bickford, John H. "Examining Historical (Mis) Representations of Christopher Columbus within Children's Literature." *Social Studies Research and Practice* 8, no. 2 (2013): 1–24.

Blair, Sean, and Neal J. Roese. "Balancing the Basket: The Role of Shopping Basket Composition in Embarrassment." *Journal of Consumer Research* 40, no. 4 (2013): 676–691. https://doi.org/10.1086/671761.

Blinder, Alan. "Michael Slager, Officer in Walter Scott Shooting, Gets 20-Year Sentence." *New York Times*, December 7, 2017. www.nytimes.com.

Blumer, Herbert. "Social Problems as Collective Behavior." *Social Problems* 18, no. 3 (January 1, 1971): 298–306. https://doi.org/10.2307/799797.

Bonilla-Silva, Eduardo. "The Invisible Weight of Whiteness: The Racial Grammar of Everyday Life in Contemporary America." *Ethnic and Racial Studies* 35, no. 2 (2012): 173–194. https://doi.org/10.1080/01419870.2011.613997.

———. "The Linguistics of Color Blind Racism: How to Talk Nasty about Blacks without Sounding 'Racist.'" *Critical Sociology* 28, no. 1–2 (2002): 41–64. https://doi.org/10.1177/08969205020280010501.

Bonilla-Silva, Eduardo, and David Dietrich. "The Sweet Enchantment of Color-Blind Racism in Obamerica." *Annals of the American Academy of Political and Social Science* 634, no. 1 (2011): 190–206. https://doi.org/10.1177/0002716210389702.

Bonilla-Silva, Eduardo, Amanda Lewis, and David G. Embrick. "'I Did Not Get That Job Because of a Black Man . . .': The Story Lines and Testimonies of Color-Blind Racism." *Sociological Forum* 19, no. 4 (2004): 555–581. https://doi.org/10.1007/s11206-004-0696-3.

Brown, Keffrelyn D., and Anthony L. Brown. "Silenced Memories: An Examination of the Sociocultural Knowledge on Race and Racial Violence in Official School Curriculum." *Equity and Excellence in Education* 43, no. 2 (2010): 139–154. https://doi.org/10.1080/10665681003719590.

"Bully, n.1." In *Oxford English Dictionary*. Oxford: Oxford University Press, 1989. www.oed.com.

Burton, Nsenga. "Double Standard: Bike 'Thief' Experiment Highlights Racism." *The Root*, September 27, 2010. www.theroot.com.

Bush, George W. "President's Statement on the U.N. International Day in Support of Victims of Torture." whitehouse.gov. June 26, 2003. https://georgewbush-whitehouse.archives.gov.

———. "President's Statement on the U.N. International Day in Support of Victims of Torture." whitehouse.gov. June 26, 2004. https://georgewbush-whitehouse.archives.gov.

Cahill, Spencer E. "Children and Civility: Ceremonial Deviance and the Acquisition of Ritual Competence." *Social Psychology Quarterly* 50, no. 4 (1987): 312–321. https://doi.org/10.2307/2786816.

Cahill, Spencer E., William Distler, Cynthia Lachowetz, Andrea Meaney, Robyn Tarallo, and Teena Willard. "Meanwhile Backstage: Public Bathrooms and the Interaction Order." *Urban Life* 14, no. 1 (April 1, 1985): 33–58. https://doi.org/10.1177/0098303985014001002.

Cahill, Spencer E., and Robin Eggleston. "Managing Emotions in Public: The Case of Wheelchair Users." *Social Psychology Quarterly* 57, no. 4 (1994): 300–312. https://doi.org/10.2307/2787157.

Campo-Flores, Arian, and Lynn Waddell. "Jury Acquits Zimmerman of All Charges." *Wall Street Journal*, July 14, 2013, sec. US.

Carey, Benedict, and Jan Hoffman. "Lessons in the Delicate Art of Confronting Offensive Speech." *New York Times*, October 12, 2016. www.nytimes.com.

Caron, Mark D., Susan Krauss Whitbourne, and Richard P. Halgin. "Fraudulent Excuse Making among College Students." *Teaching of Psychology* 19, no. 2 (April 1, 1992): 90–93. https://doi.org/10.1207/s15328023top1902_6.

Case, Kim A., and Annette Hemmings. "Distancing Strategies: White Women Preservice Teachers and Antiracist Curriculum." *Urban Education* 40, no. 6 (November 1, 2005): 606–626. https://doi.org/10.1177/0042085905281396.

Casey, Erin A., and Kristin Ohler. "Being a Positive Bystander: Male Antiviolence Allies' Experiences of 'Stepping Up.'" *Journal of Interpersonal Violence* 27, no. 1 (January 1, 2012): 62–83. https://doi.org/10.1177/0886260511416479.

Cauley, Kashana. "Mark Meadows and the Victim Card." *New York Times*, March 1, 2019. www.nytimes.com.

Cavan, Sherri. "Having Been Goffman's Student I Am Drawn to Voltaire's Dictum, 'To the Living We Owe Respect, to the Dead We Owe Only the Truth.'" Bios Sociologicus: Erving Goffman Archives, November 30, 2008. https://digitalscholarship.unlv.edu/goffman_archives/10.

Cavanagh, Kate, R. Emerson Dobash, Russell P. Dobash, and Ruth Lewis. "'Remedial Work': Men's Strategic Responses to Their Violence against Intimate Female Partners." *Sociology* 35, no. 3 (August 2001): 695–714. https://doi.org/10.1017/S0038038501000359.

CBS New York. "Pine Bush Residents Rally after Anti-Semitic Bullying Claims." November 10, 2013. https://newyork.cbslocal.com.

Cecelski, David S., and Timothy B. Tyson, eds. *Democracy Betrayed: The Wilmington Race Riot of 1898 and Its Legacy*. Chapel Hill: University of North Carolina Press, 1998.

Chandler, David. *Voices from S-21: Terror and History in Pol Pot's Secret Prison*. Berkeley: University of California Press, 2000.

Chanen, David. "Fear-Based Training for Police Officers Is Challenged." *Star Tribune*, July 11, 2018. www.startribune.com.

Christensen, Emma. "Etiquette: How To Tell Someone There's Food in Their Teeth." Kitchn. Accessed August 16, 2018. www.thekitchn.com.

CIA Inspector General. "Counterterrorism Detention and Interrogation Activities." May 2004. irp.fas.org.

Clay, Rebecca A. "Trend Report: Psychology Is More Popular Than Ever." APA.org, November 2017. www.apa.org.

Clinton, Bill. "Transcript." CNN, August 17, 1998. www.cnn.com.

Cloud, David S. "General Says Prison Inquiry Led to His Forced Retirement." *New York Times*, June 17, 2007, sec. Washington. www.nytimes.com.

CNN. "Read and Search: White House Transcript of Trump's First Phone Call with Ukrainian President." November 15, 2019. www.cnn.com.

Coates, Ta-Nehisi. "The Case for Reparations." *Atlantic*, June 2014. www.theatlantic.com.

Cohen, Stanley. "Government Responses to Human Rights Reports: Claims, Denials, and Counterclaims." *Human Rights Quarterly* 18, no. 3 (1996): 517–543.

———. *States of Denial: Knowing about Atrocities and Suffering*. Malden, MA: Polity Press, 2001.

Colorado Public Radio Staff. "Colorado Civil War Soldier Statue Torn Down at the Capitol." Colorado Public Radio, June 25, 2020. www.cpr.org.

Commission on Presidential Debates. "October 19, 2016 Debate Transcript." Commission on Presidential Debates, October 19, 2016. www.debates.org.

Conley, Dalton. *You May Ask Yourself: An Introduction to Thinking like a Sociologist*. New York: W. W. Norton, 2017.

Connolly, Matt. "There's Only One Way to Respond to Wrath of Dabo, Clemson Players Say: Learn from It." *Charlotte Observer*. Accessed October 30, 2019. www.charlotteobserver.com.

Cook, Kevin. *Kitty Genovese: The Murder, the Bystanders, the Crime 1 .. Changed America*. New York: W. W. Norton, 2014.

Corney, Charlotte. "Do Ostriches Really Bury Their Head in the Sand?" *BBC Science Focus Magazine*, 2021. www.sciencefocus.com.

Correll, Joshua, Bernadette Park, Charles M. Judd, and Bernd Wittenbrink. "The Police Officer's Dilemma: Using Ethnicity to Disambiguate Potentially Threatening Individuals." *Journal of Personality and Social Psychology* 83, no. 6 (December 2002): 1314–1329. https://doi.org/10.1037/0022-3514.83.6.1314.

Costa, Robert, and Philip Rucker. "Woodward Book: Trump Says He Knew Coronavirus Was 'Deadly' and Worse Than the Flu While Intentionally Misleading Americans." *Washington Post*, September 9, 2020. www.washingtonpost.com.

Cote, Greg. "Latest Hot Button Top 10." Random Evidence Blog, 2017. blogs.herald.com.

Cowley, Stacy, and Matthew Goldstein. "Accusations of Fraud at Wells Fargo Spread to Sham Insurance Policies." *New York Times*, December 9, 2016, sec. Business. www.nytimes.com.

Craggs, Tommy. "Trump: 'I Said It, I Was Wrong, and I Apologize.'" *Slate Magazine*, October 8, 2016. https://slate.com.

Cressey, Donald R. "The Criminal Violation of Financial Trust." *American Sociological Review* 15, no. 6 (1950): 738–743. https://doi.org/10.2307/2086606.

Cromwell, Paul, and Quint Thurman. "The Devil Made Me Do It: Use of Neutralizations by Shoplifters." *Deviant Behavior* 24, no. 6 (November 1, 2003): 535–550. https://doi.org/10.1080/713840271.

Cummings, William. "After Denying Racism, Videos of Meadows Vowing to Send Obama 'Home to Kenya' Resurface." *USA Today*, February 28, 2019. www.usatoday.com.

Danner, Mark. "Abu Ghraib: The Hidden Story." *New York Review of Books*, October 7, 2004. www.nybooks.com.

———. "Frozen Scandal." *New York Review of Books*, December 4, 2008. www.nybooks.com.

Darley, John M., and Bibb Latané. "Bystander Intervention in Emergencies: Diffusion of Responsibility." *Journal of Personality and Social Psychology* 8, no. 4 (April 1968): 377–383. https://doi.org/10.1037/h0025589.

Dean, Michelle. "Contracts of Silence." *Columbia Journalism Review*, 2018. www.cjr.org.

Del Rosso, Jared. "From Claims to Chains: The Materiality of Social Problems." *American Sociologist* 50, no. 2 (June 1, 2019): 247–254. https://doi.org/10.1007/s12108-019-9405-9.

———. "'Its Own Kind of Torture': Denial, Acknowledgment, and the Debate about Force Feeding at Guantánamo Bay." *Sociological Forum* 33, no. 1 (2018): 53–72. https://doi.org/10.1111/socf.12399.

———. *Talking about Torture: How Political Discourse Shapes the Debate.* New York: Columbia University Press, 2015.

———. "Textuality and the Social Organization of Denial: Abu Ghraib, Guantánamo, and the Meanings of US Interrogation Policies." *Sociological Forum* 29, no. 1 (March 1, 2014): 52–74. https://doi.org/10.1111/socf.12069.

———. "The Textual Mediation of Denial: Congress, Abu Ghraib, and the Construction of an Isolated Incident." *Social Problems* 58, no. 2 (May 2011): 165–188. https://doi.org/10.1525/sp.2011.58.2.165.

———. "The Toxicity of Torture: The Cultural Structure of US Political Discourse of Waterboarding." *Social Forces* 93, no. 1 (September 1, 2014): 383–404. https://doi.org/10.1093/sf/sou060.

Del Rosso, Jared, and Jennifer Esala. "Constructionism and the Textuality of Sociology Problems." *Qualitative Sociology Review* 11, no. 2 (2015): 34–45.

Del Rosso, Jared, and Blake Nordstrom-Wehner. "Team Grade Anarchy: A Conversation about the Troubled Transition of Grading." *Teaching and Learning Together in Higher Education* 1, no. 30 (2020): 1–10.

"Denial, n." In *Oxford English Dictionary*. Oxford: Oxford University Press, 2021. www.oed.com.

Department of Defense. "Transcript: Defense Department Operational Update Briefing." May 4, 2004. https://archive.defense.gov.

DiAngelo, Robin. "Nothing to Add: A Challenge to White Silence in Racial Discussions." *Understanding and Dismantling Privilege* 2, no. 1 (2012): 2–17.

———. *White Fragility: Why It's So Hard for White People to Talk about Racism.* Boston: Beacon Press, 2018.

DiAngelo, Robin, and Özlem Sensoy. "Getting Slammed: White Depictions of Race Discussions as Arenas of Violence." *Race*

Ethnicity and Education 17, no. 1 (January 1, 2014): 103–128. https://doi.org/10.1080/13613324.2012.674023.

Disis, Jill. "Donald Trump Won't Say Vulgar Remarks Reference 'Sexual Assault.'" CNN, October 10, 2016. www.cnn.com.

Du Bois, W. E. Burghardt. *Black Reconstruction in America, 1860–1880.* New York: Simon and Schuster, 1935.

Duncan, Birt L. "Differential Social Perception and Attribution of Intergroup Violence: Testing the Lower Limits of Stereotyping of Blacks." *Journal of Personality and Social Psychology* 34, no. 4 (1976): 590–598. https://doi.org/10.1037/0022-3514.34.4.590.

Durkheim, Emile. *The Rules of Sociological Method: And Selected Texts on Sociology and Its Method.* New York: Free Press, 1895.

Dworkin, Terry Morehead, and Melissa S. Baucus. "Internal vs. External Whistleblowers: A Comparison of Whistleblowering Processes." *Journal of Business Ethics* 17, no. 12 (1998): 1281–1298.

Dwyer, Jim. "When Fists and Kicks Fly on the Subway, It's Snackman to the Rescue." *New York Times*, April 12, 2012, sec. New York. www.nytimes.com.

Eberhardt, Jennifer L., Phillip Atiba Goff, Valerie J. Purdie, and Paul G. Davies. "Seeing Black: Race, Crime, and Visual Processing." *Journal of Personality and Social Psychology* 87, no. 6 (December 2004): 876–893. https://doi.org/10.1037/0022-3514.87.6.876.

Echlin, Helena. "Is There Something in My Teeth?" Chowhound. Accessed October 12, 2018. www.chowhound.com.

Egan, Matt. "Workers Tell Wells Fargo Horror Stories." CNN, September 9, 2016. www.money.cnn.com.

Eliasoph, Nina. *Avoiding Politics: How Americans Produce Apathy in Everyday Life.* New York: Cambridge University Press, 1998.

Eligon, John, and Dan Levin. "In Minneapolis, Looking for Police Recruits Who Can Resist Warrior Culture." *New York Times*, July 21, 2020, sec. US. www.nytimes.com.

Ellison, Jeremiah Bey. "'Woe Is You,' White People Say. What We Need Is a Remedy." *New York Times*, April 15, 2020. www.nytimes.com.

Esala, Jennifer J. "Communities of Denial: The Co-construction of Gendered Adolescent Violence." *Deviant Behavior* 34, no. 2 (February 1, 2013): 97–114. https://doi.org/10.1080/01639625.2012.707543.

Evangelist, Gittel, and James Nani. "Pine Bush Residents Rally to Dispute Bias Accusations." *Times Herald Record*, November 11, 2013. www.recordonline.com.

Farrow, Ronan. "From Aggressive Overtures to Sexual Assault: Harvey Weinstein's Accusers Tell Their Stories." *New Yorker*, October 23, 2017. www.newyorker.com.

———. "Harvey Weinstein's Army of Spies." *New Yorker*, 2017. www.newyorker.com.

———. "How an Élite University Research Center Concealed Its Relationship with Jeffrey Epstein." *New Yorker*, September 6, 2019. www.newyorker.com.

Feagin, Joe R., and Bernice McNair Barnett. "Success *and* Failure: How Systemic Racism Trumped the *Brown v. Board of Education* Decision." *University of Illinois Law Review* 2004, no. 5 (2004): 1099–1130.

Federal Bureau of Investigation. "Emails between Valerie Caproni and Others." *The Torture Database*, 2003. www.thetorturedatabase.org.

Fein, Esther B. "Angry Citizens in Many Cities Supporting Goetz." *New York Times*, January 7, 1985, sec. NY / Region. www.nytimes.com.

Feinstein, Dianne. "Letter to Secretary of Defense Chuck Hagel." June 19, 2013. www.feinstein.senate.gov.

Finley, Taryn. "Existing while Black." *Huffington Post*, 2018. www.huffingtonpost.com.

Fischer, Peter, Tobias Greitemeyer, Fabian Pollozek, and Dieter Frey. "The Unresponsive Bystander: Are Bystanders More Responsive in Dangerous Emergencies?" *European Journal of Social Psychology* 36, no. 2 (March 1, 2006): 267–278. https://doi.org/10.1002/ejsp.297.

Fischer, Peter, Joachim I. Krueger, Tobias Greitemeyer, Claudia Vogrincic, Andreas Kastenmüller, Dieter Frey, Moritz Heene, Magdalena Wicher, and Martina Kainbacher. "The Bystander-Effect: A Meta-analytic Review on Bystander Intervention in Dangerous and Non-dangerous Emergencies." *Psychological Bulletin* 137, no. 4 (July 2011): 517–537. https://doi.org/10.1037/a0023304.

Fitzgerald, Kathleen J. "A Sociology of Race/Ethnicity Textbooks: Avoiding White Privilege, Ahistoricism, and Use of the Passive Voice." *Sociological Focus* 45, no. 4 (2012): 338–357.

Flitter, Emily. "The Price of Wells Fargo's Fake Account Scandal Grows by $3 Billion." *New York Times*, February 21, 2020, sec. Business. www.nytimes.com.

Forman, Tyrone A. "Color-Blind Racism and Racial Indifference: The Role of Racial Apathy in Facilitating Enduring Inequalities." In *The Changing Terrain of Race and Ethnicity*, edited by Maria Krysan and Amanda E. Lewis, 43–66. New York: Russell Sage Foundation, 2004.

Forman, Tyrone A., and Amanda E. Lewis. "Racial Apathy and Hurricane Katrina: The Social Anatomy of Prejudice in the Post–Civil Rights Era." *Du Bois Review: Social Science Research on Race* 3, no. 1 (March 2006): 175–202. https://doi.org/10.1017/S1742058X06060127.

Forsyth, William. "Status of the Independent Special Counsel's Investigation into Michigan State University's Handling of the Larry Nassar Matter." Michigan: Department of Attorney General, 2018. https://gray-arc-content.s3.amazonaws.com/WILX/MSU_Investigation_Status_Update_641680_7.pdf.

Franklin, John Hope. "'Birth of a Nation': Propaganda as History." *Massachusetts Review* 20, no. 3 (1979): 417–434.

Franta, Benjamin. "Shell and Exxon's Secret 1980s Climate Change Warnings." *Guardian*, September 19, 2018, sec. Environment. www.theguardian.com.

Frenkel, Sheera, Nicholas Confessore, Cecilia Kang, Matthew Rosenberg, and Jack Nicas. "Delay, Deny and Deflect: How Facebook's Leaders Fought through Crisis." *New York Times*, March 4, 2019, sec. Technology. www.nytimes.com.

Friend, Ronald, Yvonne Rafferty, and Dana Bramel. "A Puzzling Misinterpretation of the Asch 'Conformity' Study." *European Journal of Social Psychology* 20, no. 1 (January 1990): 29–44. https://doi.org/10.1002/ejsp.2420200104.

Gaertner, Samuel L., and John F. Dovidio. "The Subtlety of White Racism, Arousal, and Helping Behavior." *Journal of Personality and Social Psychology* 35, no. 10 (October 1977): 691–707. https://doi.org/10.1037/0022-3514.35.10.691.

Gaertner, Samuel L., John F. Dovidio, and Gary Johnson. "Race of Victim, Nonresponsive Bystanders, and Helping Behavior." *Journal of Social Psychology* 117, no. 1 (June 1982): 69–77. https://doi.org/10.1080/00224545.1982.9713409.

Gallagher, Charles A. "Playing the White Ethnic Card: Using Ethnic Identity to Deny Contemporary Racism." In *White Out: The*

Continuing Significance of Racism, edited by Ashley W. Doane and Eduardo Bonilla-Silva, 145–158. New York: Routledge, 2003.

Gallo, Marcia M. *No One Helped: Kitty Genovese, New York City, and the Myth of Urban Apathy*. Ithaca, NY: Cornell University Press, 2015.

Galloway, Stephen. "Guillermo del Toro on Seeing a UFO, Hearing Ghosts and Shaping 'Water.'" *Hollywood Reporter*, December 21, 2017. www.hollywoodreporter.com.

Gamson, William. "A Stranger Determined to Remain One." Bios Sociologicus: The Erving Goffman Archives, April 28, 2009. https:// digitalscholarship.unlv.edu/goffman_archives/25.

Gardner, Carol Brooks. "Passing By: Street Remarks, Address Rights, and the Urban Female." *Sociological Inquiry* 50, no. 3/4 (June 1980): 328–356.

Garfinkel, Harold. "Conditions of Successful Degradation Ceremonies." *American Journal of Sociology* 61, no. 5 (1956): 420–424.

———. "Studies of the Routine Grounds of Everyday Activities." *Social Problems* 11, no. 3 (1964): 225–250. https://doi.org/10.2307/798722.

Ghoshal, Raj Andrew. "Transforming Collective Memory: Mnemonic Opportunity Structures and the Outcomes of Racial Violence Memory Movements." *Theory and Society* 42, no. 4 (July 1, 2013): 329–350. https://doi.org/10.1007/s11186-013-9197-9.

Gibson, Janice T., and Mika Haritos-Fatouros. "The Education of a Torturer." *Psychology Today* 20, no. 11 (November 1986): 50–58. http://dx.doi.org/10.1037/e400772009-004.

Goffman, Erving. *Behavior in Public Places: Notes on the Social Organization of Gatherings*. New York: Free Press, 1966.

———. "Embarrassment and Social Organization." *American Journal of Sociology* 62, no. 3 (November 1, 1956): 264–271. https://doi. org/10.1086/222003.

———. *Interaction Ritual: Essays on Face-to-Face Behavior*. New York: Pantheon, 1982.

———. "On Face-Work." *Psychiatry* 18, no. 3 (August 1, 1955): 213–231.

———. *The Presentation of Self in Everyday Life*. New York: Anchor, 1959.

———. *Relations in Public Microstudies of the Public Order*. New York: Basic Books, 1971.

———. *Stigma: Notes on the Management of Spoiled Identity*. New York: Simon and Schuster, 2009.

Goldenberg, Suzanne. "Memos Show FBI Agents Complained about Abuses at Guantánamo Bay." *Guardian*, December 22, 2004, sec. World. www.theguardian.com.

Goldstein, Dana. "Two States. Eight Textbooks. Two American Stories." *New York Times*, January 12, 2020, sec. US. www.nytimes.com.

Goode, Erich, and Nachman Ben-Yehuda. "Moral Panics: Culture, Politics, and Social Construction." *Annual Review of Sociology* 20, no. 1 (1994): 149–171. https://doi.org/10.1146/annurev. so.20.080194.001053.

Goodman, J. David, Jesse McKinley, and Danny Hakim. "Cuomo Aides Spent Months Hiding Nursing Home Death Toll." *New York Times*, April 28, 2021. www.nytimes.com.

Goodwin, Charles. "Professional Vision." *American Anthropologist* 96, no. 3 (1994): 606–633. https://doi.org/DOI:10.1525/ aa.1994.96.3.02a00100.

Gourevitch, Philip, and Errol Morris. *The Ballad of Abu Ghraib*. New York: Penguin, 2009.

———. "Exposure." *New Yorker*, March 17, 2008. www.newyorker.com.

Graham, David A. "Rumsfeld's Knowns and Unknowns: The Intellectual History of a Quip." *Atlantic*, March 27, 2014. www.the-atlantic.com.

Gurung, Regan A. R., Jana Hackathorn, Carolyn Enns, Susan Frantz, John T. Cacioppo, Trudy Loop, and James E. Freeman. "Strengthening Introductory Psychology: A New Model for Teaching the Introductory Course." *American Psychologist* 71, no. 2 (February 2016): 112–124. https://doi.org/10.1037/a0040012.

Gusfield, Joseph R. *The Culture of Public Problems: Drinking-Driving and the Symbolic Order*. Chicago: University of Chicago Press, 1984.

Hafner-Burton, Emilie M. "Sticks and Stones: Naming and Shaming the Human Rights Enforcement Problem." *International Organization* 62, no. 4 (2008): 689–716. https://doi.org/10.1017/ S0020818308080247.

Harari, Herbert, Oren Harari, and Robert V. White. "The Reaction to Rape by American Male Bystanders." *Journal of Social Psychology* 125, no. 5 (October 1985): 653. https://doi.org/10.1080/00224545.1985.9712039.

Hart, Timothy, and Callie Rennison. "Reporting Crime to the Police, 1992–2000." Washington, DC: US Department of Justice, 2003. www.bjs.gov.

Heffernan, Margaret. *Willful Blindness: Why We Ignore the Obvious at Our Peril*. New York: Bloomsbury, 2012.

Hegedus, Nathan. "Man Could Get Life for Hoax." *Times Herald Record*, October 20, 2001. www.recordonline.com.

Heinonen, Anna. "Neutralizing Disciplinary Violence: A Typology of Parents' Use-of-Violence Accounts." *Victims and Offenders* 10, no. 3 (2015): 270–292. https://doi.org/10.1080/15564886.2014.947545.

Hewitt, John P., and Randall Stokes. "Disclaimers." *American Sociological Review* 40, no. 1 (1975): 1–11. https://doi.org/10.2307/2094442.

Hilts, Philip J. "Scientists Say Cigarette Company Suppressed Findings on Nicotine." *New York Times*, April 29, 1994, sec. US. www.nytimes.com.

Hiltzik, Michael. "A New Study Shows How Exxon Mobil Downplayed Climate Change When It Knew the Problem Was Real." *Los Angeles Times*, August 22, 2017. www.latimes.com.

Hinton, Alexander Laban. *Man or Monster: The Trial of a Khmer Rouge Torturer*. Durham, NC: Duke University Press, 2016.

Hoffmann, Carlee, and Claire Strom. "A Perfect Storm: The Ocoee Riot of 1920." *Florida Historical Quarterly* 93, no. 1 (2014): 25–43.

Holstein, James A., and Jaber F. Gubrium. "A Constructionist Analytics for Social Problems." In *Challenges and Choices: Constructionist Perspectives on Social Problems*, edited by James A. Holstein and Gale Miller, 187–208. New York: Aldine de Gruyter, 2003.

Holstein, James A., and Gale Miller. "Social Constructionism and Social Problems Work." In *Challenges and Choices: Constructionist Perspectives on Social Problems*, edited by James A. Holstein and Gale Miller, 151–172. New York: Aldine de Gruyter, 1993.

Huggins, Martha K., Mika Haritos-Fatouros, and Philip G. Zimbardo. *Violence Workers: Police Torturers and Murderers Reconstruct Brazilian Atrocities*. Berkeley: University of California Press, 2002.

Hughes, Siobhan, and Richard Rubin. "Republican Lawmakers Air Unease over Donald Trump." *Wall Street Journal*, March 1, 2016. www.wsj.com.

Hurd, Carlos F. "'*Post-Dispatch* Man, an Eye-Witness, Describes Massacre of Negroes.'" *St. Louis Post-Dispatch*, July 3, 1917. www.stltoday.com.

Hyde, Lewis. *A Primer for Forgetting: Getting Past the Past*. New York: Farrar, Straus and Giroux, 2019.

Hylton, Wil S. "Prisoner of Conscience." *GQ*, August 1, 2006. www.gq.com.

Ibarra, Peter R., and John I. Kitsuse. "Vernacular Constituents of Moral Discourse: An Interactionist Proposal for the Study of Social Problems." In *Reconsidering Social Constructionism: Debates in Social Problems Theory*, edited by James A. Holstein and Gale Miller, 25–58. New York: Routledge, 1993.

Irwin, John. "Goffman Was by Far the Smartest, Most Interesting, Complex, Though, at Times, Snide or Disparaging Individual I Have Ever Known." Bios Sociologicus: The Erving Goffman Archives, August 7, 2008. https://digitalscholarship.unlv.edu/goffman_archives/38.

Isacsson, Alfred. "The Rumor at Pine Bush." *New York History* 44, no. 2 (1963): 139–144.

Izadi, Elahe. "Pledge of Allegiance Reading in Arabic Sparks Controversy at New York School." *Washington Post*, March 19, 2015. www.washingtonpost.com.

Jackson, Richard. "Constructing Enemies: 'Islamic Terrorism' in Political and Academic Discourse." *Government and Opposition* 42, no. 3 (2007): 394–426. https://doi.org/10.1111/j.1477-7053.2007.00229.x.

———. "Language, Policy and the Construction of a Torture Culture in the War on Terrorism." *Review of International Studies* 33, no. 3 (2007): 353–371.

John Brown Anti-Klan Committee. "Smash the Klan." 1977. https://freedomarchives.org/Documents/Finder/DOC37_scans/37.SmashKlanPressPkt1977.pdf.pdf.

Johnson, John M. "Horror Stories and the Construction of Child Abuse." In *Images of Issues: Typifying Contemporary Social Problems*, edited by Joel Best, 17–32. New York: Routledge, 1995. https://doi.org/10.4324/9781351310284-4.

Johnson, Kirk. "Goetz Is Cleared in Subway Attack; Gun Count Upheld." *New York Times*, June 17, 1987, sec. NY / Region. www.nytimes.com.

Johnson, Roberta Ann. "Whistleblowing and the Police." *Rutgers University Journal of Law and Urban Policy* 3, no. 1 (2006): 74–83.

Jones, Anthony R., and George R. Fay. "Fay Report: Investigation of 205th Military Intelligence Brigade's Activities in Abu Ghraib

Detention Facility." Washington, DC: Department of Defense, 2004. www.thetorturedatabase.org.

Jonsson, Patrik. "Zimmerman Jury of Peers Is Jury of (Mostly White) Women." *Christian Science Monitor*, June 20, 2013. www.csmonitor.com.

Kalab, Kathleen A. "Student Vocabularies of Motive: Accounts for Absence." *Symbolic Interaction* 10, no. 1 (1987): 71–83. https://doi.org/10.1525/si.1987.10.1.71.

Karp, David A. "Hiding in Pornographic Bookstores: A Reconsideration of the Nature of Urban Anonymity." *Urban Life and Culture* 1, no. 4 (January 1973): 427–451. https://doi.org/10.1177/089124167300100405.

Katz, Jack. "Concerted Ignorance: The Social Construction of Cover-Up." *Urban Life* 8, no. 3 (October 1, 1979): 295–316. https://doi.org/10.1177/089124167900800303.

Kendi, Ibram X. "The Heartbeat of Racism Is Denial." *New York Times*, January 13, 2018, sec. Opinion. www.nytimes.com.

Kilgannon, Corey. "Anthrax Joke 'Not Funny.'" *New York Times*, October 20, 2001, sec. NY / Region. www.nytimes.com.

King, Kim M. "Neutralizing Marginally Deviant Behavior: Bingo Players and Superstition." *Journal of Gambling Studies* 6, no. 1 (March 1, 1990): 43–61. https://doi.org/10.1007/BF01015748.

Klemsrud, Judy. "Women in Ku Klux Klan Move into the Male Power Structure." *New York Times*, May 22, 1975. https://timesmachine.nytimes.com/timesmachine/1975/05/22/83677312.html?pageNumber=44.

Kobrin, Solomon. "The Conflict of Values in Delinquency Areas." *American Sociological Review* 16, no. 5 (1951): 653–661. https://doi.org/10.2307/2087358.

Kolata, Gina, and Roni Caryn Rabin. "'Don't Be Afraid of Covid,' Trump Says, Undermining Public Health Messages." *New York Times*, October 5, 2020. www.nytimes.com.

Kramer, Michael R., and Kathryn M. Olson. "The Strategic Potential of Sequencing Apologia Stases: President Clinton's Self-Defense in the Monica Lewinsky Scandal." *Western Journal of Communication* 66, no. 3 (September 1, 2002): 347–368. https://doi.org/10.1080/10570310209374741.

Krieg, Gregory. "12 Times Donald Trump Declared His 'Respect' for Women." CNN, October 7, 2016. www.cnn.com.

Kumar, Akshaya. "Confronting the Shameless." Human Rights Watch, December 28, 2016. www.hrw.org.

Landay, Steve, Jeff Holland, and Jonathan Landay. "Trump Summoned Supporters to 'Wild' Protest, and Told Them to Fight. They Did." Reuters, January 7, 2021. www.reuters.com.

Lankenau, Stephen E. "Panhandling Repertoires and Routines for Overcoming the Nonperson Treatment." *Deviant Behavior* 20, no. 2 (March 1, 1999): 183–206. https://doi.org/10.1080/016396299266551.

———. "Stronger Than Dirt: Public Humiliation and Status Enhancement among Panhandlers." *Journal of Contemporary Ethnography* 28, no. 3 (1999): 288–318. https://doi.org/10.1177/089124199129023451.

Latané, B., and J. M. Darley. *The Unresponsive Bystander: Why Doesn't He Help?* New York: Meredith, 1970.

Latané, Bibb, and Steve Nida. "Ten Years of Research on Group Size and Helping." *Psychological Bulletin* 89, no. 2 (March 1981): 308–324. https://doi.org/10.1037/0033-2909.89.2.308.

Lee, Cynthia Kwei Yung. "Race and Self-Defense: Toward a Normative Conception of Reasonableness." *Minnesota Law Review* 81 (1996): 367–500.

Lee, Jooyoung. "Escaping Embarrassment: Face-Work in the Rap Cipher." *Social Psychology Quarterly* 72, no. 4 (December 2009): 306–324. https://doi.org/10.1177/019027250907200405.

Lemert, Charles. *Social Things: An Introduction to the Sociological Life.* Lanham, MD: Rowman and Littlefield, 2012.

Leonardo, Zeus. "The Color of Supremacy: Beyond the Discourse of 'White Privilege.'" *Educational Philosophy and Theory* 36, no. 2 (2004): 137–152. https://doi.org/10.1111/j.1469-5812.2004.00057.x.

Leonardo, Zeus, and Ronald K. Porter. "Pedagogy of Fear: Toward a Fanonian Theory of 'Safety' in Race Dialogue." *Race Ethnicity and Education* 13, no. 2 (July 1, 2010): 139–157. https://doi.org/10.1080/13613324.2010.482898.

Lerer, Lisa. "Joe Biden Jokes about Hugging in a Speech, Then Offers a Mixed Apology." *New York Times*, April 6, 2019, sec. US. www.nytimes.com.

Lerer, Lisa, and Sydney Ember. "Democratic Frustration Mounts as Biden Remains Silent on Sexual Assault Allegation." *New York Times*, April 29, 2020, sec. US. www.nytimes.com.

Leung, Rebecca. "Abuse at Abu Ghraib." CBS News, May 5, 2004. www.cbsnews.com.

Levin, Bess. "6 Ways Wells Fargo Made Its Employees' Lives a Living Hell." *Vanity Fair*, April 10, 2017. www.vanityfair.com.

Liu, Pauline. "Pine Bush and the Pledge: What Is National Foreign Language Week?" *Times Herald Record*, March 28, 2015. www.recordonline.com.

Loewen, James W. *Lies My Teacher Told Me: Everything Your American History Textbook Got Wrong.* New York: New Press, 2018.

Lofland, John. "Erving Goffman's Sociological Legacies." *Urban Life* 13, no. 1 (April 1, 1984): 7–34. https://doi.org/10.1177/0098303984013001002.

Lofland, Lyn H. "Self-Management in Public Settings: Part II." *Urban Life and Culture* 1, no. 2 (July 1, 1972): 217–231. https://doi.org/10.1177/089124167200100205.

López, Ian Haney. *Dog Whistle Politics: How Coded Racial Appeals Have Reinvented Racism and Wrecked the Middle Class.* New York: Oxford University Press, 2015.

Lorde, Audre. "The Uses of Anger." *Women's Studies Quarterly*, October 1, 1981. https://academicworks.cuny.edu/wsq/509.

Loseke, Donileen. *Thinking about Social Problems: An Introduction to Constructionist Perspectives.* New York: Routledge, 2017. https://doi.org/10.4324/9781315135601.

Luban, David. "Liberalism, Torture, and the Ticking Bomb Essay." *Virginia Law Review* 91, no. 6 (2005): 1425–1462.

Mague, Anthony. "College Coaching Scandals Raid Nation." *Daily Orange*, January 21, 2004. www.dailyorange.com.

Mak, Aaron. "Facebook's New TV Ad Doesn't Inspire a Lot of Confidence." *Slate Magazine*, April 27, 2018. www.slate.com.

Manning, Rachel, Mark Levine, and Alan Collins. "The Kitty Genovese Murder and the Social Psychology of Helping: The Parable of the 38 Witnesses." *American Psychologist* 62, no. 6 (September 2007): 555–562. https://doi.org/10.1037/0003-066X.62.6.555.

Marche, Stephen. "Is Facebook Making Us Lonely?" *Atlantic*, April 2, 2012. www.theatlantic.com.

Margolis, Eric, and Mary Romero. "'The Department Is Very Male, Very White, Very Old, and Very Conservative': The Functioning of the Hidden Curriculum in Graduate Sociology Departments." *Harvard Educational Review* 68, no. 1 (April 1, 1998): 1–33. https://doi.org/10.17763/haer.68.1.1q3828348783j851.

Markovitz, Andrei S., and Mark Silverstein. "Introduction: Power and Process in Liberal Democracies." In *The Politics of Scandal: Power and Process in Liberal Democracies,* edited by Andrei S. Markovitz and Mark Silverstein, 1–14. New York: Holmes and Meier, 1988.

Martin, Laura. "'Eskimo Words for Snow': A Case Study in the Genesis and Decay of an Anthropological Example." *American Anthropologist* 88, no. 2 (1986): 418–423.

Maruna, Shadd, and Heith Copes. "What Have We Learned from Five Decades of Neutralization Research?" *Crime and Justice* 32 (January 1, 2005): 221–320. https://doi.org/10.1086/655355.

Mastrofski, Stephen D. "Controlling Street-Level Police Discretion." *Annals of the American Academy of Political and Social Science* 593 (2004): 100–118.

Mayer, Jane. "A Deadly Interrogation." *New Yorker,* November 6, 2005. www.newyorker.com.

McCaghy, Charles H. "Drinking and Deviance Disavowal: The Case of Child Molesters." *Social Problems* 16, no. 1 (July 1, 1968): 43–49. https://doi.org/10.2307/799524.

McGoey, Linsey. "The Logic of Strategic Ignorance." *British Journal of Sociology* 63, no. 3 (2012): 533–576. https://doi.org/10.1111/j.1468-4446.2012.01424.x.

McKee, Maralee. "How to Handle the Three Most Common Embarrassing Situations!" Etiquette School of America, April 19, 2015. www.mannersmentor.com.

McKinley, Carol. "Sand Creek Massacre Statue to Replace Torn Down Soldier Monument at Colorado's Capitol." Colorado Public Radio. Accessed April 14, 2021. www.cpr.org.

McKinley, Jesse, Danny Hakim, and Alexandra Alter. "As Cuomo Sought $4 Million Book Deal, Aides Hid Damaging Death Toll." *New York Times,* March 31, 2021. www.nytimes.com.

McLean, Bethany. "How Wells Fargo's Cutthroat Corporate Culture Allegedly Drove Bankers to Fraud." *Vanity Fair,* 2017. www.vanity-fair.com.

Merton, Robert K. "Social Structure and Anomie." *American Sociological Review* 3, no. 5 (1938): 672–682. https://doi.org/10.2307/2084686.

Milgram, Stanley. "The Experience of Living in Cities." *Science* 167, no. 3924 (1970): 1461–1468.

Milliken, Frances J., Elizabeth W. Morrison, and Patricia F. Hewlin. "An Exploratory Study of Employee Silence: Issues That Employees Don't Communicate Upward and Why." *Journal of Management Studies* 40, no. 6 (2003): 1453–1476. https://doi.org/10.1111/1467-6486.00387.

Mills, C. Wright. "Situated Actions and Vocabularies of Motive." *American Sociological Review* 5, no. 6 (1940): 904–913. https://doi.org/10.2307/2084524.

———. *The Sociological Imagination*. New York: Oxford University Press, 2000.

Mills, Charles. "White Ignorance." In *Race and Epistemologies of Ignorance*, edited by Shannon Sullivan and Nancy Tuana, 11–38. Albany: State University of New York Press, 2007.

Mitchell, Alison. "Clinton Impeached." *New York Times*, December 20, 1998. www.nytimes.com.

Modigliani, Andre. "Embarrassment and Embarrassability." *Sociometry* 31, no. 3 (1968): 313–326. https://doi.org/10.2307/2786616.

Monahan, Brian, and Joel Best. "Clocks, Calendars, and Claims: Uses of Time in Social Problems Rhetoric." Paper presented at the Annual Meeting of the Society for the Study of Social Problems, New York, NY, August 2019.

"Mooch, v." In *Oxford English Dictionary Online*. New York: Oxford University Press. Accessed August 2, 2019. www.oed.com.

Moore, Wilbert E., and Melvin M. Tumin. "Some Social Functions of Ignorance." *American Sociological Review* 14, no. 6 (1949): 787–795. https://doi.org/10.2307/2086681.

Moqbel, Samir Naji al Hasan. "Hunger Striking at Guantánamo Bay." *New York Times*, April 14, 2013, sec. Opinion. www.nytimes.com.

Morgenson, Gretchen. "Wells Fargo Forced Unwanted Auto Insurance on Borrowers." *New York Times*, July 27, 2017, sec. Business. www.nytimes.com.

Morris, Errol, dir. *The Fog of War*. Sony Pictures Classics, 2003.

Morrison, Elizabeth Wolfe, and Frances J. Milliken. "Organizational Silence: A Barrier to Change and Development in a Pluralistic World." *Academy of Management Review* 25, no. 4 (2000): 706–725. https://doi.org/10.2307/259200.

————. "Speaking Up, Remaining Silent: The Dynamics of Voice and Silence in Organizations." *Journal of Management Studies* 40, no. 6 (2003): 1353–1358. https://doi.org/10.1111/1467-6486.00383.

Mueller, Jennifer C. "Producing Colorblindness: Everyday Mechanisms of White Ignorance." *Social Problems* 64, no. 2 (May 1, 2017): 219–238.

National Association for the Advancement of Colored People. "The Massacre of East St. Louis." *Crisis*, September 1917.

NBC Sports Boston. "Kraft Apologizes for Allegations in Statement." March 23, 2019. www.nbcsports.com.

New York Times. "Brett Kavanaugh's Opening Statement: Full Transcript." September 26, 2018, sec. US. www.nytimes.com.

————. "Denver Police Scandal Widens; New Disclosures Are Awaited." October 3, 1961.

————. "Louis C.K. Responds to Accusations: 'These Stories Are True.'" November 11, 2017, sec. Arts. www.nytimes.com.

————. "Queens Woman Is Stabbed to Death in Front of Home." March 14, 1964, sec. Archives. www.nytimes.com.

————. "37 Who Saw Murder Didn't Call the Police." March 27, 1964.

————. "Tortures and Tortures." July 8, 1902. http://timesmachine.ny-times.com/timesmachine/1902/07/08/101958086.html.

————. "Transcript: Donald Trump's Taped Comments about Women." October 8, 2016, sec. US. www.nytimes.com.

————. "Why Surrender on the Subway?" January 4, 1985, sec. Opinion. www.nytimes.com.

Nir, Sarah Maslin. "Frances Bay, Actress Known for 'Old Lady' Roles, Dies at 92." *New York Times*, September 18, 2011, sec. Television. www.nytimes.com.

Norgaard, Kari Marie. *Living in Denial: Climate Change, Emotions, and Everyday Life.* Cambridge, MA: MIT Press, 2011.

————. "'People Want to Protect Themselves a Little Bit': Emotions, Denial, and Social Movement Nonparticipation." *Sociological Inquiry* 76, no. 3 (2006): 372–396. https://doi.org/10.1111/j.1475-682X.2006.00160.x.

Obama, Barack. "Remarks by the President at the National Defense University." whitehouse.gov, May 23, 2013. https://obamawhitehouse.archives.gov.

Oeur, Freeden. "Recognizing Dignity: Young Black Men Growing Up in an Era of Surveillance." *Socius* 2 (January 1, 2016). https://doi.org/10.1177/2378023116633712.

Olick, Jeffrey K., and Joyce Robbins. "Social Memory Studies: From 'Collective Memory' to the Historical Sociology of Mnemonic Practices." *Annual Review of Sociology* 24 (1998): 105–140.

Orbuch, Terri L. "People's Accounts Count: The Sociology of Accounts." *Annual Review of Sociology* 23, no. 1 (1997): 455–478. https://doi.org/10.1146/annurev.soc.23.1.455.

Orwell, George. "Politics and the English Language." In *The Collected Essays, Journalism, and Letters of George Orwell*, edited by Sonia Orwell and Ian Angos, 127–140. New York: Harcourt, Brace, Jovanovich, 1968. https://faculty.washington.edu/rsoder/EDLPS579/HonorsOrwellPoliticsEnglishLanguage.pdf.

Palazzolo, Joe, Michael Rothfield, and Lukas I. Alpert. "*National Enquirer* Shielded Donald Trump from *Playboy* Model's Affair Allegation." *Wall Street Journal*, November 4, 2016. www.wsj.com.

Panh, Rithy, dir. *S21: The Khmer Rouge Killing Machine*. First Run Features, 2004.

Paschal, Olivia, and Madeleine Carlisle. "Read Ta-Nehisi Coates's Testimony on Reparations." *Atlantic*, June 19, 2019. www.theatlantic.com.

Patel, Ameeta, and Lamar Reinsch. "Companies Can Apologize: Corporate Apologies and Legal Liability." Business Communication Quarterly 66, no. 1 (March 2003): 9–25. https://doi.org/10.1177/108056990306600103.

Paugh, Patricia C. "Making Sense of 'Conflicting Observations': Teachers, Tests, and the Power of Collaborative Inquiry in Urban Schools." *New Educator* 2, no. 1 (January 2006): 15–31. https://doi.org/10.1080/15476880500486095.

Payne, B. Keith. "Prejudice and Perception: The Role of Automatic and Controlled Processes in Misperceiving a Weapon." *Journal of Personality and Social Psychology* 81, no. 2 (August 2001): 181–192. https://doi.org/10.1037/0022-3514.81.2.181.

Payne, Leigh A. *Unsettling Accounts: Neither Truth nor Reconciliation in Confessions of State Violence*. Durham, NC: Duke University Press, 2008.

Pérez, Raúl. "Learning to Make Racism Funny in the 'Color-Blind' Era: Stand-Up Comedy Students, Performance Strategies, and the (Re)Production of Racist Jokes in Public." *Discourse and Society* 24, no. 4 (July 1, 2013): 478–503. https://doi.org/10.1177/0957926513482066.

Peters, Jeremy W. "Trump Campaign Tried to Seat Bill Clinton's Accusers in V.I.P. Box." *New York Times*, October 10, 2016, sec. US. www.nytimes.com.

Peters, Justin. "The Slate Guide to Crime: How to Drink in Public." *Slate Magazine*, March 12, 2013. www.slate.com.

Picca, Leslie, and Joe Feagin. *Two-Faced Racism: Whites in the Backstage and Frontstage*. New York: Routledge, 2007.

Pierre, Joe. "'I'm Sorry If I Caused Offense': How Not to Apologize." *Psychology Today*, October 29, 2017. www.psychologytoday.com.

Piliavin, Jane Allyn, John F. Dovidio, Samuel L. Gaertner, and Russell D. Clark III. *Emergency Intervention*. New York: Academic Press, 1981.

Pollner, Melvin. *Mundane Reason: Reality in Everyday and Sociological Discourse*. New York: Cambridge University Press, 2010.

Powell, Brian. "Radio Fight! Le Batard vs. Bilas." *Awful Announcing* (blog), April 7, 2008. https://awfulannouncing.com.

Prasad, Vasundhara. "If Anyone Is Listening, #MeToo: Breaking the Culture of Silence around Sexual Abuse through Regulating Non-disclosure Agreements and Secret Settlements Notes." *Boston College Law Review* 7 (2018): 2507–2550.

Prather, Sr., H. Leon, and Kenneth Davis. *We Have Taken a City: The Wilmington Racial Massacre and Coup of 1898*. Rutherford, NJ: Fairleigh Dickinson University Press, 2006.

Purnick, Joyce. "Ward Declares Goetz Didn't Shoot in Self-Defense." *New York Times*, February 22, 1985, sec. NY / Region. www.nytimes.com.

Rabin, Roni Caryn. "New York Sues Sackler Family Members and Drug Distributors." *New York Times*, March 28, 2019, sec. Health. www.nytimes.com.

Rafalovich, Adam. "Making Sociology Relevant: The Assignment and Application of Breaching Experiments." *Teaching Sociology* 34, no. 2 (April 2006): 156–163. https://doi.org/10.1177/0092055X0603400206.

Rasenberger, Jim. "Kitty, 40 Years Later." *New York Times*, February 8, 2004, sec. NY / Region. www.nytimes.com.

Reaves, Brian A. "State and Local Law Enforcement Training Academies, 2013." Washington, DC: US Department of Justice, July 2016. www.bjs.gov.

Rejali, Darius. *Torture and Democracy*. Princeton, NJ: Princeton University Press, 2009.

Rezvani, Selena. "Four Ways to Stop Saying 'Um' and Other Filler Words." *Forbes*, 2014. www.forbes.com.

Roberts, Sam. "Sophia Farrar Dies at 92; Belied Indifference to Kitty Genovese Attack." *New York Times*, September 2, 2020, sec. New York. www.nytimes.com.

Roig, Miguel, and Marissa Caso. "Lying and Cheating: Fraudulent Excuse Making, Cheating, and Plagiarism." *Journal of Psychology* 139, no. 6 (November 1, 2005): 485–494. https://doi.org/10.3200/JRLP.139.6.485-494.

Romero, Mary. "Sociology Engaged in Social Justice." *American Sociological Review* 85, no. 1 (February 1, 2020): 1–30. https://doi.org/10.1177/0003122419893677.

Romo, Vanessa. "NYPD Judge Recommends That the Officer Involved in Eric Garner's Death Be Fired." NPR.org, August 2, 2019. www.npr.org.

Rosenthal, A. M. *Thirty-Eight Witnesses: The Kitty Genovese Case.* Berkeley: University of California Press, 1999.

Rucker, Philip, and Jenna Johnson. "Trump on Turks and Kurds: 'Like Two Kids in a Lot, You've Got to Let Them Fight.'" *Washington Post*, October 17, 2019. www.washingtonpost.com.

Rumsfeld, Donald. "Allegations of Mistreatment of Iraqi Prisoners." US Senate Committee on Armed Services (2004). www.govinfo.gov/content/pkg/CHRG-108shrg96600/html/CHRG-108shrg96600.htm.

Rupert, Maya. "I'm Done Debating Racism with the Devil." *Slate Magazine*, October 4, 2017. www.slate.com.

Rutenberg, Jim. "A Long-Delayed Reckoning of the Cost of Silence on Abuse." *New York Times*, October 22, 2017, sec. Business. www.nytimes.com.

Sadri, Mahmoud, and Ahmad Sadri. "Doppelganger: Twins' Disruption of the Assumptions of Constancy and Uniqueness of Self in Everyday Life." *Symbolic Interaction* 17, no. 2 (June 1, 1994): 203–223. https://doi.org/10.1525/si.1994.17.2.203.

Saletan, William. "Death Is Good: Trump's Sadistic Argument for Betraying the Kurds." *Slate Magazine*, October 25, 2019. www.slate.com.

Sanders, Clinton R. "Excusing Tactics: Social Responses to the Public Misbehavior of Companion Animals." *Anthrozoös* 4, no. 2 (June 1, 1990): 82–90. https://doi.org/10.2752/089279391787057288.

Sanger, David E. "Callers Support Subway Gunman." *New York Times*, December 25, 1984, sec. NY / Region. www.nytimes.com.

Savage, Charlie. "Amid Hunger Strike, Obama Renews Push to Close Cuba Prison." *New York Times*, April 30, 2013, sec. US. www.nytimes.com.

Schatz, Bryan. "'Are You Prepared to Kill Somebody?' A Day with One of America's Most Popular Police Trainers." *Mother Jones*. Accessed September 21, 2020. www.motherjones.com.

Scheff, Thomas J. *Goffman Unbound! A New Paradigm for Social Science*. New York: Routledge, 2015.

Schelling, Thomas. "If There Were a Nobel Prize for Sociology and/or Social Psychology, Goffman Would Deserve to Be the First One Considered." Bios Sociologicus: The Erving Goffman Archives, August 18, 2015. https://digitalscholarship.unlv.edu/goffman_archives/97.

Schonfeld, Zach. "The Curious Case of a Supposed Karl Rove Quote Used on The National's New Album 'Sleep Well Beast.'" *Newsweek*, September 8, 2017. www.newsweek.com.

Schwartz, John. "Exxon Misled the Public on Climate Change, Study Says." *New York Times*, August 23, 2017, sec. Climate. www.nytimes.com.

———. "New York Sues Exxon Mobil, Saying It Deceived Shareholders on Climate Change." *New York Times*, October 24, 2018, sec. Climate. www.nytimes.com.

Scott, Marvin B., and Stanford M. Lyman. "Accounts." *American Sociological Review* 33, no. 1 (1968): 46–62. https://doi.org/10.2307/2092239.

Scully, Diana, and Joseph Marolla. "Convicted Rapists' Vocabulary of Motive: Excuses and Justifications." *Social Problems* 31, no. 5 (June 1, 1984): 530–544. https://doi.org/10.2307/800239.

Seu, Irene Bruna. "'Doing Denial': Audience Reaction to Human Rights Appeals." *Discourse and Society* 21, no. 4 (2010): 438–457.

Shalin, Dmitri N. "Interfacing Biography, Theory and History: The Case of Erving Goffman." *Symbolic Interaction* 37, no. 1 (February 1, 2014): 2–40. https://doi.org/10.1002/symb.82.

Shane, Scott. "Drone Strikes Reveal Uncomfortable Truth: US Is Often Unsure about Who Will Die." *New York Times*, April 23, 2015, sec. World. www.nytimes.com.

Shapiro, Thomas, Tatjana Meschede, and Sam Osoro. "The Roots of the Widening Racial Wealth Gap: Explaining the Black-White Economic Divide." Waltham, MA: Institute on Assets and Social Policy, February 2013. https://drum.lib.umd.edu/bitstream/handle/1903/24590/racialwealthgapbrief.pdf?sequence=1.

Sharp, Shane, and Gregory T. Kordsmeier. "The 'Shirt-Weenie': A Note on Teaching the Power of Face-Work and Tact in Social Interaction." *Teaching Sociology* 36, no. 4 (October 1, 2008): 359–365. https://doi.org/10.1177/0092055X0803600405.

Shaw, Clifford R., and Henry Donald McKay. *Juvenile Delinquency and Urban Areas: A Study of Rates of Delinquency in Relation to Differential Characteristics of Local Communities in American Cities.* Chicago: University of Chicago Press, 1972.

Shear, Michael D. "'I'm Not a Racist,' Trump Says in Denying Vulgar Comment." *New York Times,* January 15, 2018, sec. US. www.nytimes.com.

Shotland, R. Lance, and Charles A. Stebbins. "Bystander Response to Rape: Can a Victim Attract Help?" *Journal of Applied Social Psychology* 10, no. 6 (December 1, 1980): 510–527. https://doi.org/10.1111/j.1559-1816.1980.tb00729.x.

Simmel, Georg. *The Sociology of Georg Simmel.* Edited by Kurt H. Wolff. New York: Free Press, 1950.

Simpson, Kevin. "Denver Cop and Robber Reconciles His Troubled Past." *Denver Post,* February 15, 2010. www.denverpost.com.

Skolnick, Jerome. "Corruption and the Blue Code of Silence." *Police Practice and Research* 3, no. 1 (January 1, 2002): 7–19. https://doi.org/10.1080/15614260290011309.

Smith, Ben. "The Times Took 19 Days to Report an Accusation against Biden. Here's Why." *New York Times,* April 13, 2020. www.nytimes.com.

Smith, Dorothy E. "Texts and the Ontology of Organizations and Institutions." *Studies in Cultures, Organizations and Societies* 7, no. 2 (January 1, 2001): 159–198. https://doi.org/10.1080/10245280108523557.

———. *Texts, Facts and Femininity: Exploring the Relations of Ruling.* Brunswick, NJ: Routledge, 2002.

Smith, Greg. "Incivil Attention and Everyday Intolerance: Vicissitudes of Exercising in Public Places." *Perspectives on Social Problems* 9 (1997): 59–82.

Snook, Richelle. "Facing the Consequences: The Rhetoric of Denial during the #MeToo Movement." Unpublished thesis, University of Denver, Colorado, 2020.

Snow, David A., Cherylon Robinson, and Patricia L. McCall. "'Cooling Out' Men in Singles Bars and Nightclubs: Observations on the Interpersonal Survival Strategies of Women in Public Places." *Journal of Contemporary Ethnography* 19, no. 4 (1991): 423–449.

Solnit, Rebecca. "All the Rage." *New Republic*, September 24, 2018. www.newrepublic.com.

———. *Call Them by Their True Names: American Crises*. Chicago: Haymarket Books, 2018.

———. *Hope in the Dark: Untold Histories, Wild Possibilities*. Chicago: Haymarket Books, 2016.

———. *Whose Story Is This? Old Conflicts, New Chapters*. Chicago: Haymarket Books, 2019.

Sontag, Susan. *Regarding the Pain of Others*. New York: Picador, 2004.

———. "Regarding the Torture of Others." *New York Times Magazine*, May 23, 2004. www.nytimes.com.

Spanierman, Lisa B., and Nolan L. Cabrera. "The Emotions of White Racism and Antiracism." In *Unveiling Whiteness in the 21st Century: Global Manifestations, Transdisciplinary Interventions*, edited by Veronica Watson, Deirdre Howard-Wagner, and Lisa Spanierman, 9–28. Lanham, MD: Lexington, 2015.

Spector, Malcolm, and John I. Kitsuse. *Constructing Social Problems*. New Brunswick, NJ: Routledge, 2000.

Spelman, Elizabeth V. "Managing Ignorance." In *Race and Epistemologies of Ignorance*, edited by Shannon Sullivan and Nancy Tuana, 119–131. Albany: State University of New York Press, 2007.

Spiegel, Alix. "How Politicians Get Away with Dodging the Question." NPR.org, October 3, 2012. www.npr.org.

StackExchange. "Is There Any Idiom or Proverb Discouraging Knowledge?" English Language and Usage Stack Exchange, 2016. https://english.stackexchange.com.

———. "What Is an Alternative Phrase to 'Swept under the Rug?'" English Language and Usage Stack Exchange, 2017. https://english.stackexchange.com.

Standish, Katerina. "Learning How to Hope: A Hope Curriculum." *Humanity and Society* 43, no. 4 (November 1, 2019): 484–504. https://doi.org/10.1177/0160597618814886.

Stanger, Allison. *Whistleblowers: Honesty in America from Washington to Trump.* New Haven, CT: Yale University Press, 2019.

Steel, Emily. "Employers Who Talk Up Gender Equity, but Silence Harassment Victims." *New York Times*, May 1, 2019, sec. Business. www.nytimes.com.

Stephens, Bret. "Staring at the Conservative Gutter." *Wall Street Journal,* March 1, 2016. www.wsj.com.

Stern, Mort. "What Makes a Policeman Go Wrong? An Ex-member of the Force Traces the Steps on Way from Law Enforcement to Violating." *Journal of Criminal Law, Criminology, and Police Science* 53, no. 1 (1962): 97–101. https://doi.org/10.2307/1141572.

Stewart, James B. "Consider the Sources." *New York Times*, July 4, 1999. https://archive.nytimes.com.

Stoddard, Ellwyn R. "Informal Code of Police Deviancy: A Group Approach to Blue-Coat Crime." *Journal of Criminal Law, Criminology and Police Science* 59, no. 2 (1968): 201–213. https://doi.org/10.2307/1141940.

Stolberg, Sheryl Gay, and Nicholas Fandos. "Brett Kavanaugh and Christine Blasey Ford Duel with Tears and Fury." *New York Times*, September 27, 2018, sec. US. www.nytimes.com.

Stop Street Harassment. "Unsafe and Harassed in Public Spaces: A National Street Harassment Report." Reston, VA: Stop Street Harassment, 2014.

Sue, Derald Wing, Gina C. Torino, Christina M. Capodilupo, David P. Rivera, and Annie I. Lin. "How White Faculty Perceive and React to Difficult Dialogues on Race: Implications for Education and Training." *Counseling Psychologist* 37, no. 8 (November 1, 2009): 1090–1115. https://doi.org/10.1177/0011000009340443.

Sutton, Barbara, and Kari Marie Norgaard. "Cultures of Denial: Avoiding Knowledge of State Violations of Human Rights in Argentina and the United States." *Sociological Forum* 28, no. 3 (September 1, 2013): 495–524. https://doi.org/10.1111/socf.12035.

Swidler, Ann. "Culture in Action: Symbols and Strategies." *American Sociological Review* 51, no. 2 (1986): 273–286. https://doi.org/10.2307/2095521.

Sykes, Gresham M., and David Matza. "Techniques of Neutralization: A Theory of Delinquency." *American Sociological Review* 22, no. 6 (1957): 664–670. https://doi.org/10.2307/2089195.

Taguba, Antonio M. "AR 15-6 Investigation of the 800th Military Police Brigade." Washington, DC: Department of Defense, 2004. www.thetorturedatabase.org.

Task Force on Detainee Treatment. "Transcript of Interview with Alberto Mora (Former General Counsel of the Navy)." Constitution Project, April 24, 2012. https://detaineetaskforce.org.

Tavuchis, Nicholas. *Mea Culpa: A Sociology of Apology and Reconciliation*. Stanford, CA: Stanford University Press, 1991.

Temkin, Jennifer, Jacqueline M. Gray, and Jastine Barrett. "Different Functions of Rape Myth Use in Court: Findings from a Trial Observation Study." *Feminist Criminology* 13, no. 2 (April 2018): 205–226. https://doi.org/10.1177/1557085116661627.

Thompson, Alex I. "'Sometimes, I Think I Might Say Too Much': Dark Secrets and the Performance of Inflammatory Bowel Disease." *Symbolic Interaction* 36, no. 1 (February 1, 2013): 21–39. https://doi.org/10.1002/symb.50.

Thompson, John. "Scandal and Social Theory." In *Media Scandals: Morality and Desire in the Popular Culture Marketplace*, edited by Stephen Hinerman and James Lull, 34–64. Oxford, UK: Polity Press, 2005.

Thompson, John B. *Political Scandal: Power and Visibility in the Media Age*. Malden, MA: Blackwell, 2000.

Tracy, Marc. "Joe Paterno Knew of Sandusky Abuse in 1976, According to Court Testimony." *New York Times*, July 12, 2016, sec. Sports. www.nytimes.com.

Turkle, Sherry. *Alone Together: Why We Expect More from Technology and Less from Each Other*. New York: Basic Books, 2011.

Turner, K. B., David Giacopassi, and Margaret Vandiver. "Ignoring the Past: Coverage of Slavery and Slave Patrols in Criminal Justice Texts." *Journal of Criminal Justice Education* 17, no. 1 (April 1, 2006): 181–195. https://doi.org/10.1080/10511250500335627.

TV Tropes. "Bystander Syndrome." Accessed November 20, 2018. https://tvtropes.org.

Twohey, Megan, Jodi Kantor, Susan Dominus, Jim Rutenberg, and Steve Eder. "Weinstein's Complicity Machine." *New York Times*, December 5, 2017, sec. US. www.nytimes.com.

Varki, Ajit, and Danny Brower. Denial: Self-Deception, False Beliefs, and the Origins of the Human Mind. New York: Hachette Book Group.

Vaughan, Diane. *The Challenger Launch Decision: Risky Technology, Culture, and Deviance at NASA*. Chicago: University of Chicago Press, 1996.

———. *Controlling Unlawful Organizational Behavior: Social Structure and Corporate Misconduct*. Chicago: University of Chicago Press, 1985.

———. "Regulating Risk: Implications of the *Challenger* Accident." *Law and Policy* 11, no. 3 (1989): 330–349.

Villano, Matt. "The Scent of a Co-worker." *New York Times*, June 11, 2006, sec. Business Day. www.nytimes.com.

Wall Street Journal. "Trump Stokes the Transition Panic." September 24, 2020, sec. Opinion. www.wsj.com.

Washington Post. "13 Times Trump Said the Coronavirus Would Go Away." YouTube, April 30, 2020. www.youtube.com/watch?v=r8yOv4PwttM.

———. "Tlaib Calls Meadows Use of HUD Official 'Racist Act.'" Accessed April 4, 2019. www.youtube.com/watch?v=o4pe7WOMKE4.

———. "Transcript of Mark Zuckerberg's Senate Hearing." Accessed April 10, 2019. www.washingtonpost.com.

Weiland, Noah, Maggie Haberman, Mark Mazzetti, and Annie Karni. "Trump Was Sicker Than Acknowledged with Covid-19." *New York Times*, February 11, 2021. www.nytimes.com.

Weinstein, Harvey. "Statement from Harvey Weinstein." *New York Times*, October 5, 2017, sec. US. www.nytimes.com.

Weiser, Benjamin. "Swastikas, Slurs and Torment in Town's Schools." *New York Times*, November 8, 2013. www.nytimes.com.

Weiser, Benjamin, and Nate Schweber. "Swastika on a Bathroom Stall: Anti-Semitism Still Plagues Upstate School District." *New York Times*, March 1, 2019. www.nytimes.com.

Whearley, Bob. "Exposé of Police Burglaries Marked City's 'Year of Shame.'" *Denver Post*, December 26, 1961. www.denverpost.com.

White, Jenny, Albert Bandura, and Lisa A. Bero. "Moral Disengagement in the Corporate World." *Accountability in*

Research 16, no. 1 (February 27, 2009): 41–74. https://doi. org/10.1080/08989620802689847.

Whitesides, John, and Andy Sullivan. "Biden Comes Out Swinging at Debate, Clashes with Ryan." Reuters, October 12, 2012. www.reuters. com.

Wikipedia. "Bystander Effect." November 19, 2018. https://en.wikipedia. org.

Winerip, Michael. "Stepping Up to Stop Sexual Assault." *New York Times*, December 20, 2017, sec. Education. www.nytimes.com.

Wingfield, Adia Harvey. "Are Some Emotions Marked 'Whites Only'? Racialized Feeling Rules in Professional Workplaces." *Social Problems* 57, no. 2 (2010): 251–268. https://doi.org/10.1525/ sp.2010.57.2.251.

——. "The Modern Mammy and the Angry Black Man: African American Professionals' Experiences with Gendered Racism in the Workplace." *Race, Gender and Class* 14, no. 1/2 (2007): 196–212.

Winter, Tom. "Robert Kraft Prostitution Charges Dropped by Florida Prosecutors." NBC News, September 24, 2020. www.nbcnews.com.

Wirth, Louis. "Urbanism as a Way of Life." *American Journal of Sociology* 44, no. 1 (1938): 1–24.

Woolgar, Steve, and Dorothy Pawluch. "Ontological Gerrymandering: The Anatomy of Social Problems Explanations." *Social Problems* 32, no. 3 (February 1, 1985): 214–227. https://doi.org/10.2307/800680.

Wright, Erik Olin. "Real Utopias." *Contexts* 10, no. 2 (May 1, 2011): 36–42. https://doi.org/10.1177/1536504211408884.

Yahoo! News. "Trump: 'I've Done More for the Black Community Than Any Other President' with the 'Possible Exception of Abraham Lincoln.'" September 23, 2020. https://news.yahoo.com.

Zagorin, Adam, and Michael Duffy. "Inside the Interrogation of Detainee 063." *Time*, June 19, 2005. www.time.com.

Zaveri, Mihir. "Judge Who Asked Woman in Sexual Assault Case If She Closed Her Legs Faces Suspension." *New York Times*, April 8, 2019, sec. New York. www.nytimes.com.

Zerubavel, Eviatar. "Dmitri Shalin Interview with Eviatar Zerubavel about Erving Goffman Entitled 'Studying with Erving Goffman.'" Bios Sociologicus: The Erving Goffman Archives, November 28, 2008. https://digitalscholarship.unlv.edu/goffman_archives/78.

———. *The Elephant in the Room: Silence and Denial in Everyday Life.* New York: Oxford University Press, 2007.

———. *Hidden in Plain Sight: The Social Structure of Irrelevance.* New York: Oxford University Press, 2015.

———. "The Social Sound of Silence: Toward a Sociology of Denial." *Shadows of War: A Social History of Silence in the Twentieth Century,* January 1, 2010, 32–44. https://doi.org/10.1017/CBO9780511676178.003.

INDEX

ABOUT THE AUTHOR

JARED DEL ROSSO is Associate Professor of Sociology and Criminology at the University of Denver, where he researches and teaches on collective denial. His work in this area has been published in *Social Forces*, *Social Problems*, and *Sociological Forum*. His first book, *Talking about Torture: How Political Discourse Shapes the Debate*, was published in 2015.